BEARS
IN THEIR OWN WORDS

BEARS
IN THEIR OWN WORDS

*Chicago Bear Greats Talk About
the Team, the Game, the Coaches,
and the Times of Their Lives*

RICHARD WHITTINGHAM

CB

CONTEMPORARY
BOOKS

CHICAGO

Library of Congress Cataloging-in-Publication Data

Whittingham, Richard, 1939-
    Bears: In their own words / Richard Whittingham.
       p.   cm.
    ISBN 0-8092-4035-1 (cloth)
        0-8092-3849-7 (paper)
    1. Chicago Bears (Football team)—History.   2. Football
players—United States—Biography.   I. Title.
GV956.C5W46   1991
796.332′64′0977311—dc20   91-23837
                                            CIP

This book is dedicated to the memories of George Halas,
who gave pro football the Chicago Bears;

The legion of Bears, who made it all so enjoyable these
past seventy-some years;

And Richard Youhn, who was their most devoted fan.

Variations of the interviews with Red Grange, Sid
Luckman, and Joey Sternaman appeared previously
in the book *What a Game They Played* © 1984
by Richard Whittingham (New York: Harper & Row).

Copyright © 1991 by Richard Whittingham
All rights reserved
Published by Contemporary Books, Inc.
180 North Michigan Avenue, Chicago, Illinois 60601
Manufactured in the United States of America
International Standard Book Number: 0-8092-4035-1 (cloth)
                                    0-8092-3849-7 (paper)

Contents

Acknowledgments

The author and publisher wish to thank the Chicago Bears organization, especially club president Michael McCaskey and director of community development Patrick McCaskey, for their cooperation and support in the preparation of this book.

Special appreciation is also extended to all those former Chicago Bears who graciously sat for interviews so their stories and experiences of life with the Bears could be told here.

And special thanks are offered to Irv Kupcinet, who took time from his extraordinarily busy schedule to share the many memories he has of his good friend George Halas.

Introduction

Mike Ditka summed up the Chicago Bears as well as anyone could when he said in 1985, "There are teams that are fair-haired and there are teams that aren't. There are teams named Smith and teams named Grabowski. . . . We're a Grabowski."

For decades the Bears have been known as the Monsters of the Midway, with valid reason. Since their inception in 1920 they have been the roughest, toughest franchise around. It was bred into them during the forty years George Halas stalked the sideline, cursing, cajoling, inspiring, taunting, and forever showing a fearlessness that proved rabidly contagious to his players. It is sustained today, with the volatile Mike Ditka patrolling the same area.

Even in the leanest years the Bears were a team to contend with, and opposing players took their bumps and bruises with them back to Green Bay, New York, Detroit, Baltimore, and sundry other NFL cities . . . remembering awful, bloody Sundays . . . even Sundays when they had returned home victorious.

To have built such a reputation, one that has withstood more than seventy years of contentious, raucous, free-spirited

1

competition in that gladiatorial arena known as the National Football League, the Bears had to have a unique cast of characters, spirited on one hand and capable of terrifying Attila's Huns on the other.

In the pages that follow, the most memorable of former Bears, or Monsters, tell their own stories—what it was like to be there, what went on behind the scenes, what they saw, thought, enjoyed, and endured.

Here they tell the tales of life with the Bears: George Trafton breaking Fred Chicken's leg in Rock Island in the early 1920s and then running for his life with the game receipts, Red Grange and George Halas meeting Babe Ruth in New York and President Calvin Coolidge in Washington on their historic barnstorming tour of 1925, a twenty-one-year-old Sid Luckman in his Brooklyn apartment listening to Halas tell him that he and Jesus Christ were the only two people he'd pay $6,000 to play for the Bears, Gale Sayers remembering that rookie-year day when he scored 6 touchdowns and talking of his friend the late Brian Piccolo, Doug Atkins and his uncontained antics, Dan Hampton recounting the ever-building fury that surged through him and his teammates down in New Orleans the night before Super Bowl XX . . .

The Bears are legendary. They are one of only two teams that have been around since the birth of the NFL (only the Chicago/St. Louis/Phoenix Cardinals can also make that claim). They were the Decatur Staleys that inaugural year, became the Bears in 1922, and have been a Chicago institution ever since.

The team and the league itself were the dreams of George Halas. He was there at the historic meeting in Canton, Ohio, when the NFL was founded. He and his partner, Ed "Dutch" Sternaman, guided the Bears through the financially painful and unheralded first decade of play—5,000 was considered a decent box office in those days—then Papa Bear, on his own, saw them through the Depression, World War II, the war with the AFL, and the incredible boost in popularity after television adopted the game, to the phenomenon so many millions watch and love today.

The Bears have always been instrumental in the shaping and sustaining of the National Football League: George Halas and the numerous rule changes and innovations he brought to the game, Red Grange and the Bears traveling the country in 1925 and putting pro football on the proverbial map, the great contests from the fabled "Sneakers" game of 1934 to the unparalleled 73-0 rout of the Redskins in 1940 to the widest margin of victory in Super Bowl history when the Midway Monsters systematically destroyed the New England Patriots 46-10 on that wonderful Sunday in January 1986.

The Bears have had more than their share of certified NFL legends: George Halas, Red Grange, Bronko Nagurski, Sid Luckman, Bulldog Turner, Gale Sayers, Dick Butkus, Walter Payton, to name just a few. And they have had some of the wildest, most amusing and controversial characters the game of professional football has ever seen. The escapades, the pranks, the feuds, the personal whims and superstitions, and the agonies and ecstasies, all the crazy, happy, sad things that transpired in the locker room, at training camp, during the games and after them; this is Bear lore from those who helped shape it.

The history of the Bears is recounted in the pages that follow by the men who were there. George Halas, Red Grange, and Joey Sternaman tell what it was like in the 1920s when helmets were leather and the ball was much fatter. Sid Luckman, George McAfee, Ed Sprinkle, Hugh Gallarneau, and George Connor remember the golden era of championships in the 1940s. Mike Ditka, Gale Sayers, Doug Buffone, and Johnny Morris talk of the years that led to the dynastic 1980s. And Jim McMahon, Dan Hampton, and Gary Fencik provide insights into the team that dominated the NFC Central in the last decade and went so joyfully to the Super Bowl. Many others tell their own unique Bear stories as well.

It was a pleasure and a privilege to be part of this Bear reunion, and I wish to thank all the former Bears who shared their stories with me so that they could then be shared with professional football fans everywhere. And it is a reunion—one that Papa Bear would have loved to have been at. I think the words that his daughter, Virginia Halas McCaskey, spoke after the triumph at Super Bowl XX are equally appropriate to the reunion of memories here: "Dad would relish this. . . . Dad would have loved it all. The Bears were his life. . . . He's upstairs cheering, taking notes. . . ."

And once again from Mike Ditka, who always seems to capture the quintessence of the Chicago Bears, in words he spoke around the same time: "Winning the Super Bowl doesn't tell the story of the Chicago Bears. The Super Bowl trophy is sort of like an ornament on a Christmas tree . . . it's beautiful, but what's holding it up is the tree, and the tree is the Chicago Bears."

Mike Ditka

Mike Ditka hardly needs an introduction. He is the man who virtually established the position of tight end in the National Football League and played it so well for the Bears, Eagles, and Cowboys that he earned the game's highest honor, enshrinement in the Pro Football Hall of Fame in Canton, Ohio.

He is the volatile coach, the advocate of down-to-earth, fundamental football, who took the Bears to Super Bowl XX after the 1985 season and produced six Central Division championships in seven years, five of them consecutive (1984–88, 90).

He is the man who, with a phrase or a sentence, can freeze a player with fear or break an audience into laughter.

Raised in Aliquippa, Pennsylvania, Ditka played his college ball at Pittsburgh and was named to the All-America team his senior year (1960). A defensive end/linebacker/tight end in those days, he also maintained a 40-yard punting average over three years at Pitt.

Ditka was the first-round (fifth pick) draft choice of the Bears in 1961. His first year he caught 56 passes and was named NFL Rookie of the Year. During his six years with the Bears he was chosen for the Pro Bowl five times. His all-time

Bear records include most touchdown receptions in a game, 4 (against the Los Angeles Rams in 1963, shared with Harlon Hill, who caught 4 against the 49ers in 1954); most consecutive games, 1+ receptions, 49; most TD receptions as a rookie, 12 (tied with Harlon Hill, who did the same in 1954).

Ditka's overall stats during his twelve-year NFL playing career (1961–72) are: 427 pass receptions for 5,812 yards and 43 touchdowns, an average gain of 13.6 yards per reception, 153 total games played, and punishing key blocks that are too numerous to be counted.

After his playing days were over, Ditka joined the coaching staff of the Dallas Cowboys and worked under Tom Landry there for nine years. He rejoined the Bears as head coach in 1982 and has become the second winningest coach in Bear history, trailing only George Halas, the NFL's all-time winningest coach.

I was tremendously proud to put on the Bear uniform, and I say that in all honesty. I knew very little about the Bears until I was drafted by them in 1961 because I, of course, was from Pennsylvania and mostly followed the Pittsburgh Steelers and Philadelphia Eagles. But the more I found out about the Bears, the more I liked; they played the kind of football that I believed in, and Coach Halas taught the kind of football I believed in. The Bears were the Monsters of the Midway, or the bullies, or whatever you want to call them, and that's the way I thought the game was supposed to be played.

It was intriguing too when you look back and realize that I was a twenty-one-year-old kid coming into the National Football League, and the head coach was sixty-five years old. Nobody ever assumed anything about his age, however; it did not matter, because we all knew he was the boss. To see him in action you would have thought George Halas was maybe in his fifties, but certainly not sixty-five.

I was with the College All-Stars in 1961, and we scrimmaged the Bears. I did not make any friends with them. I ran over a couple of guys, which did not sit well. We played the Philadelphia Eagles, who had won the NFL title the year before. We had some very good ballplayers.

I think the first friend I made later was Bill George. Bill was a Pennsylvania kid from the coal mine area of western Pennsylvania. He kind of took me under his wing and helped me a little bit. And I remember Larry Morris and some of the guys. Harlon Hill was a lot of help to me. Harlon was a great guy. It was toward the end of his career, and he took a good amount of time to work with me. He was also playing, and I think they were planning on converting him to tight end. I think they even tried him on defense because his days as a wide receiver were over, but in his day he was one of the great wide receivers.

I didn't have an agent when I came to Chicago. I don't have an agent now. I don't believe in agents. I know what I'm worth and what I'm not worth, and I wouldn't fool anybody about that. My agent was myself and my dad. You know, it was kind of interesting, though, because you knew you were being taken, but you didn't really mind it. I guess that's the best way to put it. I was very flattered at the time to be drafted into the NFL when I was coming out of college. I didn't know if I would play in the National Football League. It was actually George Allen who signed me—he was the assistant defensive coach for them at the time. He said, "You know, I'm paying you more money than the Bears have paid any rookie since Red Grange," or something like that, and you knew he was lying, but still you had to laugh. It was terrible, but that's the way it went.

My first impression of George Halas was that he was *the* leader—that's the one thing that stood out. What he said went; he was the boss, period. I saw him as being in control, very authoritative. He was the guy who got his way almost all the time, dealing with the Bears or the NFL.

I came to our first training camp pretty well ready. At Pitt we worked as hard as anybody. We had John Michael Olsen as our coach, and John was a stickler for hard work and tough training. So we were used to working hard, and therefore training camp was not that difficult for me.

There was, of course, a difference from college football. At

Pitt I'd played a lot of defense and blocked a lot. Catching passes was rarely on the agenda. With the Bears my job was to catch balls and block, and that was a big change for me. So, when I got with the Bears in '61, I went to Chicago early and worked out. That was the year the Bears traded for Bill Wade. Sid Luckman was there as an assistant coach, and Sid really helped me tremendously in becoming a receiver. He took the time to work with me and teach me how to catch a ball. Not that I couldn't catch the ball—I led the team at Pitt in receiving my senior year with 14 catches or so, which tells you pretty much what our passing game was like. Sid guided me, and Bill Wade worked with me, throwing the ball to me; we just did it over and over. We worked with some of the defensive backs—I can remember Richie Petibon coming in at that time and some other guys, and we really had a good group. We worked out down at Soldier Field in those days even though we played at Wrigley Field. We'd work about three, four weeks in the summer, and it really helped me for training camp.

It was a different game then too. We were all part of football as a sport, and it's not that anymore; it's big business. We were part of pro football when it was played more for the love of the game, and we played hard together on the field and off the field, and we had fun.

We were much more together as a group in those days— even guys who didn't ordinarily associate with other guys that much. It was nothing for all of us to meet at a place and have a beer together or a sandwich. I think we did much more of that than the players do today.

There was also a strong camaraderie. Maybe there wasn't a great love, but there was always a great respect between our offense and defense. I always felt that. We knew that we were a team that won because of our defense, yet offensively we tried to do the things we had to do.

Another thing I remember from when I first came to the Bears involves Joe Fortunato. One of the things I did that first summer when I came to Chicago early, besides catching passes and working out, I watched a lot of game film. One day I was watching a film of the Bears playing the Lions, and I remember

Tight end Mike Ditka (89) goes high in the air to snare a touchdown pass from Bill Wade (9) in a 1962 game against the Minnesota Vikings at Wrigley Field. Other Bears in the photograph are Herm Lee (70), Bob Wetoska (63), Mike Pyle (50), Ted Karras (67), and Rick Casares (35).

Fortunato rushing a passer. Jim Gibbons was Detroit's tight end, and he was on the right end's side. Joe got outside of him and kind of gave Gibbons the clothesline and took him all the way to the quarterback with him and just dropped them both. Coach Halas happened to be in the room at the time, and he said, "Did you see that?"

I said, "Yeah, do they always do that to the tight ends?"

And he said, "Not if you don't let them."

I said, "Well, I'll try not to let them then." Fortunato was just a big, impressive guy and a helluva football player.

Our finest season, of course, was 1963. The first thing I remember about that season was when we played the Giants in the preseason. We beat them, and after the game Coach Halas called me in and asked me about where I thought we could go that year. I said I thought we could win it all.

I also remember the '63 games against Green Bay, which were tremendous games. We won both [at Green Bay, 10-3, at Wrigley Field, 26-7]—not an easy chore when they had Vince Lombardi on the sideline and players like Starr, Nitschke, Taylor, Kramer, and Davis on the field.

The game in Pittsburgh, of course, was memorable, and even the tie at the end of the year against the Vikings, when we had to do that, and then the game when we had to win against Detroit when Davey Whitsell intercepted a pass and saved that game. After all those games and the things that happened in them, the championship game against the Giants was almost anticlimactic, but it was a great game—the league's top offense [Giants] against the best defense in the NFL [Bears].

The play that everybody seems to remember about me was in the Steelers game that year. [Ditka took a short pass and rambled 63 yards, shedding at least five tacklers to set up the game-tying field goal.] I don't really know that it was the best, because if it had been the best play I ever made, I would have scored a touchdown, and I would have outrun that last guy. I was very tired at that point. That play was near the end of the game, and I'd played the whole game. I remember that because Wade wanted me to run a deep pattern, and I said, "No, I can't," and I told him what play to run. I said, "I'll hook up about 12 yards down, you throw me the ball, and maybe I can get across midfield." Then I felt, if we hit another pass or two maybe we could score a touchdown or at least kick another field goal. Then, when the last guy hit me, all those other guys missed me, but I started running out of gas, and I went down. I mean the first guy who missed me was the guy who finally tackled me. So you know I wasn't going too fast, let's face it. On the play after that, after we got down there—I had come out of the game— Wade threw a perfect pass to Bo Farrington, hit him right between the numbers in the end zone, but he dropped it. So we had to kick a field goal to tie it then. When you think about the little things that made that season, it's kind of crazy. At any rate, we ended up half a game ahead of Green Bay and went out and whipped the Giants for the title.

We had some great players then. Bill George: he definitely was one of the all-time great players. Doug Atkins: there's no question in my mind about him either. Dick Butkus: I don't think he had a peer at that position, middle linebacker. He played the position ferociously. Bill George played it a little differently. So did Joe Schmidt of Detroit. But Butkus, Ray Nitschke of Green Bay, and Jack Lambert of Pittsburgh, they kind of played it like "I'm just going to kick the shit out of these guys; I've got no friends on the other side; don't take any prisoners." That's the way they played it. And I kind of respected them for that.

There were other damn good players too: Joe Fortunato and Larry Morris were great linebackers, Ed O'Bradovich did a great job at defensive end, Fred Williams and Stan Jones at tackle. In the secondary we had Rosey Taylor, Richie Petibon, Bennie McRae, and Davey Whitsell. So you know it was a very solid football team. We had J. C. Caroline backing up in the offense. And one of the game's great running backs and a very under-rated player, Willie Galimore. I'd seen him after he had about five knee surgeries, but he could still fly. I never saw anybody cut and run like he could. He was very similar to Gale Sayers, but actually I thought he was faster than Gale. I don't know that he could cut as well as Gale, but they were very similar. Then, of course, we had Joe Marconi at fullback and Rick Casares, and we had Rudy Bukich and Bill Wade at quarterback. We had a good football team. On the line were Bob Wetoska and Ted Karras and Herm Lee, and those guys were good football players. There was Mike Pyle at center. It was a solid football team. Bo Farrington was one wide receiver, and Johnny Morris was the other. Passing we couldn't match up in personnel maybe with Baltimore, who had Johnny Unitas and Raymond Berry, but we got the job done.

Galimore and Farrington were killed at the next training camp. It was a terrible shock. You're with the guys one night, leave a meeting with them, you have a bite to eat with them, and then it's over, forever. They went over to the country club to watch the Olympics and eat pizza later. And coming back somebody had misplaced a road sign, and they ran off the road, hooked a wheel, and the car flipped over. They both were killed. I can remember the shock going through that training camp, and it was terrible.

The toughest guys I played against? Ray Nitschke of the Packers—he was as tough as there was. Willie Wood, up in Green Bay, was a really rugged defensive back. I had great respect for Willie. And, of course, I had to play against Herb Adderley. Another was a kid out of the 49ers, Jimmy Johnson, a great defensive back. Through my career most of the trouble seemed to come from the Packers, guys like Willie Davis. Another of the toughest guys I played against was Bill Pellington, at Baltimore—he'd knock people down with his fist.

Gino Marchetti—I respected him so much. He was just a great football player. I mean if you can block Marchetti and you can block Willie Davis, you can block anybody. They were really exceptional players. Another one was Alex Karras over in Detroit. He was pretty damn tough. There was a linebacker out of San Francisco who came later, and he played through the seventies, Dave Wilcox. He came later—that was '64; he played against us at the end of my Bear career, and then when I was at Dallas and still playing. He was a very underrated football player.

I had a couple good run-ins with Sam Huff of the Giants, but I had great respect for Sam because he played the game the way I did. He just played hard like I did, and we both felt you can't worry about who gets mad at you out there as a result. If they get mad at you, they get mad at you. Sam didn't have to be big, he played so well; he wasn't small, though—I think he played linebacker at about 230 or 235.

The two best teams of my time were the Packers and the Colts. Baltimore, talent-wise, might even have been better than the Packers. They finally won the NFL championship in 1964.

It was really something, however, to go against the Packers in those days. It's always been a great rivalry between the Bears and Green Bay. But we had a good rivalry too with Baltimore in those days, when we went once a year to Memorial Stadium and they came once here to Chicago. In fact we had a lot of intense rivalries: Detroit, of course, then Minnesota became a rivalry.

I came back to the Bears in 1982. George Halas called me. I had written him a letter some years before and told him if the opportunity ever arose I would really appreciate at least talking about the possibility of coaching the Bears. And so he called me, and he asked if I would come in and have a talk. Actually, he didn't call me first; he called the Cowboys for permission to talk to me, and Tex Schramm, the president of the Cowboys, told me that I could. Then Halas called me at home one night and said, you do this, fly in, and come to my apartment. Don't tell anyone about it. So that's what I did.

We sat down and talked. It was very informal, at the kitchen table. At the time all the fair-haired guys were coming in, the new geniuses of football. I think Mr. Halas was trying to check me out to see if I was one of them, and so he asked me what my philosophy of football was. I kind of laughed, and I said, "You know I don't think that's important. First of all, my philosophy is the same as yours, and that's strictly to win. How we do it—we have our methods and we have our ideas, but if you're asking me am I going to go out and throw the ball all over the ballpark like it's a wounded duck, no, I'm going to play football and teach good, basic fundamentals."

Then he offered me a two-year contract, but I said I wouldn't take a two-year contract; it would have to be a three-year contract, period. I said two years wasn't enough. And it wouldn't have been. He said, "Fine," and gave me the other year. It was not a very lucrative contract, but it didn't matter. That was never important; the opportunity was what was important.

He gave me that opportunity, and I'm forever grateful. It's just a shame that he couldn't have stayed around to see all the good things that have happened to the Bears in the 1980s and now the nineties. But I think he knows they happened. I think he had an inkling they were going to happen. I really do. It's also a shame he didn't get a chance to see the '85 team, because it may have been as good a Bear team as there ever was.

In the beginning, when I first got out of playing the game, I wanted to stay with it, coaching. I managed to do that. But I knew it would be a while before I was ready to take on a head coaching job. In fact I never wanted to be head coach per se. I had a good job, assistant coach with the Dallas Cowboys, and that's a pretty secure job if you do your job. It was good because the Cowboys had won and were a very stable organization. I was working for Tom Landry and Tex Schramm, two people I loved and respected.

Everybody started talking about head coaching jobs when Dan Reeves, another of our assistants at Dallas at the time, got the Denver Broncos job.

The only job I ever wanted was the Bears job. Nobody was going to call me from New York or Atlanta or any of those kinds of teams. I was committed to the Bears type of football—the kind George Halas had fostered. Anybody can think what they want to think or write what they want to write—it was just meant to be. That's all there was. You can call it fate, whatever you want to call it, but that's how it was meant to be. I don't think if anybody ever wrote a script they would have written it with the sense of destiny I felt, beginning with my coming to Chicago in '61 and my travels and my return in '82 twenty years later.

The year 1985 was, of course, truly special. I thought we would be a pretty good football team. I thought we would be a team that would never knuckle under to anybody. I knew we were going to be tough. And then everything just came together.

We won most of the early games really with offense; our defense was kind of not sure yet. They were still getting their feet wet, and everybody had kind of picked on that defense. Other teams knew when we were blitzing and this and that, but then once the defense cranked it up it didn't matter if they knew or not, because nobody could stop them. As the season went along, our cornerbacks got more confidence, our people covered receivers like blankets—they had a lot of confidence. By the end of the year you could see from the other teams playing us that they didn't want any part of those guys, nor did they want any part of our defensive line or linebackers—Hampton, Dent, Perry, McMichael and Singletary, Marshall and Otis Wilson. Those guys were just awfully good. And they were brutal.

We just surged to the Super Bowl, and that, I tell you, is the best feeling there is. I mean of all the feelings I've ever had, to be the head coach of a Super Bowl-winning football team, that's the finest, because that's a total team effort. That's nothing I did, and it's nothing any one individual on a team did; it was a collective effort of everybody in the organization from top to bottom. There were so many people to thank, even people who were gone, like Jim Finks; he had helped put the pieces in place by his excellent draft picks. And Jerry Vainisi and Bill McGrane from the front office. It was a terrific organization from the top to the bottom. It seemed like everybody worked for a common goal that year, and that's what we're going to try to get back. That's such a hard thing to reestablish once you have done it, because people get caught up in the whole idea of why you win or how important they were in the scheme of things instead of realizing that they were just *part* of the reason, not the whole reason.

Of course the history-making thing would have been to beat Miami down there in 1985, but they just outcoached us, that's all. Don Shula did it—he outcoached us. Not that they outplayed us. Our guys were really playing hard; they just outcoached our ass. I'm willing to admit that, period.

Then, I think, if we hadn't lost that game, I'm not sure we would have gone all the way. I thought that regenerated everything, that just pissed everybody off: staff, players, everybody. And we went out and rededicated ourselves. When we hit the playoffs, we shut out two teams, just rolled over them. We hit, did everything right. We peaked at the right time. And we haven't done it since, although I believe we've had just as good a team.

We, of course, had Walter Payton that year. As a football player he was simply the best, the best I've ever seen as a complete player. I'm talking about the whole package—what you give to the game, what you take from the game, your attitude on and off the field, how you handle the media and the press, how you play the game. He played the game with great enthusiasm and fervor, and he was exceptional. Walter was a great runner, and he was also a great blocker. He did everything—he could have played defense if we'd put him over there, and he'd have played it pretty darn good.

Now we have to face the nineties. The chief goal I have is to see the organization come together again as it was in '85. I would like to see the Bears back in the Super Bowl one more time. That's what we're judged on—we're judged on winning. A professional in football is not judged on anything but the previous week's performance. You're as good as your last game, just like you're as good as your last time at bat in baseball. In 1989 we didn't do very well. We lost 10 out of our last 12 games after starting out as good as anybody, and that's pretty hard to take. That's not going to happen again. We used it to refuel the ball club, especially the veteran part of it, because it is a good team, a worthy team. We hope it sank in with some of those kids, but that's my job—to make it sink in, to make them understand what's at stake, what they are, in fact, capable of. In our sport we want to be able to say, "Hey, there was one time, one year, in the National Football League that we played for the very best there was—we were the world champions." Not too many people can say that. The significance when you wear that Super Bowl ring is something extraordinary. We're in a game today where the players make so damn much money that the conquest becomes like a side issue—it's not as important.

I think today we have to be careful not to lose sight of football as a great sport. I don't know that you can change it, because TV dictates when you play at night, in the morning, in the afternoon, Monday, Wednesday, Thursday, Saturday, Sunday.

I'm not saying that's necessarily wrong; the game has become very big and reaches tens of millions of people each week of the season, and everybody is entitled to his piece out of the game. Yet I still go back and say that our game, the game played in the National Football League, is a very good product, and I don't think there are a lot of reasons to be changing everything every year. We go in and we meet, and we try to change rules and make this or that happen. It's a good product; let's be careful we don't take what is good about the product and get rid of it. This game has been played for a long time—seventy-some years—and will be played for seventy more. We should not spend our time worrying about making the game shorter or speeding it up or that kind of bullshit. If it's a good game, it's a good game. Think of all the great individual games we've been fortunate to watch; think of the great performances, the great plays, the great team efforts—*that's* NFL football.

We have to be careful not to lose sight of the game itself and the glory connected with it.

Mike Ditka, Bear tight end (1961–66) and head coach (1982–present). For his playing career as the first of the great tight ends, Ditka was honored with induction into the Pro Football Hall of Fame in 1988. As head coach Ditka has taken the Bears to the playoffs six times and, of course, brought Chicago the NFL championship after the 1985 regular season with a triumph in Super Bowl XX.

Bad Loser

Dan Reeves, coach of the Denver Broncos (1981–present), often tells this story about coming to understand Mike Ditka, coach of the Chicago Bears (1982–present), when in 1968 Ditka, then a tight end, joined Reeves, a halfback, on the roster of the Dallas Cowboys:

"We were playing gin rummy one night, and after Ditka lost a couple of hands he picked up a chair and threw it across the room. All four legs stuck in the wall. All I could say was, 'God, this guy hates to lose.' "

Well, He Did Throw a Clipboard, But . . .

John Schulian, writing for the *Chicago Sun-Times* in 1982 under the headline "Hiring Ditka Would Be Madness":

Again and again, you are confronted with visions of him [Mike Ditka] throwing clipboards and cursing officials when he should be sending in the next play on offense or calling the next defense. He is, after all, a creature of brute force, the quintessential Midway monster, and such is not the stuff head coaches are made of. But if Ditka still wants to come back to Chicago, finding a position for him shouldn't be difficult. Even at his age, he would be a better tight end than any of the stiffs the Bears have there now.

Red Grange

Grantland Rice gave him the name the "Galloping Ghost." Damon Runyon said of him, "On the field he is the equal of three football players and a horse." Countless writers since have said he was to football what Babe Ruth was to baseball, Jack Dempsey to boxing. Certainly Harold "Red" Grange is a certified sports legend.

A three-time All-American at Illinois, Red Grange filled college football stadiums wherever he performed. Just how good the redhead was is forever preserved in the statistics of the 1924 Illinois–Michigan game. Before the game Fielding Yost, Michigan's famed coach, whose team was ranked number one in the nation that year, shrugged off Grange's talent: "All Grange can do is run," he said. That was true: against Michigan Red ran for 5 touchdowns, 4 of them in the first quarter. By the end of the game he had gained 402 yards on 21 carries. And to disprove Yost he also threw 6 pass completions, one of them for a touchdown, as Illinois annihilated top-ranked Michigan 39–14.

Under the tutelage of the game's first agent and one of its all-time masterful entrepreneurs, C. C. Pyle, Grange became a pro in 1925, signing with the Chicago Bears. The biggest name in football had defied the college mentors like

Amos Alonzo Stagg and his own coach Bob Zuppke, both of whom denounced with special vitriol the game that was played for money, and in so doing he gave it a boost in popularity and a sense of respectability that it never should have been denied in the first place.

Grange certainly reaped the spoils, splitting with Pyle gate receipts of about $250,000 from the 1925 Red Grange/ Chicago Bears tour and pocketing perhaps another $100,000 from endorsements, personal appearances, and motion picture contracts—all in an age when his fellow ballplayers were earning between $50 and $200 a game.

Pyle and Grange launched the first American Football League in 1926, with Red the drawing card for the New York Yankees. While with that team he injured his knee and would never again be the dazzling runner who had brought so many millions of people to their feet in both college and pro football stadiums.

George Halas lured Grange back into the game in 1929, and he played with the Bears through the 1934 season. He was, in the words of Halas, "the game's greatest runner until he hurt his knee and after that the game's best defensive back."

Something of what Red Grange was to football can be gleaned from the headline in a Chicago newspaper when his kid brother, Gardie, an end for the Bears, caught a game-winning touchdown in 1931: "Red Grange's Brother Beats Giants on Pass."

Red Grange, one of sports' all-time great legends, died January 28, 1991.

I was in about the seventh grade when I first started to play football. It was in Wheaton, Illinois, a little town about twenty-five miles west of Chicago. Now it really wasn't football that we played; it was a game like it. We called it "Run, sheep, run." There would be two or three guys in the middle of a field, who were to be the tacklers, and a goal at either end; usually the goals were sidewalks. All the rest of us would line up at one goal and on a signal run to the other. If you were tackled, you would have to stay out in the middle and become a tackler. It would go until the last player was tackled. I used to get my pants and socks torn up all the time, and of course my folks were not fond of the game, for legitimate reasons, but that was where I first got a taste of running and tackling, and I found I really liked it.

One of my first nicknames was the "Wheaton Iceman." The reason I got it was because every summer while I was in school I used to deliver ice. In those days folks didn't have electric refrigerators. The ice truck would come by and deliver ice. Practically every day I'd carry these big blocks of ice in from the truck to people's houses. I started in my sophomore year of high school, mainly because I needed the money. Most of the kids around there worked in the summer. I carried blocks of ice up to maybe a hundred pounds. What it did, without my knowing it, was to develop my leg muscles. I mean I'd make about fifty calls a day on an average, up and down stairs with these huge blocks of ice, and it built my legs up.

It was in high school that I played football in an organized way for the first time. In my first year I played right end. The way it happened was pretty simple. I went out for the team as a freshman, and on the first day our coach called all the new kids together and asked them what they played. He said to me, "Kid, what do you want to play?"

And I said, "Well, what do you need?"

"We've got ten men back from last year," he told me. "All we need is a right end."

"Well, I'm a right end," I said, and that was it. I made it as a starter at that position.

The next year we lost most of our backfield, and the coach felt I could run, so he moved me [to halfback]. And I played halfback ever since.

It was Charlie Pyle, however, who got me to join the pros. His initials were C.C., which some writer later said stood for "Cash and Carry." But Charlie was the most impressive man I ever met in my life, and I've met millions of people, presidents and everything else.

Charlie Pyle stood about 6'1" and weighed maybe 190 pounds. He had been an excellent boxer, had taken it up as a kid, and he could take care of himself, believe me. At the same time, he was a very dapper guy, sort of a peacock strutting in spats and carrying a cane, the most immaculate dresser I've ever seen. I don't think he ever wore anything twice, and he would go the barbershop at least a couple of times a week. He was a real, true dandy.

Charlie was in the theater business. He owned three movie houses, two of them in Champaign and another over in Kokomo, Indiana. I met him at the Virginia Theater in Champaign one night in 1925 when I was a senior. An usher came to my seat and said, "Mr. Pyle would like to see you in his office." Well, I'd heard of him, and I knew he was the one who gave out free tickets to his theater to those of us on the football team, so I went up to his office with the usher. When I opened the door, the first thing he said to me, before I could even sit down, was "Red, how'd you like to make $100,000?" I thought he was crazy. That was like saying a million today. But I said naturally I would—who wouldn't?

Then he said, "Well, I've got an idea. Sit down." And he explained it to me. He wanted me to join up with a pro team, and we would make a tour of the country after the regular pro season. He said we would go to cities where they had pro teams and play them, as well as to others where they never got to see pro football. He thought the Chicago Bears would be the ideal team to go with and said if I were truly interested in the scheme he would work it out with them. He would be my personal manager, handle all the financial and promotional things for me. He was like the agents of today, but he was also the promoter of the tour. Charlie ran the whole thing.

As it turned out, there were two tours. The first went out east to places like New York, Boston, and Washington; the second went from Florida to California.

It wasn't all that easy, though. Pro football was pretty questionable in those days. Most of the college coaches and a lot of the sportswriters were very down on it. "Football isn't meant to be played for money," Zup [Bob Zuppke, Grange's coach at Illinois] said to me.

On the other hand, nobody seemed to mind that baseball players made money by playing the game. So I told Zup, "You get paid for coaching it. Why should it be wrong for me to get paid for playing it?" No matter what, he was still opposed to it, and we didn't really talk to each other for a number of years after I agreed to play with the pros. That's just the way it was in those days. College football would draw seventy or eighty thousand to a game, but the pros might not get more than four or five thousand. It was a different time altogether.

Needless to say, I went with Charlie Pyle and the Bears. I played my last game in Columbus, Ohio, against Ohio State. It was kind of a madhouse, because there were all these rumors that I was going to go pro right after it. I had to sneak out of the hotel there, down the fire escape, and I got a cab and went to the railroad station. Then I went to Chicago and checked into the Belmont Hotel under an assumed name. Charlie was over at another hotel setting up the deal with George Halas and Dutch Sternaman, the two owners of the Bears. The next day I signed the contract. I signed first with Charlie, making him my manager, and then we both signed the deal with the Bears. You see, I couldn't sign anything before that, not while I was playing college ball. A lot of people and a good number of newspaper writers said that I had signed a contract beforehand, but that just wasn't true. It made a good story, I guess. But that day in Chicago was the first time I met Halas or Sternaman. I'd known of them, of course; in fact they had gone to Illinois themselves, about five or six years ahead of me.

The first game I played for the Bears was on Thanksgiving Day in 1925, against the Chicago Cardinals. It wasn't part of the tours, just a regular-season game. My first impression was how much bigger the pro players were. A college lineman ordinarily weighed only about 190 pounds back then. The pros were all 230 or 240. It was a big difference.

After that, a week or two later, we went on our first tour. Out in New York we played the Giants at the Polo Grounds, and more than seventy thousand were in the stadium. There were hundreds of others up on Coogan's Bluff watching it too. That was the biggest crowd ever to attend a professional football game up to that time. I believe the proceeds that the Giants got

were enough to save the team. You see, the Giants had lost a lot
of money that year. It was their first year in the NFL, and Tim
Mara, who owned them, dropped plenty until that game.

I have another memory of that game in New York. We were
staying at the Astor Hotel over on Times Square. Babe Ruth,
who was at the height of his prestige and glory, called on me
during the two or three days I was there. I was very flattered
that he would take the time and effort. I remember he said to
me, "Kid, I'll give you a little bit of advice. Don't believe
anything they write about you, good or bad. And further, get
the dough while the getting is good, but don't break you heart
trying to get it. And don't pick up too many checks!" He told me
that, but he was a guy who would spend money right and left.
What a guy to give that kind of advice.

On the second tour we went out to California. That's the
first time real pro football was ever played in the West. I don't
think they'd ever gone west of Rock Island, Illinois, before that.
We met all kinds of people out there: the Hearst family (at their
fabulous estate San Simeon), the Wrigleys on Catalina Island,
the Hollywood stars like Douglas Fairbanks and Harold Lloyd.
They were all good football fans too.

Charlie Pyle arranged for me to make a couple of movies
out there as well. The first was called *One Minute to Play.* It was
about a halfback who was ineligible to play in the big game of
the year. Then, in the last few minutes, it is learned that he
really is eligible, that what caused the ineligibility was just
something cooked up by gamblers to keep him out of the game.
And naturally, as Hollywood would have it, he goes out and wins
the game in the last minute.

That was the movie where Charlie Pyle proved his show-
manship. It was being made in June in Hollywood. For the major
scene they needed a crowd of about three thousand to fill the
stadium to make the big game look realistic. And the game was
supposed to be the last one of the season in the Midwest. Well,
it was about a hundred degrees in Hollywood in June, hardly a
typical November day in Michigan or such. Also they would have
to pay extras $15 or $20 for a day's work—that's $45,000 or
$50,000 in salaries just to produce a crowd. So Charlie came up
with this scheme. He got hold of Wildcat Wilson, an All-Ameri-

can from out there and a very popular football player in California. Between the two they rounded up enough players for a football game. I was to captain one team and Wilson the other. Then Charlie took out an ad in the Los Angeles papers to announce this big exhibition game. In it he said that everyone who wore a coat and hat would be let in free. Well, more than three thousand showed up, and it was about a hundred degrees, but they were there in coats and hats and scarves, perspiring through four quarters. Charlie got it all for the price of a couple of ads, and I think he paid each of the players $25.

The other movies I made were *Racing Romeo*—that was in 1927—and two years later there was *Galloping Ghost*. Pyle arranged for all of it, engineered the deals. He also handled all the premium deals. There was a Red Grange candy bar, autographed footballs, a Red Grange doll, clothes, even a ginger ale and a yeast foam malted milk [named for Grange].

Grantland Rice was with us for a while on the tours. He was a great writer, not just on football but on all sports in those days. He was known and read all over the country. I had a lot of respect for him as a sportswriter. Damon Runyon was there too. And Westbrook Pegler. I knew Pegler very well in those days. He was a great guy personally, but he was brutal when he wrote. As he used to say, nobody would read him if he didn't tear things down. That was his style. He never wrote a good thing about anyone, I don't think. When somebody would complain about what he wrote about him, Pegler would just say, "Hell, don't worry about it, another million people know your name every time I tear you down." He did have a tremendous following around the country.

The Bears had a wonderful team at the time I joined them. Little Joey Sternaman was the quarterback, and there was never a better one than him. He could run with the ball, he was smart, he could pass, he could kick. Laurie Walquist was the other halfback, and he had played at Illinois before too and was very good. But the best, the very best player I ever encountered, was one I played with later on the Bears, Bronko Nagurski. We played in the same backfield for about five years. Bronk was big, about 240 pounds, and fast. He could do everything on a football field. And he had respect for all his fellow players. If he gained some yards running, he'd pat his blockers on the back. Everybody liked to play with Bronk, on his side; I'm not sure they liked to play against him, though.

On the other side of the fence there were players like Ernie Nevers, one of the finest I ever played against. Ernie came out of Stanford University and played with the Chicago Cardinals against us. Nevers was probably the first and best of the triple-threat backs. He could run, kick, and pass. He played out of the double wingback offense, and he was a star through and through. Guys like Nevers and Nagurski would have played the game for nothing. They were insulted if they were taken out of a game, even if it was just for a few minutes or because of an injury.

Another great back of that time who should also be remembered was Paddy Driscoll. He played with the Cardinals and then with me at the Bears. Paddy was a runner, a passer, and a great dropkicker. He could drop-kick it through the uprights anywhere from the 50-yard line in. And he was a good defensive player as well.

All these guys, who were the big stars of the day, could also block and tackle. In my time they stressed blocking and tackling. It was the first line of business, and you had to do it well if you were going to be any good at the game. Because you played sixty minutes, you had to master both. You learned those things in high school then. And when I'm asked who were the hardest tacklers I ran up against, my answer is all of them, because I can't remember anybody who stuck around the pros who wasn't a hard tackler. I've got the bumps and pains to prove it.

And certainly one of the most memorable characters of the time as well as one of the finest players was Johnny Blood. I ordinarily played against him, but we played together and roomed together a couple of times too. After the regular season was over, we used to barnstorm in those days, and Johnny and I did it together. Johnny was a great pass receiver, and there was never any better runner in the open field than Johnny. Quick as a rabbit. He was a character, though, but a likable one. Money was never an objective for him. He didn't care about it and usually blew it as fast as he got it. I remember one time a girl asked him for an autograph after a game, and he said, "Sure," then cut himself on the wrist, took her pencil, and signed her program in blood. It took a couple of stitches to close up his wrist afterwards. Johnny Blood was also one of the smartest persons I ever met. He could talk with anybody about literature and poetry, and he could recite Shakespeare and practically every poet who ever lived. He liked that almost as much as he did raising a little hell.

George Halas was our player/coach, and he was certainly a tough cookie. But if you wanted to play, wanted to work, he'd go to hell for you. There was no fooling around with George. If football was anybody's life, it was his. You worked, gave your all, and he would give you anything he had; if you didn't, he didn't want you around. But he built the Bears. When I joined them, George would lug equipment around, write the press releases, sell tickets, then run across the road and buy tape and then help our trainer, Andy Lotshaw, tape the other players' ankles.

I remember an incident that happened in 1934 that George was a part of that kind of tells you what he was like. It involved Johnny Sisk, one of our backs, who they called "Big Train." Sisk didn't like to practice and would complain about injuries in order to get out of it. But he was always ready to go on game days. Johnny came out this one day and told Halas he couldn't practice because he'd hurt his knee in the game the previous Sunday. He hobbled around to show Halas. Well, George watched him limp around for a little while and then told him to go sit in the stands until practice was over. An hour or two later, after the practice session, everyone went into the dressing room to shower. Except George. A little later Sisk went out to get into his new car. Halas was out there watching him limp along. Well, when Johnny started up his car, a smoke bomb exploded. Naturally it scared hell out of him, and he jumped out of the car and came flying back to the clubhouse—he was a sprinter, and he was really moving. George just looked at him and said, "OK, John, six laps."

Originally I had signed with the Bears only for the two tours. I hadn't given much thought to playing for them after that. My destiny, so to speak, was in Charlie Pyle's hands in 1925. So when it was all over, I went with the AFL, the new pro league. Charlie started that league himself, got it all organized. I signed with the team in New York, the Yankees, which played in Yankee Stadium. There were teams in many cities.

It was while I was playing in New York that I hurt my knee. The Yankees became part of the NFL in 1927, and we were playing in a game against, of all teams, the Chicago Bears at Wrigley Field. I had my cleat dug into the ground, and it was kind of a wet day, and somebody fell over my knee. It was nothing deliberate, just one of those things. I was hit from the side by somebody, and boom, out went the knee. Knees and shoulders, those are the two places a ballplayer got hurt the most seriously in those days. I got it in both places and have the aches to prove it. But the knee injury that day in Chicago, it was by far the worst.

After that injury I came back, but I could never do again what I'd been able to before. I was just an ordinary back after that; the moves were gone forever. I wore a brace with steel hinges on both sides. The injury not only slowed me down, but I couldn't make the turns anymore. In other words I became a straight runner, one who doesn't try to get away from tacklers but instead just opts to run into them. And even if a player's knee gets well, he never gets well up in the head. He always protects it. I know I did. And as a result you are never the same runner again.

I was out of football for a year after the injury. I thought I'd never play again. But George Halas talked to me about it. "Why don't you get yourself up and in shape and give it a try again?" he asked. I decided I would, and it worked out all right. I guess I was about 70 percent of the football player I'd been, but I worked on playing defense, and that became a strong point with me. The secret of offense is pulling the defense out of position, and I worked hard so that never, or at least seldom, would that happen to me. I stayed where I was supposed to, and I was a good tackler. I played for the Bears for six years after my knee went out, and we did pretty well, won a couple of championships.

In 1934 I decided it was finally time to get out of the game.

Actually for a year I knew it was time. Every football player knows when his time is up. It was during a game against the New York Giants that year when I took a handoff and there was a big hole. I got into the open field, but I was caught from behind by a lineman. I realized before I'd reached midfield that I was through. My legs kept getting heavier and heavier. I knew I'd never reach the end zone, but I knew I'd reached the end.

So, I went to George Halas and told him, "This is my last year," and that was it. I stayed around with the Bears for three years as an assistant coach, but I didn't really like that role and was glad to get out of it. George and I parted good friends, just like we'd always been since 1925, when we first met in that hotel in Chicago with Charlie Pyle.

I did stay with the game as an announcer and commentator for ten years, though, and I did enjoy that. I never lost my desire to watch the game. I worked with Bob Elson in Chicago for a long time on radio. And I was with Lindsay Nelson on national television. I had my own show after the Bear games in Chicago.

All in all it was a great sport to be involved with. I hope the players today get as much out of it as I did.

Meeting the President

The Bears' 1925 whirlwind exhibition tour of the United States, which featured Red Grange, the most famous name in football, put professional sport on the proverbial map. Certainly a highlight of that odyssey occurred in the nation's capital. As the Galloping Ghost himself tells it:

"We went to Washington. . . . The senator from Illinois, McKinley I believe it was, arranged for us to meet the president, Calvin Coolidge. We were taken in, and I was there with George Halas. The senator introduced me as 'Red Grange, who plays with the Bears.'

"Coolidge shook my hand and said, 'Nice to meet you, young man. I've always liked animal acts.' "

Kicking to Grange

When Red Grange made his pro football debut on Thanksgiving Day in 1925, the Bears were playing their intracity rival, the Chicago Cardinals, and the game ended in a scoreless tie. Grange not only was held to 36 yards rushing but also was unable to exercise one of his other notorious threats, returning punts.

The Cardinals' triple-threat tailback Paddy Driscoll, who would later play for the Bears (1926–29), punted many times that day, but he always kept it away from Grange, kicking either to Joey Sternaman or out of bounds. "Kicking to Grange," Driscoll said before the game, "is like grooving one to Babe Ruth."

After the game was over and Grange had made his uneventful debut, Driscoll stopped at the seats behind the Cardinal bench to talk to his wife. As the other players headed for the locker rooms, there was a lot of booing. "I hate to hear the fans boo a young man like Grange," Driscoll said. "It wasn't his fault he couldn't break one today."

"Don't feel sorry for Grange," his wife said. "It's you they're booing."

Charter member of the Pro Football Hall of Fame, halfback Red Grange played for the Bears in 1925 and was the feature of the two barnstorming tours of the country the Bears made after that year's regular season. Grange also starred for the Bears from 1929 through 1934.

1933 Championship Game

The first in NFL history
At Chicago, Wrigley Field, December 17, 1933

New York Giants		Chicago Bears
Red Badgro	LE	Bill Hewitt
Len Grant	LT	Link Lyman
Butch Gibson	LG	Jules Carlson
Mel Hein	C	Ookie Miller
Pottsville Jones	RG	Joe Kopcha
Steve Owen	RT	George Musso
Ray Flaherty	RE	Bill Karr
Harry Newman	QB	Carl Brumbaugh
Ken Strong	LH	Keith Molesworth
Dale Burnett	RH	Gene Ronzani
Bo Molenda	FB	Bronko Nagurski
Steve Owen	Coach	George Halas

Giants	0	7	7	7	—	21
Bears	3	3	10	7	—	23

Touchdowns—Giants: Red Badgro, Max Krause, Ken Strong; **Bears:** Bill Karr (2)
Field Goals—Bears: Jack Manders (3)
PATs—Giants: Ken Strong (3); **Bears:** Jack Manders, Carl Brumbaugh

Jim McMahon

In 1982 Jim McMahon gained the distinction of becoming the first quarterback the Bears had drafted in the first round since they selected Bob Williams of Notre Dame back in 1951. The Bears were looking for a quarterback who could take them to the NFL championship game, a contest they had not entered in almost two decades, not since the world championship of 1963.

McMahon came with the credentials: a consensus All-American from the volatile offense of Brigham Young and the holder of 56 NCAA Division I records for passing and total offense.

He had little trouble snatching the starting job at quarterback, taking over in the first game after the NFL players' strike of '82 and introducing Chicago Bear fans to a passing game they had not seen in years. McMahon was named NFC Rookie of the Year by the UPI and was awarded the Bears' Brian Piccolo Award by his teammates.

Jim McMahon had his dazzling moments on the field as well as a raft of injuries and controversies and a quarterback productive output that had not been seen in Chicago since Hall of Famer Sid Luckman hung up his cleats in 1950. In his

seven years with the Bears, McMahon swirled through Chicago like a twister across the Kansas plains. There was never
a dull moment.

At the end of his career with the Bears, McMahon had
posted an overall record as a starter of 49–17, including the
unforgettable triumph in Super Bowl XX. His best single
season was that championship year, 1985, when he completed 178 of 313 passes for 2,392 yards and 15 touchdowns.
His most productive days were November 1, 1987, when he
passed for 311 yards against the Denver Broncos, and a week
later, when he completed 23 passes against the Tampa Bay
Buccaneers, both career highs.

McMahon has the highest career quarterback rating
(80.4) in Bear history and also holds the club record for
completion percentage (57.8 percent). He stands second
only to Sid Luckman in the team record books for number
of pass completions and pass attempts and third in touchdown passes after Luckman and Bill Wade.

Before leaving for the Philadelphia Eagles after the 1988
season, McMahon racked up totals of 874 completions on
1,513 attempts, 11,203 yards gained passing, and 67 touchdowns against 56 interceptions. And he rushed for a total of
1,284 yards (5.4-yard average).

I was about ten years old when I first started to play organized football. We had a Little League program out in San
Jose, California. I remember the first day of practice; the
coach had everybody line up on the line, and whoever threw the
football the farthest was the quarterback. I threw it the farthest,
and that's how I became a quarterback.

After I played two years of high school ball in California,
my family moved to Roy, Utah, and I finished up playing the last
two years there. If I'd stayed in California, I would probably have
been more highly recruited. As it was, I took a look at the Utah
schools and Nebraska, Oklahoma State, Las Vegas. But I wanted
to play baseball in college too, and Brigham Young had a good
baseball program. That and the fact it was close to home where

my parents could continue to watch me play were the biggest reasons I went to BYU.

BYU wasn't what I thought college life was going to be like. If you're not a Mormon there, you hardly exist as far as they're concerned. I knew a lot of people who went there and didn't stay more than a year. They just couldn't handle the constant pressure of the religion thing: every class began with a prayer, and you had to take fourteen credit hours of the Mormon religion. And there weren't a whole lot of things a guy could do for social life if he didn't believe in what they believe in.

The school there was about 98 percent Mormon, but as far as the athletic teams—football and baseball, the two I played—they were made up mostly of non-Mormons. And I didn't have any problems with the guys on the team or the coaching staff for that matter.

Our head coach was LaVell Edwards, who had been there since 1972 and became one of the winningest coaches in college football. I got along with him all right, although there were times when we had our differences. There were people there who were always saying something that got back to him—it seemed every Monday that I came back to school somebody had said I was at a party somewhere in Roy or Provo, here or there, or I did this or that. The majority of it wasn't true.

At BYU all the plays were sent in from the sideline, but I had a lot of freedom to change plays there, and I did it quite often. We did have a great offensive system out there under Edwards, and we became known for it, but in the early years our football program didn't really get much respect because they didn't consider our conference [Western Athletic Conference] all that good—which I think was ridiculous. In my first two years there Arizona and Arizona State were in our conference before they moved to the PAC-10. It wasn't until 1984, when BYU won the NCAA national championship, that the program got the recognition it deserved. When I was there, we got little respect, but I contend the BYU team that won the NCAA title in '84 couldn't have touched some of the teams we had when I was there.

When the Bears drafted me in 1982, my happiest feeling at

first was that I wasn't going with the Colts, who were still in Baltimore. They had the pick just before the Bears that year, and all indications I got prior to the draft were that the Colts were going to take me. My agent at the time, Jerry Argovitz, had a player with the Colts, Curtis Dickey, a running back, and he was having some hellish contract problems. Argovitz basically told them, "Don't draft McMahon, because you're never going to sign him." So they passed on me and took Art Schlichter instead.

After I was drafted by the Bears, they brought me to Chicago with all the hoopla to meet everybody—the organization people, the press, and the other media. I don't remember exactly when it was that I first met George Halas—sometime later during contract negotiations. I think he probably wasn't too happy with me or my agent around that time. But when I did meet him, he basically told me that I was too small, I had a bad arm, a bad knee, that I couldn't see very well, and I ought to just go to Canada, because I wouldn't make it in the NFL. If I got $200 a game, I'd be overpaid.

At any rate, he offered me a contract, which was horseshit. That year the NFL had some kind of a July deadline that they'd never had before or since. If you didn't sign before the deadline, you couldn't play. That was also the first year of the USFL. So I took the Bears' contract, threw it back, and said, "I'm not signing this."

I went and talked to George Allen, the coach of the Chicago Blitz in the USFL, and he offered me a contract verbally. I told him, "Look, I've got two days to make a decision. You put it in writing, and I'll play for the Blitz." He went back to the owners, and I guess nothing ever got done.

So I felt I was stuck, and I ended up signing with the Bears. Later I found out that two of the top draft picks who came out the same year, Marcus Allen, who went with the Raiders, and Darrin Nelson, who went with the Vikings, hadn't signed by the July deadline but still got to play and sign later on. So it kind of pissed me off.

I remember too, when I did sign the contract, Argovitz and I gave them a piece of paper that said we reserved the right to sue the Bears because I was signing under duress. And that, I think, got both Halas and Jim Finks pretty pissed off themselves.

Halas said it was the most money he'd ever offered to anybody, but it was a ridiculous contract. As an agent Argovitz had about eleven people that year, and I was the highest pick. I think he had six or seven in the first round and a couple more in the second round. And all those guys, even the ones in the second round, got more money than I did. So I wasn't real happy with the contract. I was stuck with it, is the way I felt.

Training camp came up pretty suddenly after I signed. I hadn't thought I was going to be with the Bears—I felt I was going to end up with the Blitz, and therefore I'd have a couple more months to get in shape. But then all the stuff about the deadline hit the fan, and I signed and went to camp, and I wasn't in very good shape.

The first thing we had to do was a mile-and-a-half run, and I still remember all the press sitting up in the stands watching us. We only had to run it in twelve minutes, which ordinarily would have been a breeze, but I was never a distance guy anyway. We had to run two miles in college, but I usually never showed up for those. Anyway, it was about ninety degrees and 90 percent humidity that day, and after the second lap I just was delirious. I didn't even know where I was. The only guy I beat was Noah Jackson [a guard], who went about 275 pounds. And I beat him by only a couple of seconds.

Ditka was standing there by the track, and every time I passed him I could hear him mumbling something about "That's what you get for playing golf all summer" and things like that. So it wasn't a very good opening day for me.

Once I got into it at the Bears, I was kind of disappointed, because I was used to playing a wide-open type of offense. The stuff we had in Chicago was just so basic. Here we were in pro football, and everything was so elementary it was scary. But I think a lot of it had to do with the personnel we had at the time. Walter Payton had been there for six or seven years before I came, and he was *the offense*. For a long time they hadn't had a quarterback who thought for himself when he was on the field.

Whatever the play that was called from the sideline, that was the play that was run.

I remember it was the third game of the season my rookie year, my first start, just after the players' strike of '82 ended. I changed a play at the line of scrimmage. We were very predictable then. It was third down and eight, and the play came in for a sweep to the right. Their whole defense shifted, knowing we were going to run the sweep to the right. So I just audibled for a simple run play away from it. When I did, Noah Jackson, our left guard, kind of looked back over his shoulder at me, very surprised, and said, "What?"

I said, "Just block somebody; we're coming at you."

Well, we got 9 yards and a first down. Back in the huddle Jackson said to me, "Youngster, do you have any more surprises for me?"

I told him, "Hey, just keep your ears open from now on, and you might hear anything."

I was so used to changing plays that it was just natural for me. I think it is a quarterback's job to find a weakness in the defense and exploit it. But the other Bears were surprised when I did it. I guess they didn't have anybody there before who would change plays like that.

I got along well with the offense from the start. Kenny Margerum, one of the wide receivers, who had come up the year before, was a good friend of mine. He'd played at Stanford, and we had played together on a couple of all-star teams while we were in college. Kenny was friends with all the guys on offense, like Keith Van Horne, Jay Hilgenberg, Jeff Fisher, Danny Neal. Neal was the center and kind of the elder statesman of the offensive line at the time. This was his eighth season, I believe. I got in pretty good right off the bat because I knew Kenny, and he was friends with all the others. Neal even took me aside later and said to keep doing what I was doing, that they hadn't had somebody who really took charge since he'd been there. "Just keep it up," he said.

It was Mike Ditka's first year as head coach too. I could tell right off that he was the type of coach who truly wanted to win and also really understood the game. But I think he had more of a tight end's perspective of offense than a quarterback's, and I think that was evident in his play calling.

I also felt he wanted me to play from day one because the guys we had, Bob Avellini and Vince Evans, had been there for years and really hadn't done much. But I didn't have a very good training camp. I was having problems picking up the language of calling plays. From Little League until I got to the Bears, even numbers in play calling were always to the right; with the Bears they were to the left, and it took me a while to adjust to that.

I didn't deserve to start opening day, and I didn't. Avellini did, and Evans came in later, when he wasn't accomplishing anything. Then Evans started the next game, but he couldn't get anything going, and so I played the second half. Then the strike came, and when it was over I got the nod to start. I started the rest of the games that year.

That first game got off to a very bad start for me. We were playing the Lions at Soldier Field, and two of my first three passes were intercepted, and one was run back for a touchdown. I thought for sure I was going to get the hook, but I didn't. I was really glad Ditka stayed with me, and it did finally work out. Near the end of the game I hit our tight end, Emery Moorehead, down the middle for a big gainer that got us to the 3-yard line, where we kicked a field goal to win the game, 20-17.

The most impressive player at the Bears was, without a doubt, Walter Payton. He was great. I got along well with him my whole career with the Bears. He was class. As time went on, I think it was a relief to him to know that I was not just going to keep him running all the time, getting him beat up play after play. I would change plays to ease things up. Some of the pressure was finally taken off him because we started throwing the football more and using him more out of the backfield rather than having him get his head beat in time after time running the football. I think we might have added a few years to his career when I got there because we didn't have to run him so much anymore. At the same time, I think he could probably still play in the league today, the kind of shape he keeps himself in.

That's what always intrigued me about Walter: the tremendous shape he was always in. He missed only one game in thirteen years, and when you consider the work he did on the field during all those years—it speaks for itself. He was just a tremendous player, took that kind of pounding year in and year out, and was ready to go every week.

I was not so durable. The first major injury I got was in a game against Denver in the second game of the season in 1984. I broke my hand and bruised my back on the same play. That's when I really got the first taste of the trainers and the doctors there. I came off the field, and my back hurt so bad that I didn't really notice my hand; but finally I looked down and saw this big knot on it and realized it hurt just to move my fingers. They looked at it and said it was probably just a bruise. Eventually, however, they took me to the hospital toward the end of the game for an x-ray and found it was in fact broken. And it was my throwing hand. They didn't cast it—just put a splint on it and told me to be sure not to tell anybody it was broken. I thought, why, but what's the big deal. But that night I was in so much pain from it I went to a hospital and got it casted. When I came to practice the next day, the trainer kept asking me why I had the cast on. "Because the damn thing's broken," I said. I left the cast on until Friday and then took it off to see if I could practice. I got a shot of Novocain, which numbed it, and I went out to practice and threw the ball OK. Then I put the cast back on until Sunday, took it off, got a shot of Novocain, and played. I did that for seven weeks, until I got a worse injury that put me out for the rest of the season.

It was in the tenth game of the season against the Los Angeles Raiders. It was on a third down, and I took off out of the pocket running. I got hit from behind and got kind of turned around. I was trying to make a move on the guy in front of me when the guy behind me caught up and turned me around. The doctor said later that what he thought happened was when the guy turned me around my kidney came out from under the rib cage and was exposed, and it got hit solid with a guy's helmet. I was sandwiched, and the ribs just cut into the kidney in four or five places and tore the bottom part of it off.

It hurt like hell. I've blown my shoulders out and my knees, but I never felt anything like that. I didn't really know what I was doing, and I got up and kept playing. There were about two minutes left to play in the half. I audibled a deep pass, but I guess Willie [Gault] didn't hear the audible, because he was nowhere in sight where I threw the ball. It was intercepted. He probably couldn't hear the audible, because I wasn't talking very loud and was having a helluva time breathing.

When I went in at halftime, I told the doc, "I can't breathe." I said, "I got hit in the kidney." He said, "It's probably just a bruise." I went over to Steve Fuller, my backup at the time, and told him to make sure he was ready to play because I didn't know how much farther I could go. I went back out for the second half, called one play, and the guys in the huddle told me to get out of there. They knew there was something very wrong because I could barely talk to them.

So I went to the sideline and sat there for a couple of minutes. Then I went into the locker room and into the bathroom because I felt I had to go and nothing but blood came out. Our weight coach, Clyde Emrich, was in there with me. And he said, "I gotta go get an ambulance."

Instead of just going to the ambulance right away, I took a shower, took my time, because I knew if I went to the hospital I wouldn't shower for a week.

By the time I got to the hospital I was pretty delirious, yelling at everybody and telling them to give me something for the pain, but they couldn't until they diagnosed what exactly was wrong with me. At first I think they thought it was a broken rib that punctured a lung, because I couldn't breathe. I kept telling them it was my kidney. I guess what was happening was that the internal bleeding was putting pressure on my lungs, and that's why I was having trouble breathing. By about nine o'clock that night they finally figured out what it was: a lacerated kidney.

Then they put me on morphine, and I was just drugged out for about ten days. I remember the doctor coming in that night while I was still bleeding fairly heavily to tell me they were going to give me a transfusion because they were going to have to operate and take the kidney out. I was at least aware enough to know what that meant. If they did that, my career would have been over. You can't play with just one kidney; they won't insure you. I begged the doctor to give me another day, and he did, and the bleeding subsided. And that was it. I had to rest for a couple of months and made a full recovery.

The next year was the one to remember, 1985. I think the third game, that Thursday night one up in Minnesota, was the milestone of the season. I think we knew after that we were on our way and nobody was going to stop us. We showed we could turn it around if we had to. We had won our first two games of the season easily, beating Tampa Bay and the Patriots, but the Vikings were always tough up there in the Metrodome, and everybody knew it.

I'd been in the hospital in traction a couple of days that week because of a back injury, and I didn't get out to practice until Wednesday, the day before the game. When I got out there, I just kind of stood around, because they didn't want me doing anything. Well, the ABC-TV guys were there, including Joe Namath, who had always been an idol of mine. I went up and sat in the bleachers with him, talking, and I guess Ditka got pretty upset because I wasn't watching the practice. I knew what the hell we were doing, I knew the game plan, but he was pissed anyway.

At the same time I had a leg infection in my calf. I'd gotten a turf burn, and it got infected and was swollen. On the plane up to Minneapolis, Ditka came over and told me I wasn't going to play.

So when they had the team meeting up in Minnesota, I stayed in my hotel room and kept my leg elevated, which I was supposed to do. But I got a call from one of the coaches, and he said, "Get your butt down here. Ditka's mad as hell you aren't here." I went down to the meeting, and Ditka chewed me out. I'd figured, Why be at the meeting if I'm not playing and my leg's infected and I'm supposed to keep it elevated? It was just one of those points Ditka and I didn't see eye to eye on.

Before the game I got to the locker room early like I always do and got taped. I went through pretty much my normal pregame routine, and we went out for warm-ups, and I was throwing the ball well, feeling OK. So I went up to Ditka and started to say something. He raised his hand in front of me, "Don't even say it," he said. "You're not going to play."

I said, "Well, I just wanted to let you know I'm ready if you need me." He nodded, that's all, but I think he was glad I came up to him with that.

The first half didn't go all that well, and the start of the second wasn't any better. We were losing 17-9, and you could sense it on the sideline, the looks on the guys' faces—this could be our toughest competition in the NFC Central [the Vikings were 2-0-0 at the time too], and we were on national television at the same time, and we just didn't seem to have it, couldn't get anything going.

So I was in Ditka's ear most of the time on the sideline about putting me in. Steve wasn't playing all that bad; it's just that the team wasn't getting anything done. We needed a spark, a change. Finally Ditka looked over at me and said, "Get your ass in there and throw a screen pass."

So I called a screen pass. But as I was dropping back I stumbled. They were blitzing, and I saw the linebackers coming as I was regaining my balance. What I also saw suddenly was Willie [Gault] running free down the middle, so I just unloaded it to him, and it was a 70-yard touchdown. We were shocked ourselves, not to mention all the Viking fans in the stadium. I got back to the sideline, and Ditka said, "What did you call?" I told him I called a screen pass. And he said, "Why did you throw it to Willie?"

"Because he was open," I said.

Well, that gave us the spark. The defense intercepted a pass for us, and we scored again on our first play. We were on their 25-yard line. It was a bootleg, and my first two receivers were covered. Usually, on that play, you know you're going to have either the running back in the flat or the tight end crossing, but neither of those guys was open. Then I just caught Dennis [McKinnon] getting behind somebody in the end zone and threw it to him, and he grabbed it, and suddenly we'd gone from losing 17-9 to winning 23-17.

The defense held again, and we got the ball back. We just missed on an option screen—on that I could either throw the ball deep or toss it out to the screen back. I threw deep but missed Willie [Gault]. But then Dennis McKinnon got loose, and we teamed on a 43-yarder and another touchdown and put the game away. The final was 33-24. It wasn't only a decisive game; it was just a lot of fun for all of us.

Without a doubt we had the most talented team in the league that year on both sides of the football. Our defense played great. They got a lot of attention and a lot of headlines, deservedly, but I think our offense got overlooked. That year we were the highest-scoring team in the NFC [456 points, 28.5 per game average]. We had the most yards gained in a season and the most first downs in all Bear history that year. I think we had the best time percentage holding the ball in the entire league.

I had a lot of good receivers on that team. Everybody knew they were a potential receiver on every play. The opposing defense always dictates who you throw the ball to. I told them [the Bear receivers], "I don't care what pass is called, or if we don't throw to you in practice all week before the game, it doesn't mean you ain't going to get the ball in the game on Sunday. Because if the defense does something, I'm going to throw it to whoever is open." They were also a good source of information. I'd always be asking them on the sideline what happened when we did this or what happened when we did that.

I think Dennis McKinnon was probably the most reliable receiver we had besides Emery Moorehead. Willie Gault was our deep threat. He would clear out coverage, and that enabled us to hit the other guys. If he beat the defenders, we'd, of course, throw to him. And we had Walter Payton coming out of the backfield. But when you really needed a catch to be made, McKinnon was the guy to go to.

The Super Bowl that season was a ball, for the most part. Unfortunately the first thing that comes to mind is that idiot from the TV station down in New Orleans coming on and saying I'd called all women sluts. Up to that time I'd been having a grand time in New Orleans. People were treating us well, we were having a good time with them, and all of a sudden this story comes out.

On the road to Super Bowl XX, William "Refrigerator" Perry, the 320-pound-or-more defensive tackle and sometime running back, scores a touchdown against the Green Bay Packers in 1985. Looking on are quarterback Jim McMahon and tackles Keith Van Horne (78) and Andy Frederick (71).

First he said I'd done a radio interview at six o'clock in the morning at some pizza place. Well, the reporters who knew me and the players knew damn well that I wasn't going to get up and do some interview at six in the morning. Well, this guy didn't check up on the story, and he just went on the air with it.

Next thing I know we've got women picketing outside our hotel. Men are calling my room telling me I'm a dead man. It was ridiculous, but I bet 95 percent of the media there wanted to believe the story. It was news for them, true or not. I know Jerry Vainisi [the Bears' general manager] believed it. Mike McCaskey believed it.

At the time, I got woken Thursday morning by two callers who were yelling at me over the telephone. I didn't know what the hell was going on. So I came down to breakfast, and I remember the first guy I ran into was Vainisi, who said, "You really did it this time, didn't you?" I still had no idea what the hell was going on. Finally Ditka came up to me and said, "Did you say that?" I said, "Say what?" So he explained it to me, and I couldn't believe what I was hearing.

When I went back to my room, the Bears' PR guys told me I had to talk to the press, straighten the thing out. I said, "To hell with the press. They're the ones who started all this shit, not me." I did go down and meet the press about an hour later, but I don't know how much good it did.

I called my wife and told her about the crap that had come out on the news. "I don't know where they got it," I told her, "but don't believe it." She came down on Friday before the game, and I spent the night with her at her hotel. The Bears wouldn't put the wives up at our hotel; they put them in some fleabag somewhere down the street. On Saturday morning I got up and was walking back to the hotel the team was staying in, and I see in front of it all these cop cars and fire engines and all kinds of turmoil going on. I thought, Oh, shit, they just bombed my roommate [offensive guard Kurt Becker] out. As it turned out, it was a bomb threat because of the crap on the news, but no bomb, thank God. After that I was just glad to get the game over with and get the hell out of town.

I had some personality or ego conflicts with Ditka, or

maybe it was just different approaches to football. I don't really know for sure. I think much of it started to come to a head when I got hurt again in 1986. I hurt my arm in the opening game against Cleveland, and I probably should not have played anymore at that point without having it fixed. I kept telling the doctors and the trainers what was wrong with it—it was coming out of the socket when I threw the ball—but they said that couldn't be happening; it had to be something else. And for six weeks it was the same thing: one day it would feel OK, and I could throw the ball, and the next day I couldn't even move the arm.

Then all this crap started coming out about "McMahon doesn't want to play." Somebody was feeding this to the press. It was ridiculous. Hell, I'd played with a broken hand, stayed in when I had the kidney injury. That's around the time Dan Hampton jumped on me, saying, You don't practice, you don't do this, you don't do that. And here's a guy who didn't do anything in training camp. I probably could have lasted forever too if I didn't have to practice. But the guys on offense always had to practice, or they didn't play—that was Ditka's rule. But the guys on defense—if they didn't practice, they still got to play. Before that Dan and I had gotten along pretty well. I even went down to Arkansas to play in a golf tournament with him. Well, anyway, we got into a big argument at a team meeting about my practicing. I remember Jay Hilgenberg and Keith Van Horne standing up for me at the time, saying, "Look, the guy's hurt; lay off." Everybody on the offense knew I had an injury problem.

I kept trying to play during the season and was in and out of the lineup, but I'd been doing pretty well—we won the first six games that year with me starting—but it all came to an end in the Green Bay game, which was the twelfth game of that season. That was when I got blindsided by Charles Martin, their defensive end, and he dropped me long after I'd thrown the ball.

I knew somebody was behind me—I could hear him coming—but I didn't pay any attention because the ball was already down the field and I was just watching it. And then it happened so fast, I didn't know what hit me. All I know is I was down and Martin was on top of me.

I probably should have been more alert. The night before the game I was out with one of the defensive linemen from the Packers whom I'd known for a long time, from college days. He said, "You know, our coach doesn't like you very much." Their coach was Forrest Gregg. I said, "I know. I don't like him either." My friend told me that Gregg had been telling the defense all week, "If you get a shot at McMahon, hit him." And my friend warned me I'd better watch out for myself in the game the next day.

I should have known. We all should have known. This guy, Martin, comes out on the field with a towel with a bunch of numbers on it, those that he said he was going to knock out of the game. He had my number on it, Payton's, Dennis Gentry's, and Willie Gault's. The whole thing was so blatant.

I left the game after that. After it I told somebody I was going out to see Dr. Jobe, a shoulder specialist. The Bears got wind of it and said, "No, you're not going to go see him. Our doctor says you're fine; there's nothing wrong with you." I said, "Well, at least let me have another test on the shoulder." So they did what they call an MRI scan on it and found a tear in the rotator cuff.

That was the least of my problems, however. It was caused by the arm coming out of the socket up at the shoulder, and it just pulled part of the muscle off the bone. When I finally got out to see Dr. Jobe, he asked when I noticed the injury. I told him the first game of the season. He said I was very lucky I hadn't shredded the shoulder. He did the surgery, and the Bears' doctor came out to watch it. He fixed the tear in about ten or fifteen minutes, and then they moved the scope around to the front of the shoulder and found there was no joint there. So they had to open me up, and I got the surgery I should have had after the first game. And I think, after that, everybody said, "Well, shit, I guess he was hurt after all."

I started for the Bears in '88, but there was a lot of talk going around even then about trading me. Anyway, we were 7-1-0 when I pulled a hamstring in a game against New England, and that took me out, and I didn't play again until the playoffs.

I tried to get back for the Detroit game, which was the next-to-last game of the season, and I could come off injured reserve. I practiced that week, had my knee taped, but it still didn't feel right—still sore and loose. Two days before the game my attorney advised me to go to another doctor and get an opinion about whether or not I was ready to play. I went and saw Dr. Shaeffer, and he said my knee was nowhere near ready. The hamstring was still weak, and the knee joint was too loose.

So I came in the next morning and said I wasn't going to play. Everybody got all upset. I said, "Look, I planned to play this week, I want to play this week, but it's not worth risking my career."

I played in the two games of the playoffs that year, but then I was gone, traded to Philadelphia. It wasn't any big surprise at that point.

I enjoyed the friendships I made with a lot of the guys on the Bears. Those are going to last a lifetime. And I enjoyed Chicago—it's a great city. That's where my home is now, and that's where it's going to be when I retire.

Super Bowl XX

At New Orleans, Louisiana Superdome, January 26, 1986

OFFENSE

Chicago Bears		New England Patriots
Willie Gault	WR	Stanley Morgan
Jim Covert	LT	Brian Holloway
Mark Bortz	LG	John Hannah
Jay Hilgenberg	C	Pete Brock
Tom Thayer	RG	Ron Wooten
Keith Van Horne	RT	Steve Moore
Emery Moorehead	TE	Lin Dawson
Dennis McKinnon	WR	Stephen Starring
Jim McMahon	QB	Tony Eason
Walter Payton	RB	Craig James
Matt Suhey	RB	Tony Collins

DEFENSE

Dan Hampton	LE	Garin Veris
Steve McMichael	LT/NT	Lester Williams
William Perry	RT/RE	Julius Adams
Richard Dent	RE/LOLB	Andre Tippett
Otis Wilson	LLB/LILB	Steve Nelson
Mike Singletary	MLB/RILB	Larry McGrew
Wilber Marshall	RLB/ROLB	Don Blackmon
Mike Richardson	LCB	Ronnie Lippett
Leslie Frazier	RCB	Raymond Clayborn
Dave Duerson	SS	Roland James
Gary Fencik	FS	Fred Marion
Mike Ditka	Coach	Raymond Berry

Bears	13	10	21	2	—	46
Patriots	3	0	0	7	—	10

Touchdowns—Bears: Jim McMahon (2), Matt Suhey,
   Reggie Phillips, William Perry; **Patriots:** Irving Fryar
Field Goals—Bears: Kevin Butler (3); **Patriots:** Tony Franklin
PATs—Bears: Kevin Butler (5); **Patriots:** Tony Franklin
Safety—Bears: Henry Waechter tackled Steve Grogan in
   end zone

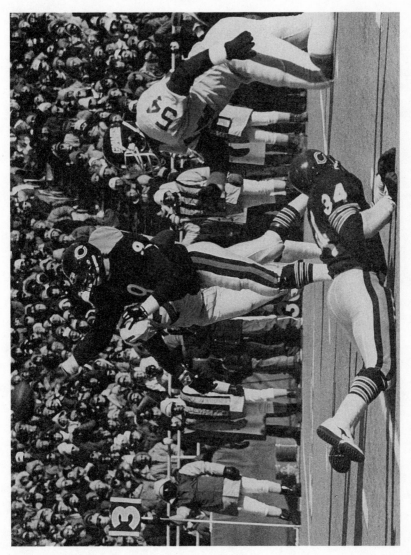

Jim McMahon fires one off in the 1985 playoff game against the New York Giants, which the Bears won, 21-0, as they surged to Super Bowl XX. McMahon took over the Bear quarterbacking duties as a rookie in 1982 and handled them expertly for seven seasons. The Bear on the turf is Walter Payton.

Gale Sayers

The Kansas Comet was a nickname that merely described the speed and grace of Gale Sayers as he streaked down a football field. It did not take into account those magnificent moves that left defenders groping air or untangling legs or those seemingly impossible cuts back across the grain—that here-one-moment, gone-the-next style of running he patented.

Sayers was an irreplaceable gemstone in the necklace of thrilling Bear running backs that was strung over the years with the likes of Red Grange, Bronko Nagurski, George McAfee, Rick Casares, Willie Galimore, Walter Payton, and Neal Anderson.

Sayers had a spectacular college career at Kansas, where over three years he maintained a rushing average of 6.5 yards per carry, and was a consensus All-American in both 1963 and 1964. He left in his wake three Big Eight records by rushing for 2,675 yards, gaining 835 yards on kickoff returns, and catching passes for 408 yards.

Selected by the Bears in the first round of the 1965 draft, he acknowledged it by turning in the most exciting rookie season ever seen in the history of the NFL. He set a league record by scoring 22 touchdowns—since exceeded by O. J. Simpson of Buffalo and John Riggins of the Redskins but never matched by a rookie—and tied the NFL record for most touchdowns in a game when he scored 6 against the 49ers that year. And there were the 96-yard kickoff return against the Vikings and the other 3 touchdowns that game, and the 80-yard screen pass he carried for a touchdown against the Rams, and the 85-yard punt return for a TD against San Francisco, and the 3 touchdown runs from scrimmage that year of 61, 50, and 45 yards, and, well, the list goes on. Gale Sayers won NFL Rookie of the Year in a landslide.

His rookie year stats: 867 yards rushing, a rushing average of 5.2 yards a carry, 660 yards on 21 kickoff returns, 238 yards on 16 punt returns, 507 yards on 27 pass receptions, combined net yards of 2,440, 22 touchdowns, and a total of 132 points scored—most of them Chicago Bear records for a rookie.

Besides the NFL record–tying, 6-touchdown day and those other sparkling moments in his rookie year, Sayers continued to hold Bear fans spellbound for the next five years. There were the 197 yards he rushed for against the Vikings in 1966, a Bear record at the time; and the day in 1968 when he broke it by gaining 205 yards against the Packers; and that 103-yard kickoff return for a touchdown on opening day 1967 against the Steelers, still the Bears' all-time standard.

Knee injuries cut short Sayers's brilliant career as one of the game's all-time great running backs, and he retired in 1971. In the last two years of his career Sayers played in only four games. But in the preceding five he managed to set or tie seven NFL records and fifteen Chicago Bear marks and was named All-Pro all five years. His lifetime average of 30.6 yards per kickoff return remains the NFL record, as does his 6 touchdowns on kickoff returns (an NFL mark shared with Ollie Matson of the Chicago Cardinals and Travis Williams of the Packers). He still owns or shares eleven all-time Bear records.

Gale Sayers was inducted into the Pro Football Hall of Fame in 1977 at age thirty-four, the youngest NFL player ever to be so honored.

After leaving the Bears, Gale went back to his alma mater, Kansas, to serve as assistant athletic director, then to Southern Illinois University as athletic director, and today is president of Crest Computer Supply Inc. of Skokie, Illinois.

Football has been part of my life almost as far back as I can remember. I started playing when I was eight years old in Omaha, Nebraska. We lived in the so-called ghetto there, but we were very sports-minded. All we did was play football, baseball, basketball—before school, at lunchtime, after school. We played in the schoolyards and some playlots, and every Saturday the kids—all ages—would go to a park there to play football.

As a little kid I started out playing end and a while later got switched to halfback. At Central High School in Omaha, I played halfback on offense and linebacker on defense. Most people thought I would stay in the state after graduating and go to the University of Nebraska, which had a very strong emphasis on football, but I chose Kansas instead, and it proved to be a very good experience for me.

I liked it at Kansas. We didn't have outstanding teams, but I got the chance to start from my sophomore season on, and I gained a lot of experience. My senior year we finished just a half game behind Nebraska for the Big Eight championship.

When I got drafted in 1965, the AFL was coming along, and they had some solid money now to offer college players and woo them away from the NFL. There was a lot of competition for players that year between the two leagues. That was the year the New York Jets of the AFL signed Joe Namath for $400,000 a year, an enormous amount of money in those days.

I was drafted in the first round of the AFL by the Kansas City Chiefs and in the first round of the NFL by the Bears. All along I had wanted to play in the National Football League. It was established and had a lot of the really great players in it. And there was little question they were playing better football in the NFL at that particular time. I just felt to better myself as a football player I needed to play in the NFL. The Kansas City Chiefs offered me a little more money than the Bears did, but I felt very comfortable choosing the Chicago Bears.

I came to Chicago after I was drafted and then for the College All-Star game and finally to report to the Bears' training camp. I met George Halas for the first time when I came up for the press conference after I'd signed my contract. I couldn't believe it; he was sixty-nine years old my first year, and he was still coaching, with all the wear and tear that comes with it, all that it can take out of a man. I mean I thought sixty-nine was an old man, but it wasn't where Coach Halas was concerned. He was able to coach and was on top of everything, and I must say it inspired me to do my best. We had some very cold winters in the mid-sixties in Chicago, and I would see him the first one on the field and the last one to leave it. He really was an inspiration to me in those years.

Pro football was not the same as college ball, but in a way I found it better for me personally. That's because of the experience of the players I was joining. When I was playing at Kansas, we had sophomore and junior linemen, very inexperienced. When I came to the Bears, although we didn't have the greatest offensive lines, the players still had six, seven, eight years of experience playing together. They worked together, and that was definitely to my advantage. It helped me as a football player.

I wasn't cocky when I came to the Bears, but I knew I could play. I saw the running backs they had then—Ronnie Bull, Jon Arnett, Andy Livingston, Ralph Kurek, Joe Marconi. I knew given time I would start, because I had more quickness than those people and more speed. I felt it was a matter of my learning the system and Mr. Halas giving me the chance to play and prove myself.

There were some definite things I needed to learn. In college we ran very few audibles, but in pro ball there were a lot of audibles to pick up, and I had to adjust to that. Another thing in the pro system that was different was that you had to do more blocking—pick up linebackers on pass plays, for example. And there was a lot more passing to backs coming out of the backfield. But other than that, if you play the game a number of years, you find it's just a matter of progression. It gets a little tougher at each step: from sandlot to high school, high school to college, college to the pros. It takes some work, but it isn't all that difficult to pick up.

Dick Butkus was drafted the same year I was; he was a number-one draft choice too. And the Bears also drafted Dick Gordon and Jimmy Jones, both good, fast wide receivers. We all became friends, coming in together. But once I got there, I considered everyone on the Bears a friend because they were my teammates. The veterans are not all that encouraging to the rookies, granted, but that's for a good reason. The rookies are there competing for their jobs. So in training camp they test you, so to speak, make you prove yourself, but that's just part of the game.

I started that year, Dick Butkus started, Dick Gordon started most of the time, and Jimmy Jones started some of the time. So that's four rookies coming in and taking jobs. But once you make the team, there's no problem; you become part of it, and everybody works together, rookies and veterans.

Andy Livingston, a big fullback who went about 235 pounds, was my first roommate. He came to the Bears in '64 but hadn't played much that year. He and I got along fine, and he ended up playing a lot more in the backfield in 1965, did a lot of blocking for me that year.

Later my roommate was Brian Piccolo. He came up the same year I did, but he wasn't drafted by the Bears. He tried out as a free agent and made the team. I still to this day can't understand it. Brian had to be the only man in the history of college football to do so well his senior year and not be drafted by a pro team—any pro team, in either the NFL or AFL. At Wake Forest, in his last year there, Brian led the nation in rushing and in scoring, but no team selected him. They thought, I heard later, that he wasn't fast enough or big enough for the pros.

The Bears took a chance on him, though. His first year Brian was redshirted because of an injury and didn't play. The next year, however, he came back and backed up me and Ronnie Bull. In 1967 he got more playing time than Ronnie and gained more yards for us. And when I was injured in '68, he started in place of me.

Brian was a good, heady football player. He may not have

had the greatest talent to begin with, but he had the instinct and the fortitude inside. He was a player who could get you those 3 or 4 yards when you really needed them, and he never made a mistake out there on the field.

We started rooming together in 1968, and the friendship blossomed. I can't remember how many basketball games and hockey games and other things we did with Brian and his wife, Joy, in those days. We were all just very close.

The year he got sick [1969] everybody was having colds, and he had this persistent cough that wouldn't go away. Eventually he went into the hospital, and they found a spot on his lung. I think it was Ed McCaskey who broke the news to me that they found the spot. We all went by to see him before they took the biopsy, and then we prayed for him, and I remember it was right before the Baltimore game Ed told me it was malignant.

Anytime you have a friend like Brian, all you do is hope and pray things will work out. But they didn't know all that much about treating cancer then—not like today—and we knew it was usually deadly, and in Brian's case unfortunately it was. It was a very difficult time.

One of the problems I think the Bears had when I got there in '65 was the age of a lot of the players. There were some great ones—Doug Atkins and Bill George, they're both in the Hall of Fame, but they were about thirty-five years old then. And Joe Fortunato and Stan Jones and Herm Lee—they were about the same. And both of our quarterbacks, Rudy Bukich and Bill Wade—they were thirty-four, both of them. I think the Bears just kind of kept them around, didn't want to trade them, didn't want to force them into retirement. You see, if you were loyal to the Old Man, he was loyal to you. And those guys had earned his respect by what they'd done in the past, which was quite a bit for the Bears. But it probably hurt the Bears in the middle sixties, and it kept a number of younger players off the roster or on the bench, where they weren't gaining any real playing experience.

I played in both Wrigley Field and Soldier Field with the Bears, and I must admit I really enjoyed Wrigley Field. You definitely had a home-field advantage in Wrigley Field, unlike Soldier Field, where the people in the stands are so far away from the field. Wrigley Field being a baseball stadium, the fans were right on top of you, behind you, behind the benches. They were close, and they were loud, and all the other teams sure knew they were in Bear territory. But the league finally said a team had to have a stadium with a capacity of at least fifty thousand, and that left Wrigley Field out, so we had to move out of there after the 1970 season.

As for the 49ers game my rookie year, the one where I scored the 6 touchdowns, I didn't feel any different before it or didn't do anything different. I do remember I was very, very concerned about the weather conditions, though. It was a really rainy, muddy day out there, and I actually didn't like playing in that kind of weather. So many things can happen; you can slip, pull a muscle, tear a hamstring—all kinds of things when the field is sloppy like that.

You must remember too that we were on a roll at the time, playing really good football. We'd won four straight games going into it. And there was a revenge factor too, because San Francisco had killed us the first game of the season, 52-24. Everything just went right for us that day, and we got our vengeance, beat 'em 61-20.

The way things were going I probably could have scored 8 touchdowns that day. But back then no one cared about records, and no one kept track of them. I didn't even know I'd tied the 6-touchdown record until after the ball game. Today they have people in the press box with record books, and they're always announcing that this player needs one more fumble to do this or that player needs to complete one more pass to do that. We were ahead by 40 points, we had the game, so who cared about scoring 7 or 8 touchdowns? We won the ball game, and that was the most important thing at that time.

That was a great game, no question. But there were a lot of terrific games, and the fact is all games were important. Each week you went out to win—that's what we showed up for; that was what it was all about.

At the other end, the worst game for me was also against the 49ers, three years later in 1968. That was the game I injured my knee. I took a pitchout from Virgil Carter, going to my left, and one of their defensive backs, Kermit Alexander, got through and threw a kind of blocking tackle at me. His shoulder caught my knee just as I was making my cut, and I went down. It wasn't intentional; it was a clean tackle. It was just one of those things that can happen in a football game.

I remember I had a lot of pain, but I got up. When I put weight on it, though, it buckled and I grabbed Kermit, and he held me up until the Bear players got there. I knew right then that it was gone. When I got to the sideline, Dr. Fox told me that I'd torn some ligaments, and that was it for me for the season.

I was having one of my better years at the time [856 yards rushing, a 6.2-yard average per carry, and 1,463 combined yardage in only eight games], and so it was even tougher to take.

I think we could have won the division that year if I could have played in the last five games. When I got hurt, we were on a winning streak, and everything seemed to be falling into place. As it was, we lost two of those last five games and ended up a game behind the Minnesota Vikings, a team we'd beaten twice that year.

Right after the ball game I had surgery on the knee. In those days they didn't have arthroscopic surgery, so I ended up in a cast for eight weeks. After the cast was taken off, you had to break down the adhesion. The leg was stiff, so you had to get in the whirlpool and work on it gradually. Later I started lifting weights. Once you got it strong enough so you could put weight on it, then you started running. It was a drawn-out process. Once I got to the point of running, it was almost the only thing I did. I ran seven days a week, and by April of 1969 I was ready to play football again. I never even put tape on it. I just went out there and played ball because I knew I was ready.

Coach Halas had retired the same year; he was seventy-three years old then, but in a lot of ways I hated to see him go. Coach [Jim] Dooley, who replaced him, did things in a little different way. He was a fine football man but probably should not have been a head coach. The same with Abe Gibron, another great football man but one that probably shouldn't have been a

With his dazzling running the fabled number 40, halfback Gale Sayers, electrified Bear fans from 1965 through 1971. In his rookie year alone he set a then NFL record by scoring 22 touchdowns and tied the single-game mark of 6 against the San Francisco 49ers. Sayers was the youngest man ever to enter the Pro Football Hall of Fame when he was inducted in 1977.

head coach either. What hurt Jim Dooley a lot too was that we had a lot of injuries around that time. I was healthy in 1969, but a lot of others weren't. He never really operated with a full complement of people. But Jim knew offense and he knew defense, and he was restricted because he didn't have a lot of talent out there on the field, and there were some pretty poor drafts around that time as well.

I think the 1969 season was as important to me as any season because that was the year I was coming back off the first knee injury. It was a big test for me, a big challenge, and I just didn't know whether it would work out for me. Well, my knee held up, and it did work out for me, because I was able to come back and lead the league in rushing [1,032 yards, and the only player to rush for more than 1,000 yards in that fourteen-game season]. It was not a good year for the team, however, because we won only one game and lost the other thirteen. I believe it was the worst year in all Bear history. But for me at least I was able to do what I set out to do, and that was to prove you could come back off a serious knee injury within one year.

I hurt my other knee in 1970. We'd won the first two games of the season, and everything was looking pretty good. But then I went down in the Detroit game, and I was out for the rest of the year.

I tried to come back in 1971, like I had in '69. I carried the ball thirteen painful times, and then the knee went out again, and I knew I was through. I just couldn't run anymore, so I retired.

Part of the problem with the later knee injuries I suffered may have been from playing on AstroTurf. I much preferred to play on natural turf, and I was not comfortable playing on an artificial surface. The players in my era never played on it before, and so it was a big adjustment, which a lot of us didn't make too well. Today's players are used to it because they play on it from grade school on up.

Still, it was a great time of my life playing for the Bears, and I had two wonderful things happen to me at the end of it. I was taken into the Hall of Fame, and I was presented for that honor by George Halas.

A Day to Remember

It was December 12, 1965, at Wrigley Field. The Bears took the field against the San Francisco 49ers and unleashed rookie running back Gale Sayers. What he did during the sixty minutes of playing time that followed electrified the Bear fans there that afternoon and electrocuted the 49ers.

The Kansas Comet scored 6 touchdowns to tie the NFL record that was shared at the time by Ernie Nevers of the Chicago Cardinals and Dub Jones of the Cleveland Browns. How he did it:

> 80-yard screen pass play (from Rudy Bukich)
> 21-yard run from scrimmage
> 7-yard run from scrimmage
> 50-yard run from scrimmage
> 1-yard run from scrimmage
> 85-yard punt return

Not surprisingly, the Bears defeated the 49ers that day by a score of 61–20.

Three postgame quotes worth remembering:

George Halas: "It was the greatest performance ever by one man on a football field; I never saw such a thing in my life."

Y. A. Tittle, a 49er assistant coach at the time: "I just wonder how many that Sayers would have scored if we hadn't set our defense to stop him."

Gale Sayers: "I had real good blocking on every play."

Notable Quotes

George Halas, on retiring as head coach of the Bears after forty seasons: "I knew it was time to quit when I was chewing out an official and he walked off the penalty faster than I could keep up with him."

Mike Ditka, while a tight end for the Bears in the 1960s, after negotiating his contract one year: "George Halas throws nickels around like they were manhole covers."

Gale Sayers, on accepting the George Halas Award in 1970 for Most Courageous Athlete of the Year because of his remarkable comeback from a serious knee injury to lead the NFL in rushing: "You flatter me by giving me this award, but I tell you here and now I accept it for Brian Piccolo. Brian Piccolo is the man of courage who should receive the award. It is mine tonight. It is Brian Piccolo's tomorrow."

Sid Luckman

A key to the character of Sid Luckman lies in the fact that he turned down several college scholarship offers at academically lesser schools and chose Columbia, where he would have to work his way through four years, because he felt he would get a much better education there. He did, and he also played a fine game of football for that Ivy League school, ending up an All-American halfback in 1938.

George Halas followed Luckman's football fortunes that senior year with more than casual interest. He saw in Luckman, who was both a fine runner and a good passer, the qualities he felt were necessary for the complex T formation he was infusing into the Bears' scheme of things. Luckman had not only the physical talents but also a brilliant, absorbent mind; he was quick to read defenses, decisive, a natural leader, and a dogged worker. Halas went after him with a passion and signed him.

The transition from a single-wing tailback to a T formation quarterback was very difficult, but after apprenticing as a halfback for part of his rookie year Luckman made it and, of course, became the game's first great T formation quarterback. In his twelve years with the Bears (1939–50) he guided them to five league championship games and four NFL titles. He was an All-Pro five times in an age when the NFL could boast quarterbacks of the caliber of Sammy Baugh, Cecil Isbell, Tommy Thompson, Bob Waterfield, and Paul Christman.

His greatest single effort was on Sid Luckman Day at the Polo Grounds in 1943, a special tribute to the Brooklynite who had done so well after leaving New York's mean streets. His mother was in the stands for one of the very rare occasions on which she watched him play the violent game of football. Gifts were bestowed before the game, and Luckman was deeply touched. Then he went out and destroyed the New York Giants by throwing an NFL record 7 touchdown passes that afternoon in a 56–7 triumph. To this day no one has thrown more touchdown passes in one game, although several passers have since tied it. He also set another NFL record by passing for 433 yards the same afternoon, a full 100 yards more than the record set by Cecil Isbell of the Green Bay Packers the year before.

When Sid Luckman retired in 1950, he had completed 904 of 1,744 passes for 14,686 yards and 137 touchdowns, all club records that still stand. Sid was inducted into the Pro Football Hall of Fame in 1965, with the third class of enshrinees.

With the same qualities that made him a masterful quarterback and team leader, he became an eminently successful businessman in Chicago after retiring from football. But even while building his business empire, he kept his hand in football as an assistant coach at various places, from the Bears to Notre Dame, teaching the intricacies of T formation quarterbacking.

Where I grew up in Brooklyn, New York, we used to play football, stickball, and baseball all the time. But football was my favorite. We played right out there on the city streets. It was in Flatbush by Erasmus Hall High School.

How I got from there to Columbia was a rather interesting story. I don't want it to sound like braggadocio, but I'd done pretty well in high school, in football and scholastically, and I had a number of college scholarship offers. Some of the people in the neighborhood around that time took me over to see the Columbia-Navy football game played at Baker Field. After the game was over, the people who had taken me there brought me in to meet the coach of Navy and then into Columbia's dressing room to meet their coach, Lou Little. I'd heard a lot about him. He'd been to the Rose Bowl with Columbia a few years earlier. And right away I could see there was something about the man; he had a certain charisma, a certain air about him. I felt from the start if I could spend four years with a man like that it would enhance my life.

I met Lou Little again, and after the second meeting I was certain Columbia was the place where I wanted to matriculate. I wanted both to play football and to get a good education. Coach Little wanted that for me too. He said football was just a means to enhance your life. When I think about it, though, I guess it was not really the university I chose, although I love it with all my heart; it was the person, Lou Little, who had such a tremendous charisma, that I really chose. It would be the same thing later, when I went to the pros. It was not the Bears I really chose; it was George Halas, another man with tremendous charisma.

As a football coach Lou Little was tremendous. It was very difficult for him. Admissions were very strict at Columbia. He couldn't get the players that other schools outside the Ivy League could. I was the biggest back he had, and I weighed only about 178 pounds then. Our line averaged only about 170 pounds. I was the tailback in the single wing. But I called the signals. It was a very unusual situation because he never had a real chance to prove how good a coach he was. The boys he had were just not on a par with the teams we were playing against.

Then I went with the Bears. It was kind of interesting how that came about too. George Halas wrote me a letter saying he might like to have me play for him in Chicago. I answered it saying I didn't have any desire to play professional football. I'd taken a lot of punishment as a tailback in college, and I knew how rough the pro game was.

Coach Halas had come up to watch Columbia play. The

Bears were playing the New York Giants the next day at the Polo Grounds, and he came with Luke Johnsos [a Bear end, 1929-37, and later assistant coach] and a few other assistant coaches. He sat in the press box, and apparently after the game he made up his mind that I could fit into his system, the T formation, which he was just beginning to develop. With it the quarterback did a lot of spinning and handing off, and as a tailback I did a lot of that. I guess he decided I might work as a quarterback in his system. You see, his quarterbacks, Carl Brumbaugh and Bernie Masterson, were getting a little old, and there weren't many people around who understood what quarterbacking was in those days. There just weren't any quarterbacks then as we know them today. Nobody else in the pros was using the T formation.

Then Coach Halas called Lou Little, who talked to me for him. Halas also made a trade sending Eggs Manske [1937, 1938-40] to the Pittsburgh Steelers and giving them his first-round draft choice for their first-round draft choice—they had the first pick that year. Then he called Lou Little again. After that he came to New York to see Lou Little, and the three of us got together. I reiterated that I hadn't the least interest in playing professionally and that I'd just gotten a wonderful job. I also told him that I, as an Ivy League player, probably was not good enough or could possibly get good enough to play pro football. He was very insistent, however, that I at least give it some serious consideration. He came back again, and by that time I'd gotten married. We had a little apartment. He came to visit with me and my wife, Estelle, at the apartment. Estelle made dinner for the three of us. Afterwards he made me a very fair and equitable offer. Later he said to me that I was the only player he had to truly talk into playing professional football. He had the contract with him, handed it to me, and I signed it. Then he walked around the table and kissed Estelle on the cheek. He sat back down and lifted up a glass of wine and said, "You and Jesus Christ are the only two people I'd ever pay that much money to." I think it was $5,000 or $6,000 at the time. But that was the most money he'd ever paid anybody except Red Grange.

Coach George Halas tousles the locks of his fair-haired quarterback, Sid Luckman. Halas converted Luckman from a single-wing tailback to a T formation quarterback in 1939.

It was a very difficult transition from playing tailback at Columbia to quarterback for the Bears. The signal calling was diametrically opposite. The spinning was very difficult because you had to be so precise and so quick. They don't do it today like we had to do it. We had counterplays and doublecounters and fakes. It was very hard for me to adjust, to get my hand under the center, and to get back and set up.

Coach Halas had made up his mind that I would play quarterback, but he started me off at left halfback. Then every day he had his former quarterback, Carl Brumbaugh, work with me for about two hours after practice. Carl taught me the setting up, the spinning, all the different ramifications and fundamentals of the T formation. We worked very hard during the day, and then at night I'd go home and study the playbook with Mrs. Luckman. I felt I had to get to know better what the guards and tackles did or were supposed to do. I wanted to have a better understanding of what the overall picture was when I was in the huddle.

Finally, during the sixth game, I got my chance at quarterback. Coach Halas loved to start players in games in the city they were from, the reason being that there was no television back then, so it gave them a chance to play before their hometown fans. He reasoned they would be fired up and do better. So he started me in the New York Giants game at halfback. There were a lot better halfbacks on our team than me in 1939, fellows like Ray Nolting and Bobby Swisher. It was a nice gesture and enabled my hometown folks to watch me play. Well, during the course of the game at the Polo Grounds, the Bears were behind 16-0. It was in the third period, and we weren't moving the ball very well. The Giants always had a great defense, with Steve Owen as their head coach and players like Mel Hein and Johnny Dell Isola and Ed Widseth. Coach Halas, who always called me "son," walked over to me on the sideline.

"Son," he said, "are you ready to go back in?"

I said, "OK, Coach."

"All right, son, I want you go back in at quarterback."

Well, that was the single most intense nervousness I've ever known in football, even more so than a world championship game. That *one* moment, in my hometown with my mother there—she saw me play only a couple of times before that—Coach Little there, all my friends, and there I was trying to be a T formation quarterback, a position I'd never played in a game before. There I was in New York, at the Polo Grounds, going up against the Giants. It was almost like a dream. And the good Lord must have put his arm around me that day. Bob MacLeod [1939-40], from Dartmouth, who I'd played against in college, was at halfback for the Bears at this particular time. He came back in the huddle and said to me, "I can beat my defender if you want to try a long one, Sid." I always liked to listen to people in the huddle, so I said, "Sure, Bob." I called a stop and go, and he went in motion. It was a play very similar to the ones they run today. Coach Halas had us running plays just like they do today, just as imaginative. Men in motion, split ends, double tight ends. Everything you can think of, he was doing in those days, fifty years ago. The T formation really should be called the Halas formation, because he made it into a science and brought it into the game of professional football. Anyway, MacLeod went in motion, made his fake on the defensive back, and then shot around him. I threw a long, wobbly pass. It was too short, and MacLeod had to come around, circle back, and he did and just took it right out of the Giants' defender's hands. It looked like a sure interception, but Bob took it away and kept right on going around him all the way for a touchdown.

A little while later I called a play to throw to another of our backs, Bobby Swisher, who was from Northwestern. It was a little screen pass, and he grabbed it and ran 65 yards for another touchdown. We still lost, 16-13, but the next day the people back in Chicago read about how I threw two touchdown passes. Everybody said, "Hey, that's great." They didn't know I really hadn't had a damn thing to do with it. It was MacLeod and Swisher who made those plays.

Then the big test came when we played Green Bay two weeks later. Coach Halas started me this time at quarterback, and we beat them 30-27. They were a real powerhouse that year and went on to win the title. That was the second most exciting, pressure-filled time I experienced in football. The pressure came from the fact I was playing at quarterback, but also because for the first time I was going against people like Don Hutson and Clark Hinkle and Arnie Herber and Cecil Isbell and Buckets Goldenberg. They'd been heroes of mine before, and I never honestly expected to be playing as a pro against them on a football field. And I looked at their line, me who had been used to playing against linemen in the Ivy League who weighed 170 or 180 pounds. And all of a sudden here are guys weighing 250 or 260. I just couldn't believe that there were those size athletes. I sort of got into the groove after the game got started, though. That was the start of my career really as a T formation quarterback, and it worked. We had a great team that year, with linemen like Joe Stydahar and Danny Fortmann and George Musso and such great runners as Bill Osmanski and Joe Maniaci and Ray Nolting and Bobby Swisher.

Halas in those days was probably the toughest coach in the game. They talk about Vince Lombardi being tough, but Halas was just as tough. And he had down all the finesse of the game as well. I remember he used to give us nineteen seconds in the huddle, said we had to be out to start the play no later than nineteen seconds, which left us eleven to get the play off. He had everything down to a science. He demanded perfection. He was a perfectionist himself, and we had to work twice as hard just to be half as good as he was. His whole life was football. He worked seven days a week, from nine in the morning until ten or eleven at night. He was truly dedicated, and he wanted total dedication from everyone associated with the team. Leadership, drive, and knowledge of the game—those were his keynotes.

We played offense and defense in those days. It was very different from today. You couldn't today—not with the kind of players you go up against who are so fast, so big, so strong. Wide receivers, for example, have such great speed. I, as a defensive back, couldn't compete with them. When you played all the time, sixty minutes, you never thought a thing about it. In high school, college, the pros, you simply played offense and defense. It was the game. We never realized that someday it would become a game of specialists. In those days there weren't any substitutions like now; if they took you out of the game, you couldn't come back during that quarter, which also meant you couldn't have any plays sent in like they do today. It was a 15-yard penalty if a play was sent in from the bench, so I had to call all the plays myself. It was truly different. I mean here I had to cover as a defensive back a receiver like Don Hutson or Jim Benton of the Cleveland Rams or later Tom Fears when the Rams were in L.A. It was a problem. And while you were doing that, you were also thinking about what you were going to do as soon as you got the ball: what kind of plays you would call, what kind of series you would plan. In other words, your mind had to be functioning all the time. You had to stay a little bit ahead of the game.

And you had to stay healthy, in good shape, to go the distance. It was a very rugged game. They hit hard, played hard. I remember some very tough tacklers: Mel Hein of the Giants, he was one of the all-time greatest; Baby Ray at Green Bay was another; and Fred Davis of the Redskins, who later played for us at the Bears [1946-51]; and Wee Willie Wilkin, another great lineman for the Redskins who was not very "wee"—he was about 6'4" and 260 pounds.

The Bears had many of the true greats of the day, however, like George McAfee. You'll never find a guy who can run better than he did. And Bill Osmanski, Bullet Bill, an incredible powerhouse; and Ray Nolting, who could hit a line as fast as any man I've ever seen. I could go on and on about the Bears of those days: Joe Stydahar, Danny Fortmann, George Musso, Lee Artoe, Dick Plasman, George Wilson, John Siegal, Norm Standlee, Joe Maniaci. They were all all-stars. And look at the pass catchers I had: Ken Kavanaugh, an uncanny football player, as were Jim Keane and Harry Clark and Dante Magnani.

I was at the right place at the right time. And I have Mr. Halas to thank for that. If I'd been a tailback or signed with another team, which I probably would not have done, I don't think I would have been able to stay in the league for twelve years as I did with the Bears. As a quarterback in the T formation, however, I was able to stay.

One of my most vivid memories is, of course, the 1940 championship game against George Preston Marshall's Red-

skins. It was the greatest display of psychological impact ever
given to a football team. That was one of the things Halas was
marvelous at. He had a great way of building you up for a game.
Well, we'd lost to the Redskins 7-3 in the regular season. The
game was played in Washington a few weeks before. We had
pretty well dominated that game; just a few breaks went against
us. Then on the last play of the game we were on the Redskins'
7-yard line. Bill Osmanski was our fullback, and I called for a
pass to him over the center. He was just about to catch the
ball—it was just a short pass over the goal line—and as he went
to grab it the defensive back knocked his hands down, and the
ball just bounced off his stomach. Well, the official was standing
right there, and it was clearly pass interference. But for some
reason or another he didn't call it. We screamed about it, but
that didn't help.

We vowed that we would even it up when we met again.
Well, that meeting was the championship game. It also was
played in Washington. We took the train from Chicago on Friday
night, and normally the boys would be playing cards or something like that. But this time everybody had his playbook out.
Nobody was laughing or horsing around. You could actually feel
the tension in the air.

We arrived in Washington on Saturday morning and went
out to practice that afternoon. Coach Halas ran us through a
very short drill, and after it we had a players' meeting. Later that
afternoon Sammy Baugh and I went on national network radio
and talked about the upcoming game. Now Sammy is a very
humble, very decent man. We wished each other luck—may the
best team win, that sort of thing. When the radio show was
over, I said, "Sammy, it's going to be quite a game."

He said, "Yeah, I know, but we're ready for you."

"We're gonna have a lot of fun out there tomorrow," I said.

The headlines in the newspapers Saturday night, however,
said the Bears were crybabies. This had come from George
Marshall. He said something to the effect that ever since they
whipped us in the regular season, all we did was cry about how
we were robbed by the officials. We were just crybabies, quitters, he said. Coach Halas, of course, saw it and took it out of

the newspapers. Then he had the pages blown up. He must have found some printing company who could do it. Anyway, around the whole dressing room when we walked in were these blown-up newspaper stories.

Then he made his classic speech, one of the most memorable of my life. He said, "Gentlemen, I know," and he looked us right in the eye, "this is the best football team ever assembled. I know it. You know it. Now I want you to prove to the American public that you are as good as *you* know you are, as good as *I* know you are. And more importantly, I want you to prove to Mr. Marshall and the Redskins that what they think of you is not true." He pointed around the room at the newspapers on the wall. "Look at this—this is what he thinks of you, what the Redskins think of you. All you great players, players who I respect, look at this. We have never cried in our lives. No one can talk that way about us."

Then it was over. And I tell you there was never such a surge for the door. I tell you we almost broke the damn door down.

He had given me some plays to run if the Redskins were using the same defense that had worked against us before. It had worked well then, and Halas wasn't going to let it happen again. If I saw a similar defensive lineup, we would compensate: McAfee in motion one way, Nolting in motion the other, whatever, to beat the defense. We knew if they used the same defense we had them. We'd planned against it the entire week before the game. And they used the same defense.

It was just one of those incredible games. We were perfectly prepared for it. Halas had seen to it. We were motivated and we won 73-0.

Another great memory was of Bronko Nagurski. When I first saw him, I saw the nearest thing to the most perfectly built, strongest human being I'd ever met. He had such tremendous power. He had played in the thirties, become a legend, then he came back to training camp in 1943. He came back to play tackle for us. The Bronk was thirty-four or thirty-five then and had been out of the game for about six years. It took him a little while to get back into the swing of things. A couple of our

coaches, Hunk Anderson and Luke Johnsos, later decided to try
him at fullback in the last couple of games. And that came back
to him too. When I handed him the ball, I could just sense the
power. He would take it with just such a great burst as he went
into the line. In one of the games against the Redskins I was
walking off the field with Sammy Baugh afterwards, and I said,
"Sammy, can you imagine what he must have been like in his
prime?"

Sammy said, "I remember. He was the most powerful human being I ever played against." And I might add Bronko
Nagurski was also one of the finest gentlemen you'd ever meet.

In 1946 the championship game we played against the New
York Giants was the most vicious football game I'd ever played in
my life. There was the toughest tackling, the fiercest blocking,
the hardest running. What happened was, somehow or other,
there was this supposed gambling situation. The night before
the game one of the Giants, Merle Hapes, a back, was suspended, and Frank Filchock, their quarterback, got in trouble,
but he was allowed to play. Steve Owen, their coach, told me
afterwards that he'd never seen a team who wanted to win a
game more than the Giants did that one. They wanted to win it
for those two fellows accused of the gambling. They wanted to
show all the fans that it was on the up-and-up. Especially Frank
Filchock, who was playing and wanted desperately to show that
he wasn't involved. They felt they had to win to save face. And
it was a real brawl. They gave us a helluva tough battle. But we
finally won it [24-14].

One of the most memorable plays I ever had in pro football
occurred in that game. We had a play called "Bingo keep it"
where I ran with the ball. Halas didn't care if I ran with the ball,
but he didn't want me to do it too much during the regular
season. In the championship game, that was another matter. If
I got a bad bruise, I'd have the rest of the year to get over it, not
just a week, like in the regular season. Well, it worked like this.
McAfee was such a tremendous threat as a runner, the best
breakaway back in the game, they always had to watch out for
him. And he had been running well off left end all day in that
championship game, and the Giants were always looking for
him. So, in the middle of the fourth period I took a time-out and

Sid Luckman (1939-50), doing what he did so brilliantly for the Bears during his twelve-year career in Chicago, is about to unleash a pass in this 1943 game against the New York Giants. Luckman was inducted into the Pro Football Hall of Fame in 1965.

went over to talk to Coach Halas. I said, "Now?" He knew the play I meant. We'd talked it over before the game.

He nodded. "Now."

So I went back out and called "Bingo keep it." When I got the snap, I faked to McAfee, who went around left end with the defense in hot pursuit. Everyone was chasing McAfee, so I just danced around right end with the ball and then along the sidelines for a touchdown—19 yards. That was one of the few times in my life I ran for a touchdown. It was a real thrill for me.

We won that game 24-14, despite how hard the Giants played. It was especially wonderful in that Coach Halas was back, his first year after spending four years in the navy. It was a great team we had, just like the dynasty before the war. I played a few more years after that, and we were in it each year, very close, but always a little short, and that game with the Giants turned out to be the last championship game I played in.

I coached with the Bears for a number of years after that, and I remained very close with my dear, dear friend George Halas until the day he died.

A Novel Way of Passing

John "Bull" Doehring, a running back for the Chicago Bears in the 1930s, was known for a rather unusual passing ability. He could throw a football behind his back as far as most players could throw one overhand. Luke Johnsos, a Bear end in those days and later a longtime assistant coach with the team, recalled one play in particular:

"Bull took a lateral and started out toward the sidelines. He was supposed to throw a long pass to me, but he was in trouble—the defense was all over him. He didn't even have room to raise his arm. I looked away, figuring the play had failed. Then I happened to look up, and there, coming straight into my hands, was the ball. I was so surprised, I dropped it. As we were walking to the dressing room later, I asked him how he got rid of the ball.

" 'Well, they were rushing me, so I threw it behind my back.'

"And that is what he had done, thrown the ball behind his back. Forty yards. Right into my mitts."

1943 Championship Game

At Chicago, Wrigley Field, December 26, 1943

Washington Redskins		Chicago Bears
Bob Masterson	LE	Jim Benton
Lou Rymkus	LT	Dom Sigillo
Clyde Shugart	LG	Danny Fortmann
George Smith	C	Bulldog Turner
Steve Slivinski	RG	George Musso
Joe Pasqua	RT	Al Hoptowit
Joe Aguirre	RE	George Wilson
Ray Hare	QB	Sid Luckman
Frank Seno	LH	Harry Clark
George Cafego	RH	Dante Magnani
Andy Farkas	FB	Bob Masters
Dutch Bergman	Coach	Hunk Anderson, Luke Johnsos, Paddy Driscoll

Redskins	0	7	7	7	—	21
Bears	0	14	13	14	—	41

Touchdowns—Redskins: Andy Farkas (2), Joe Aguirre; **Bears:** Harry Clark (2), Dante Magnani (2), Bronko Nagurski, Jim Benton

PATs—Redskins: Bob Masterson (2), Joe Aguirre; **Bears:** Bob Snyder (5)

1946 Championship Game

At New York, Polo Grounds, December 15, 1946

Chicago Bears		New York Giants
Ken Kavanaugh	LE	Jim Poole
Fred Davis	LT	Tex Coulter
Rudy Mucha	LG	Bob Dobelstein
Bulldog Turner	C	Chet Gladchuk
Ray Bray	RG	Len Younce
Mike Jarmoluk	RT	Jim White
George Wilson	RE	Jim Lee Howell
Sid Luckman	QB	Frank Filchock
Dante Magnani	LH	Dave Brown
Hugh Gallarneau	RH	Howie Livingston
Bill Osmanski	FB	Ken Strong
George Halas	Coach	Steve Owen

Bears	14	0	0	10	—	24
Giants	7	0	7	0	—	14

Touchdowns—Bears: Ken Kavanaugh, Dante Magnani, Sid
   Luckman; **Giants:** Frank Liebel, Steve Filipowicz
Field Goal—Bears: Frank Maznicki
PATs—Bears: Frank Maznicki (3); **Giants:** Ken Strong (2)

Dan Hampton

Dan Hampton's illustrious twelve-year career with the Bears ended with the playoff loss to the New York Giants on January 13, 1991. After four trips to the Pro Bowl, numerous All-Pro selections, and eleven knee operations, he had earned his place among the greatest defensive linemen the Bears had showcased over seven decades—players like Ed Healey, Joe Stydahar, George Connor, Doug Atkins.

Hampton was an All-America selection his senior year at Arkansas (1978) and was named Southwest Conference Defensive Player of the Year. He was the fourth player chosen in the 1979 draft after the Bears traded Wally Chambers to Tampa Bay to obtain that selection. He won a starting job on the defensive line in his rookie year.

Twice during his career he recorded three sacks in a single game, against the New Orleans Saints in 1980 and the Green Bay Packers in 1986. In a game with the Saints in 1982 he was credited with a career-high 16 tackles.

In the Bear record book Hampton ranks third in career sacks (78.5) behind Richard Dent and Jim Osborne. He is only the second Bear to have played in three decades (Sid Luckman played in the 1930s, 1940s, and 1950s). He was

named to the All-Pro NFL Team of the Decade, 1980s, by the
Pro Football Hall of Fame Board of Selectors.

Hampton will keep in touch with the Bears by doing
some television broadcasting of NFL games when he isn't
tending to his various business interests in Arkansas and
Chicago and his hobby, a cattle ranch in Cabot, Arkansas.

The spring of 1979 was a pretty exciting time for me. It
was the time before BLESTOE and the draft combines
were factors, and so about the top twenty-five choices
were flown around to different teams to be checked out, take
physicals, that kind of thing. Any club that was remotely interested in you as a first-round pick would bring you in.

I went to thirteen teams that spring, and the Bears were
one of the last. They didn't know a whole lot about me. I
remember their scout, Jim Parmer, coming by Arkansas that
spring, and when I heard he was there I said, "Man, the Chicago
Bears, I want to go talk to him." And I did. I asked him what
kind of time he had on me for the forty [yard sprint]. He said
5:2. Well, I had been running better than that, better than that
the year before. So I said, "Let me run for you again." We went
out, and he clocked me at 4:8. They also had me listed at 240
pounds, but I was 260. After he reported that to the Bears, they
became immediately interested in me and brought me up to
Chicago.

It was clear they were interested in drafting defensive
linemen that year. I talked to almost everyone on the staff. I
remember a lot of them, but the one that was foremost was
Buddy Ryan. Mitch Friedman, their films director, brought me
to this room, which was dark, and a film was running. There
was a guy in there watching the film, and Mitch said, "This is
Buddy Ryan, our defensive coordinator." He never turned the
light on or anything. He just said, "Sit down, big boy." So I sat
down by the desk, and he didn't say another thing for about ten
minutes.

We were watching a film from the Bears' 1978 season.
Finally he said, "See that guy, number 82? That's Alan Page

[Bear defensive tackle 1978-81]. He's one of the greatest who ever played the game." Anyway, I watched him for a few more minutes, and I could see how quick Alan was. Buddy then said, "Boy, I'd sure like to have you. I betcha I could get you to play like that someday." I was flattered that I was even mentioned by Buddy Ryan in the same sentence as Alan Page.

I knew after that I really wanted to be drafted by the Bears. But I didn't want to be disappointed, so I didn't say anything about it. I just went back to Fayetteville [Arkansas] and waited for draft day. And that morning, about ten minutes into the thing, they took me with the fourth pick. It was very exciting to me. I remember that afternoon, to work off some of the adrenaline, I went down to the weight room at Arkansas to work out. A buddy of mine there, who heard I was drafted by the Bears, gave me a book by Dick Butkus called *Stop Action*. I think I read that book three times by midnight. It was really interesting to me because I always thought Butkus was maybe the greatest ballplayer of all time. I kept thinking this was going to be my new career and I was hungry to learn all I could about the Bears. Butkus had a real sour attitude around that time, but still the book was a great insight into pro football.

I came to Chicago the next day. Dale Haupt, our defensive line coach then, picked me up at the airport and brought me downtown for the press conference. It went pretty well. I ran off a bunch of one-liners. And I got along with the media right off.

The highlight of the day, however, came later, when they took me over to the Bears' home office at 55 East Jackson and I met Papa Bear for the first time. He was bright, articulate, interesting. He was still very much the president of the Chicago Bears. I think he was eighty-four that year.

I met Jim Finks too. I respected and liked him a lot. Jim is one of those guys who kind of sits in the background and watches. He's not the gregarious type who gets out and pumps everybody's arm.

I was so excited to be part of the Bears and pro football. When I was a kid, the doctor told me I'd never play football again. I was in the sixth grade, and I fell forty-five feet out of a tree. I crushed my right heel and broke my legs in three or four places. I was in a wheelchair with a hip cast on my legs for six months. The doctor said I'd never walk comfortably, let alone run.

Then, when I was a junior in high school, some of the coaches and players talked me into coming out for the team. I didn't seem to have any problems. I was rusty, and it took a while to kind of get in the groove, but I was able to earn a scholarship after my senior year. [Hampton made national high school All-America team his senior year.] I had bad eyes in high school. I used to squint all the time. One day the coaches got on me about some kind of technique thing. I remember I said, "Well, Coach, quite honestly, I can't really tell if he's got the ball. I can't see that good." He asked me how the hell I could tackle anybody then. So I said, "Well, I just tackle everybody, and the one that struggles the hardest, I know he's the one that has the ball, and so I throw him down." I got contact lenses when I went to Arkansas.

I had scholarship offers from a lot of places, but the only place I wanted to go was Arkansas. My dad had been a big Razorback fan, and he had died when I was in the eighth grade, so it was kind of something that I thought he would really have wanted me to do. So I went up to Fayetteville, and things worked out, and by my senior year I was rocking and rolling pretty good.

Lou Holtz took over as head coach at Arkansas after my sophomore year. I remember going down to the Orange Bowl my junior year. We were 10-1-0 and ranked fourth in the nation, and we were going there to play Oklahoma, who was ranked number one. We were 10-point underdogs, but then Holtz suspended our starting running backs and our top receiver for a dorm incident. Well, that took the game completely off the board in Las Vegas.

We went ahead and won it 31-6. Afterwards the reporters were all saying that was the greatest job of coaching ever done by anyone. Holtz had us so fired up that day we hit the field like 150 miles an hour. After the game the reporters were saying to Holtz, "My God, you were such an underdog, they took you off the board in Vegas, and you're playing the mighty Oklahoma Sooners; how did you get your team so fired up?"

Holtz said, "Well, I told them simply that the last eleven guys out of the locker room had to start."

My senior year was more frustrating. We were ranked number one in the country through the first five games of the year, but then we lost to Texas, and that was the start of taking us out of the running for the national championship. As it turned out, it was a great shaping season for the pros, because there was a lot of adversity.

After the Bears drafted me, I told my agent, "Look, I'm glad to be going to Chicago. The main thing to me is I want to go to training camp, and I want to be one of the guys they can count on this year."

I thought all the guys up there would be mastodons, and I knew I wanted to play and knew I'd do whatever it took. And it would take being in training camp on time. I've always had a real open attitude, and I think that's one thing the Bears appreciated about me—that I never got hung up on money, contracts, and holdouts, no bitching and moaning.

My first coach in Chicago was Neill Armstrong. He was such a terrific guy, more of an administrator than an actual coach. He let Buddy run the defense and Ken Meyer, our offensive coordinator, run the offense. Neill was more or less a figurehead. He didn't want to step on anyone's toes, and he was a genuinely nice human being. Unfortunately he trusted the players, thinking because they were veterans they were responsible, and we didn't have that type of team. We had a bunch of kids who tried to get away with things and wouldn't do the things you had to do in order to win. And ultimately it cost Neill his job.

Training camp was so long and grinding, I found out right off. It was really different from college. That first year in Chicago we had four or five preseason games, and I had been so intent on doing everything right and worked so hard at it by the time the preseason was over I was already starting to wear down. The problem was we had lost a number of defensive linemen in training camp to injuries, and so I ended up practicing practically every play in camp and every play in the preseason games. I remember it being like a death haul and saying to myself, If I get through this year alive, it's going to be amazing.

Another observation I had that first year was that in college I could physically overpower practically everyone I lined up against, but in the pros that wasn't the case because everybody was big and strong and of All-American caliber. It became quite evident to me that technique was the make/break heart of pro football. It was the combination of physical attributes and the mental and technical skills that you could amass that would make you successful in the pros.

It took me about five games into the season before I started really figuring out how to play the game. Leverage was the key. I remember watching films of Lee Roy Selmon before the Tampa Bay game that year. I thought he was one of the best defensive ends in the game, just a terrific ballplayer. I watched how he pass-rushed: kept the leverage all the time, used his shoulders and arms, saw the moves he had.

In the first few games of that year I did not rush the passer very well. I was playing defensive end then. Buddy Ryan chided me about it. "Well, big rook, I thought you were going to be a big pass rusher for me. What happened?" It really bothered me, gnawed at me, and then suddenly it just hit me. Leverage—all those things that Selmon had down so well. I worked at it, and by the end of the year Buddy had no complaints with me.

I always had to work for what I got. And I did it that first year. It just showed me the old axiom that good things come to those who go out and work for them. From that point on I continued to improve.

I got my first sack in that game against Tampa Bay, and that's where, I guess, I created the wild-eyed style I wanted to play with. I was really pumped up for the last game of the season. We were playing St. Louis and had to win by a big point differential if we were to get into the playoffs. I played my tail off against Dan Dierdorf that day and ended up with a couple of sacks, and I forced a fumble here and there. It was a great game, and we made the differential [the Bears beat the Cardinals 42-6]. We got the wild-card spot and went up to Philadelphia, but we lost to the Eagles [27-17].

Just getting to the playoffs revved me up for the next

season. I think it was the second game of the season [1980] that we played New Orleans, and we really beat up their quarterback, Archie Manning. We killed them, 22-3, and I had three sacks that day and was named Defensive Player of the Week. So it was really a lot of fun at that point; my heart was going so strong. It was pro football, and I was really, finally a part of it.

The next year [1981] was just a disaster. Neill was kind of a lame-duck coach, and nothing seemed to come around, and on top of that my knee was bothering me most of the year. We ended up 6-10-0.

Then they brought in Mike Ditka, who breathed fire. In my college career I spent the first two years under Frank Broyles. The only time we would see him was the pregame talk, when he'd give us a little speech. That was it. He was an administrator who let Jimmy Johnson run the defense. But then they brought in Lou Holtz, who ran everything, had his fingernails in all the pies, and was a flamethrower. We went from 5-5-1 in Broyles's last year to 11-1-0 the next year under Lou Holtz and a number-two ranking in the nation.

So when Ditka came in, I was very excited. I knew what kind of effect that type of personality would have on a football team. Unfortunately we didn't have the manpower to do it right off the bat.

A new coach was allowed two minicamps. That's where I first met Ditka. He gathered us on the 50-yard line in Sun Devil Stadium out in Phoenix and said, "Gentlemen, good morning, my name is Mike Ditka. I'm the new head coach of the Chicago Bears. My goal is to go to the Super Bowl and win it. Some of you will be there; some of you won't."

Now, right off that got my attention, because for the three years I'd been with the Bears nobody on the staff had ever said anything about going to the Super Bowl, much less winning it. Until Ditka gave that little talk, it was like we were embarrassed even to think about going to the Super Bowl. Only Dallas and Oakland and Miami and Denver could talk about the Super Bowl. The Bears weren't in the tournament. We were one of the guys in the back of the bus—we would never be able to drive the thing; we were just going to ride in it.

What also caught my ear was when he said some of the players wouldn't be there. I had seen some of these players we had then lie down, and I knew we couldn't count on some of these guys to be the kind of players we had to have to go to the Super Bowl. I appreciated the fact that Ditka knew it too, because a team is only as good as its weakest link. After hearing him, I just knew that this guy saw the same kind of light at the end of the tunnel that I did.

Mike and I were never the greatest of friends. I respected him, and I suppose he respected me, and we had a good working relationship. The most important thing to me was that he came out the first day and mentioned the same goal that I had always dreamed of.

Going into Ditka's first season [1982], I was really breathing fire, and I started off the season superstrong. I was leading the team in tackles after four or five games, but then we had the strike and the season was shot. I was really disappointed we didn't do well that year—we won only three of the nine games we played.

The next year in training camp I ripped up a finger and got a bone infection in it, and it was a big old nasty thing all year that I had to wrap up like a club. Due to that I did some stupid things to get by on the field, and one time I tried a spin move on a guy in Philadelphia, and he leg-whips me and cracks my knee. At that point I just thought it was an injury that I'd come right back from. I never dreamed at the time that the knee would never be the same again.

I went and had it operated on and came back four weeks later, but the knee wasn't real strong. I played pretty well down in Tampa, played decent the next week against the 49ers, and then it started getting weaker and weaker, and by the end of the season I just couldn't go, my knee was so full of blood.

So it was in my fifth year the knee injuries began. With that the physical attributes began to dwindle, and I knew I would have to make up for that somewhere else. I would have to compensate, and that's where I became even more engrossed with technique, concentrating on quickness and studying the opposition's offenses. I was, I believe, able to stay effective for a lot of years that maybe I wouldn't have if I hadn't been obsessed with compensating. Once physical abilities start to diminish, you've got to find it someplace else.

I was really primed to make a comeback in '84. As it turned out, it was one of my favorite seasons. I think we had four quarterbacks playing for us that year [Jim McMahon, Greg Landry, Steve Fuller, Rusty Lisch] at different times, but still we made it to the NFC championship game. We got there by beating the Redskins at RFK Stadium, which was one of my favorite games of all time. Washington had won the NFC title the year before and then lost to the Raiders in the Super Bowl. It was a real battle. We did it in a convincing fashion because we were winning by only 6 points in the fourth quarter, and they had the ball inside the 50-yard line four times, but they didn't score on any of them. Our defense that day really rose to the occasion. [The final score was 23-19, the Redskins getting 2 points in the fourth quarter when Bear punter Dave Finzer stepped out of the end zone for a safety.] The next week, against San Francisco, however, we couldn't get anything going on offense or defense and got beat up out there [23-0].

But I tell you what we did. We got a taste of the soup, and now we were hungry for the main course. And we went into the 1985 season with the goal of not being denied. And, of course, we weren't.

The players as a whole were really committed to the fact that this was going to be our year. We were not going to let it go without a helluva fight. A lot of teams tried their damnedest to beat us that year—they'd give us their best shot—and we just rocked them week after week, except for that awful game down in Miami [the Bears' only loss of the year 38-24 to the Dolphins].

I worried some when the "Super Bowl Shuffle" came out. McMichael and I wouldn't do it. I was saying, "Hey, they think we're going to go, and we still have five games to go before we even get into the playoffs." But it didn't hurt. Buddy Ryan and Mike Ditka, as coaches, kept the defense and offense well focused.

All that season I used to ride with Ming [Steve McMichael] to practice, and every day we'd talk about going to the Super Bowl, how great it would be. And then, after the last playoff game, we got in the car and looked at each other, and we said, "We can finally say we're going." It was a very moving moment.

I remember especially the night before the Super Bowl. It was kind of an emotional thing, we'd been ready for so long. We had meetings that night. In ours, the defense, we were going to watch a game film, and by this time we were sick of films. As I was going in there, I said, "Hey, Ming, I cannot watch another roll of film. We got to do something."

I'm watching about the sixth play, and my heart's beating fast. I can't wait, so I just got up and kicked the projector off the little table it was sitting on. Ming, at that moment, leaped up and grabbed a chair and screamed some expletive about the Patriots and swung the chair at the chalkboard that had all these plays diagramed on it. All four legs stuck into the chalkboard. Nobody said anything, and finally I just said, "Let's get the hell out of here." We all walked out of the room, no one saying anything, and went to our rooms and went to sleep. And everybody knows what happened the next day [Bears 46, Patriots 10].

Ming was like that—wild, funny. I remember one game in 1984 after somebody wrecked us, just beat us like bad dogs. We came into the locker room, and everybody sat down, and Ming came in last and yells, "Quick, close the door, the son of a bitches are coming in after us!"

Mike Hartenstine was another very good friend. We had a lot in common, both being defensive linemen. He played twelve years for the Bears, eight of them with me. And he was my roommate all those years.

One of my other favorite seasons was 1988. We had a real combination team, a bunch of old veterans and a lot of young blood. I had a real good year too—started all eighteen games and got some All-Pro recognition. We went 12-4-0, beat the Eagles in the playoffs, and then lost to the 49ers.

In '89 I injured my left knee again and had to have surgery on it, and after the season I had surgery again on my right knee. As far as the knee injuries go, every time you get one, no matter how severe or mild it is, every time the surgeons go in that joint, they change it and it gets worse. And every rehab you have gets harder and harder. It was no big deal; don't pin a Purple Heart

Everybody's All-Pro, defensive tackle Dan Hampton (99) strikes a little fear into the heart of Kansas City's Henry Marshall before he crushes the Chiefs' wide receiver to the turf. Hampton joined the Bears in 1979 and, after twelve illustrious seasons and eleven knee operations, retired after the 1990 season.

on me. All I knew was that I had no choice in the matter—it was either fish or cut bait. And I decided to fish as long as I could.

I just refused to let the pain bother me. It was the strength and the mobility I lost in the knees that finally got me. The pain

I could handle. You break your arm five times in the same spot and see how strong it stays. In some strange and frustrating way I really didn't mind that things happened the way they did. I got twelve years in. I did a lot of good things on the field, played in a lot of memorable games, played on a championship team. The good Lord gave me a good hand, and I played it as long and as hard as I could.

I wanted to come back in 1990, one more year. But in 1989, while I was on injured reserve, I understood that the management did not want me to try a comeback, said it was time for me to retire. But the team had a terrible year, and I guess it was a combination of things, but they changed their minds.

Coach Ditka really went to bat for me. So I got to play in 1990, and I was really happy about that. And even though I didn't play super football in '90, I was able to do what I could to contribute and give my teammates maybe some of that old gnarled, grizzly attitude. And that's what I had to have for the last couple of years. Maybe I made a difference, and maybe I didn't; all I know is I tried to make a difference.

Worn No More

Eleven Chicago Bear jersey numbers have been retired over the years. They are:

3	Bronko Nagurski	42	Sid Luckman
5	George McAfee	56	Bill Hewitt
7	George Halas	61	Bill George
28	Willie Galimore	66	Bulldog Turner
34	Walter Payton	77	Red Grange
41	Brian Piccolo		

George Connor

George Connor has the distinction of being the only Chicago Bear in history to be named to the NFL All-Pro team on both offense and defense. One of the last of the certifiably great sixty-minute players, Connor was an All-Pro five times as an offensive tackle, twice as a linebacker, and once as a defensive tackle. The only other Bear in history to be named to eight All-Pro teams was Bill George.

The most famous college lineman of his day, Connor was a consensus All-American tackle for Notre Dame in 1946 and 1947 (both years Notre Dame was the NCAA national champion).

He followed a circuitous path to the Bears but made it to Chicago for his rookie year in 1948 and ended up a starter that year. Playing at 6'3" and 240 pounds, he was a vicious blocker and a mobile but notoriously bruising defensive player. He was so quick he was switched from defensive tackle to linebacker by George Halas and became the first of the both big and fast men to play that position. He was also regarded as one of the most intelligent and instinctive linemen ever to play the game.

A leg injury contributed to his decision to retire in 1955 after eight exceptional seasons with the Bears.

Connor was honored as one of the tackles on the Hall of Fame's All-Pro squad of the 1940s. He was inducted into the NFL Pro Football Hall of Fame in 1975.

Today George Connor is president of his own company, Connor Sales Corporation.

J ohnny Lujack and I came to the Bears together in 1948. We got a mixed reaction because we were out of Notre Dame and had gotten an awful lot of publicity in 1946 and '47.

I was one of the higher-paid linemen to come along in those years, and I cashed the $6,000 bonus check I got as a rookie for signing out at a certain bank on the South Side. Ray Bray and Chuck Drulis, two guards with the Bears who were in the automobile business, knew somebody at the bank, and that somebody did not have very good ethics. He told them the amount of the check from the Bears. The word spread among the players, and there was a lot of conjecture that maybe I was making more money than Bulldog Turner and Bray and a lot of other well-established Bear linemen.

When I went to my first training camp, I found out just how poorly that sat with the other players. They really gave me a bad time. We scrimmaged a lot, we had intrasquad games, and they were really after me. Most of the scars I have on my face today are from my teammates that year. But I was able to ward them off and got through the camp scrimmages with a variety of bruises, scabs, and pains.

At the end of the training camp, when the squad was set, Bulldog Turner, our All-Pro center, came up to me and said, "Kid, you're all right. You took everything we gave you. Welcome to the team."

It was a kind of strange set of circumstances that brought me to the Bears that year. I had been the number-one draft choice of the New York Giants my junior year at Notre Dame in 1946. Wellington Mara [son of Tim Mara, founder and owner of the Giants, and today the president of that franchise] contacted me. I had played out east for two years [1942–43] at Holy Cross in Massachusetts before coming to Notre Dame after the service, and that's where they had first seen me play.

At any rate, I did not want to play in New York. I wanted to play in my hometown, which was Chicago—I'd grown up on the South Side, played football for De LeSalle out there. So I went to the Chicago Cardinals first, the South Side team who played in Comiskey Park then, and told them I didn't want to play for the Giants. But the Cardinals, who had just won the NFL championship the year before—they beat the Eagles that year—didn't show any interest in me.

So I went over on Wabash Avenue to the Bears' office and saw George Halas. He said, "Kid, stick to your guns, and you'll wind up a Bear."

I went back and played my senior year at Notre Dame, and Wellington Mara came out and visited with my family and me in Chicago after the season. I convinced him, however, that I did not want to play pro ball in New York, so he traded the rights to me to Ted Collins, the owner of the Boston Yanks, who was also the manager of the singer Kate Smith. Ted Collins kept calling me, and eventually he threatened that if I didn't sign with him he'd tell the president of Notre Dame, Fr. John Cavanaugh, who was a good friend of his.

I said, "Well you just go ahead and do that, because I don't want to play in Boston any more than I wanted to play in New York." Finally he got frustrated, and he traded me to the Bears for Mike Jarmoluk, a tackle from Temple.

I negotiated my contract directly with George Halas. My father was a physician on the South Side, and one of his customers was Judge Cornelius J. Harrington of the Circuit Court of Cook County. So, before I signed the contract in Halas's office, I said, "I want to show it to my lawyer," who was Judge Harrington. I got in a cab and went out to Twenty-Sixth and California, where Judge Harrington saw me in his chambers. He looked at the contract, ruled out some clauses, and then went back downtown with me for the signing.

As it turned out, Johnny Lujack and I signed the same day. Halas scheduled a press conference but didn't tell me that Lujack was signing too, or I'd have probably gotten some more money from him. We both would have.

Years later an irony popped up; it was in the George Allen

incident, when he was an assistant coach with the Bears. Without Halas's permission Allen went out and talked with Dan
Reeves, then the owner of the Los Angeles Rams, about the head
coaching job out there. Well, Halas sued on the basis that Allen
couldn't take the job with another club because he was still
under contract to the Bears.

The case appeared in Judge Harrington's court. And I don't
know whether Halas and Judge Harrington ever got together
out of court or what, but Judge Harrington made a monumental
ruling at the time that on the prima facie evidence the contract
was binding. Halas jumped up in court, jubilant, and said, "Your
Honor, that's all I wanted to prove. I withdraw my case."

Halas proved the sanctity of a contract and then let Allen
out of it so he could go off to his head coaching job. Nobody
ever remembered that the judge had been my lawyer.

We trained at beautiful St. Joseph's College in Rensselaer,
Indiana, back then, the garden spot of America. There was one
bowling alley and, I think, one saloon. Every once in a while
we'd get out to the one golf course. And that was about it. There
was no place else to go.

On occasion we'd get an afternoon off. The singular highlight I remember was this: Sid Luckman was a Chrysler-Ply-
mouth dealer in the off-season during those years, and he had a
brand-new Chrysler convertible with wood paneling on the side.
We had this one afternoon off, and Sid said to Don Kindt, who
was a halfback of ours from Wisconsin, and me, "You want to go
for a ride?" Well, you know, when you're down in Rensselaer,
Indiana, riding in a new convertible was quite a thrill out of the
ordinary. So Don drove, and I was in the front seat next to him.
Sid was in the backseat—in those days Sid loved to get tan; he
tanned beautifully. And so he put his oil on, sitting there in the
backseat, and said to Don, "Slow down to 55½ miles an hour;
that's where I get my most even tan."

I played at 6'3", 240 pounds then, and of course we went
sixty minutes. I played tackle on offense and defense at first,
and I played on kickoffs and punts and returns. In fact everybody had to have an offensive and defensive position because we
had only thirty-one players on our team when I came up. There

were no platoons or special teams then. Most of us really loved it, but the players today, they don't even play every down on offense or defense.

I became a linebacker later, quite by accident. It was because of the great running back Steve Van Buren of the Philadelphia Eagles. They had been the scourge of the league in 1947 and 1948. In 1949 we had an outstanding defensive coach in Hunk Anderson. He was a genius. He was the only coach I ever knew who could stand on the sideline of a game and tell you everything that was going on in the game all over the field. Most of the other coaches had to wait until they saw the movies the Monday after the game.

Hunk came up to me one day and said he wanted to talk to me about Van Buren, who went about 6'1" and 210 pounds and was a truly powerful runner. The Eagles would send Joe Muha in motion, and they would pull the two guards. They would spread Pete Pihos out to split end. Then with the two guards, Pihos, and Boss Pritchard, their right halfback, providing a wave of blockers, they would give the ball to Van Buren. So Hunk said, "Kid—," he called everybody "kid" just as Halas did; Halas even called Red Grange "kid"—"did you ever play linebacker?"

I said I had, my senior year in high school. I had had a bad knee, and a lot of teams were running away from my defensive left tackle position because I couldn't move quick enough to get to them. So my high school coach at De LaSalle, Joe Gleason, made me a middle linebacker so they couldn't really run away from me.

Hunk Anderson said, "That's fine, kid; you're our left linebacker."

I said, "What do I do?"

He said, "When Pihos lines up next to the tackle at tight end, you stay in front of him. When he spreads out to split end, you go out with him. If he goes to get a drink of water or anywhere, you go with him. And then, when the interference comes around, knock everybody down that you can. I don't care if you make a tackle all day, because you'll have help coming from the inside. Just stay with Pihos wherever he goes."

Well, the long and short of it, we were the only team to beat the Eagles that year; we beat them 38-21 at Wrigley Field. In the middle of the third quarter, though, I got too smart. I thought they were going to throw a pass to Boss Pritchard, the halfback, so I had the end crash, and I went out with Pritchard. They threw a little screen pass to Pihos behind the line, and he went 38 yards for a touchdown. I didn't want to come off the field, and when I finally did, Hunk said, "You dumb so-and-so. What happened to you?"

I said, "I thought, but I'll never think again."

And that's how I became a linebacker.

Before that the linebackers were either the center or the fullback, but I was the first really big linebacker.

It was second nature to play both ways in those days. When you grew up as a kid in grade school and high school, you played offense and defense. In the pros it was no different. Our quarterback, Sid Luckman, played many years on defense and was a fine defensive back. Johnny Lujack was one of the best defensive backs in the game, although everybody remembers him as a quarterback.

A lot of the old-timers would say that we were better than these kids today because we played sixty minutes, but the other side of the coin is maybe we all got tired together. On the other hand, I don't think a player in the condition they get themselves into—they bulk up too much, and they're too heavy—I don't think they could play sixty minutes.

Our conditioning was a lot different then—no weights, no carefully planned programs. I believed in doing a lot of running. I wasn't much of an exercise guy, other than warming up. But I ran. When I was in high school and starting out, I was 5'3" and 125 pounds as a freshman. Then I grew a foot, and I realized that I had to gain some foot speed. So I ran a lot of sprints before and after practice. I did that later with the Bears too.

In the off-season at Notre Dame I was introduced to the game of handball, and it helped me tremendously as a football player. And in high school I'd played basketball—in fact I was probably a better basketball player than I was a football player.

I actually played two years of college basketball at Holy Cross, and I was on the basketball team my junior year at Notre Dame. Basketball and handball added quickness. I had the innate strength, and so I didn't have to work on that as much.

I met a lot of interesting characters along the way and made quite a few good friends. I got to be friendly with Norm Van Brocklin, who was with the Los Angeles Rams then. We played in several Pro Bowl games together, and when you're thrown together with a guy in a situation like that for ten days you get to be friends. We used to go out and have a few beers after practice, and that actually intensified our desire to play well against each other, which we did twice each season.

One year we were playing the Rams out in Los Angeles, and I was our left defensive linebacker. We were operating almost in front of the Rams' bench. Well, I used to like to manhandle the tight end and not let him off the line of scrimmage—maybe trip him a little, maybe grab his jersey a little. I would wrestle him down the field, so that made me susceptible to screen passes. In this instance I was wrestling the tight end of the Rams, and they threw a little screen pass over to my side. I came up and made the tackle, but not until about a 7-yard gain. Van Brocklin was over on the sideline, yelling in his nasal twang, "Hey, Georgie, Georgie, show 'em your Notre Dame card," laughing at me.

Later in the season we were playing in Chicago. It was a late November game, a muddy, cold day. It was third down and long, a passing situation. Now I was over on the right side linebacking, calling the defensive signals. Quarterbacks are creatures of habit; they usually look the same way every play they come up to the line of scrimmage. Van Brocklin would start to the left, then to the right. Well, while he was doing that, I timed my thing, and I blitzed. I red-dogged from the right linebacker position, and Van Brocklin, being a right-handed passer, had his back to me. Everybody was pretty well covered, and I nailed him and pushed his face into the mud. He was a pretty rough character, and he shouted, "Who the hell is this?"

I said, "Hey, Normie, want to see my Notre Dame card?" That was a lot of fun.

Bobby Layne was another great one. I played with him in

Chicago, although he didn't play much his rookie year with the Bears. He was the third of the "Three Ls"—Luckman, Lujack, and Layne. Well, Luckman was entering the twilight of his grand career in 1948, and Lujack really had a great first two years before he hurt his shoulder, so Bobby didn't get much playing time. He had played single-wing football down at Texas, and he didn't fully understand the T formation when he first came up.

George Halas later said selling Bobby Layne was the biggest mistake with the Bears he ever made. He sold him to the Boston Yanks, not the Detroit Lions, for $50,000, and when the Yanks dropped out of the league Bobby wound up with the Lions.

Bobby Layne was a great leader, and he could really direct a two-minute drill. We were playing the Lions over in Detroit, and I was the right linebacker. Bobby looked the other way, and I guessed just right. As he turned around, he couldn't hold the pass back, and I intercepted it. After the play he gave me a few words of wisdom and said, "You're not supposed to be over there, you big ape."

I said, "OK, Bobby, I'll remember that next time."

I made it to the first four Pro Bowl games, and I really enjoyed those games. To meet players from other teams and to practice with them, to get to know them—it was a lot of fun.

In those days the Pro Bowl games were held in Los Angeles at the Coliseum. We went out there and worked out for ten days. The winners got a rousing bunch of bucks, $800, and the losers got $500.

One year I was out there rooming with Johnny Lujack, and they put a third roommate in, Gordy Soltau from the 49ers, who was a great football player and became a great friend of mine. The next year, when the 49ers came to Chicago to play us, I invited Gordy to dinner. My mother was a great cook. I went down to the Windemere Hotel and picked him up and brought him home for dinner. We had a nice time, and then I dropped him back at his hotel.

Well, the Morabitos owned the 49ers at the time, and their thinking, their mentality about running a football team, was not very good, which is why the 49ers were never very good in those days. So Gordy told me on Sunday that Morabito called him in the day after we had dinner and said the team manager had seen George Connor pick him up at the hotel. Gordy said, "That's right; I went to his house for dinner and met his parents. It was an excellent dinner by the way," he added.

Morabito said, "They are the enemy. You shouldn't be fraternizing."

I could never get over that, because as a Bear you respected the guys on the other team, and once the game was over you could be friends. Gordy Soltau today is probably the best friend I have that played for another team. I could never understand the ownership of the 49ers chastising him for going out with the "enemy."

We had a really intense rivalry with the Chicago Cardinals. I had played with Bill Fischer, one of their tackles, at Notre Dame, and I grew up on the South Side with Elmer Angsman, their halfback. Elmer and I had kind of a little feud going in the games. Elmer was one of the fastest starting backs ever, a stellar performer in the "Dream Backfield" [the others: Paul Christman, Charley Trippi, Pat Harder].

One game it was fourth and goal to go on our half-yard line out at Comiskey Park, the south end of the field. I was the left linebacker, and Elmer was the right halfback. The halfbacks have to look at the quarterback so they can get the proper handoff. I waited for Elmer to look because I was pretty sure he was going to get the ball. When he did, I got a message of where he was going with it. And then I snuck over, opposite their left guard, and got down on the line of scrimmage, guessing that Elmer would run the quick trap he was so famous for. I nailed him on the 1-yard line. When he got up, he said, "Hey, George, what the hell are you doing over here?" If he had run straight, he would have made it to Seventy-Ninth Street.

We always had a lot of fun playing the Cardinals. For some reason or other they always played their best against us. They had some real hot games. The hottest was the one in 1955, when they knocked us out of the championship. That was the one out at Comiskey Park, where Ollie Matson had a career day and they ran up a score of 53-14 on us.

I have one other worthy story about playing against the Cardinals. It was at Comiskey Park during my rookie year. I had been the kickoff man at Notre Dame, and when I came up with the Bears I kicked off for them—George Blanda did not come until the next year. I didn't do too bad a job for playing the whole game; I could get it down to the goal line most of the time and into the end zone sometimes.

Before a game the team went out to do calisthenics and to warm up. The punters would punt the ball, and you would run down on the punts—things like that. When the passers started their drill, the line coach took all the linemen down into one of the end zones so they could start beating the hell out of each other. Well, I wasn't too fond of that, so I decided I would practice field goals, kicker that I was. I'd get a bag full of footballs from George Halas. He'd have me sign a promissory note, because the balls cost $25 apiece. They didn't give me a center or a holder, so I lined up the ball, put my heel into the ground like kids do in the backyard, and teed it up. I wasn't really aiming for the goalpost; I was just trying to kill some time. When the linemen's drills were over, I'd pick up the balls and sign out with Halas—he would count the balls—and then we'd go in for the pep talk, and then the game would start.

So, out at Comiskey Park that day, it was the middle of the third quarter. I was Fred Davis's substitute at that early point in the season and therefore was on the bench. All of a sudden I heard Halas hollering, "81! 81!" Well, I thought it was a play I didn't know. But it was my number that year [it was changed to 71 the following year], but it didn't dawn on me that he was calling it. Finally he shouted, "Connor, get the hell up here!" He must have been watching before the game, and I must have made a few of those practice field goals, so he said to get in there and kick a field goal.

I was thrilled. All my South Side friends were there in the stands; Bulldog Turner was over the ball; the two blocking backs were in formation; little J. R. Boone, who was a rookie like me, was down on one knee to hold, and he marked the spot. I lined up and started swinging my arms, because that's what Lou "The Toe" Groza, the great kicker for the Cleveland Browns, did, and I patterned myself after him.

The ultimate stiff arm. George Connor (1948–55), after intercepting a Los Angeles Rams pass, applies it to the face of a sorry would-be tackler. Connor, one of the most devastating sixty-minute men in the game's history, made All-Pro eight times as both an offensive and defensive player and was inducted into the Pro Football Hall of Fame in 1975.

Jack Brickhouse on WGN radio said, "Ladies and gentlemen, I think this is a trick play." I made a two-step kick, and, well, I stubbed my foot, and the ball hit Turner in the fanny, and a piece of turf about as big as a softball went over the line of scrimmage. Halas never asked me to kick a field goal again.

I think Johnny Lujack was the best all-around college football player I competed with or against. He was that good. That's unfortunately what did him in with the Bears. They played him offense and defense, and he got both shoulders hurt. And, of course, sports medicine wasn't what it is today. John was a very intense quarterback. During his first two years he was absolutely spectacular. Against the Cardinals at Wrigley Field in 1949 he passed for 468 yards, which still stands as the Bear all-time record. And we won that game 52-21.

One game I especially remember was in 1955, my last year. We played the Green Bay Packers at Wrigley Field. I made a tackle on a kickoff that people who were there still ask me about. Knowing it was my last season and with my brother on leave from the marines and at the game with my parents, I really wanted to do well that day. I had always loved covering on kickoffs—I just like the contact. So, just before the start of that game I said to myself, you've got to do something special today.

I lined up for the opening kickoff on the right side, about two players right of the kicker, George Blanda. I ran downfield, heading for the wedge, which in those days usually consisted of a couple of tackles, another lineman, and a linebacker. For lack of other names, we used to call them the Four Horsemen. They lined up on about the 15-yard line. They ordinarily defy anybody to run through them. Well, I was running down and really had the steam up as I was going into the wedge, and all of a sudden it just opened up. Al Carmichael and Veryl Switzer, who was up for rookie of the year, were the two backs at the goal line for the Packers. Switzer caught the ball, and Carmichael moved out as his personal blocker.

I was running full-speed now directly at Carmichael and couldn't see Switzer behind him. And suddenly, for some reason or other, Carmichael disappeared, and there was Switzer. I hit him at top speed with my shoulder, the ball went up in the air, and so did his helmet. A lot of people in the stands thought I had decapitated him. Bill George picked up the ball and took it into the end zone for a touchdown. Switzer was knocked out before he hit the ground.

I kept running through the end zone and then around back to the bench. Coach Halas said, "Nice tackle, kid." I was down on one knee now, rubbing my shoulder, behind the other players, because I didn't want the Packers to know it hurt. A few minutes later there was a big, resounding roar of applause. And I said to Bill George, "What's going on out there?"

He said, "Well, the back you hit, Switzer, he just got up and walked off the field under his own power."

I said, "Well, I guess I'm losing my touch; maybe I better get out of the game."

Later I talked to Max McGee, an end with the Packers, about what happened. I said, "Didn't you guys like the kid?"

McGee said, "No, we loved him. Everybody just messed up their assignments. That's all. And you just pulled off the toughest tackle I've ever seen in all my football life."

I suffered a knee injury in 1954, and it finally caught up with me. In those days the public did not know which players were injured. The teams did not have to announce it, and therefore they didn't. A lot of players were out there playing on one leg or playing all taped up for some other injury and, as a result, not doing their best, and some of the fans would boo them.

When I got injured in '54, I got a lot of doctors' opinions. Some said it was the cartilage, and others said it wasn't. I finally went to Coach Halas and said, "You know, I can't go anymore."

Halas said, "We'll see."

I had the knee operated on, and I came back in 1955, and it was the biggest challenge I ever faced in football. It hurt, and I was not playing up to par. And the fans booed me. I think the fans have a right to cheer or boo, but if you're injured they should have been told about it. Anyway, I wanted to change the boos to cheers, and that's where the challenge came in. I managed to do it, and then I left the game.

Retiring was not an overnight thing, however. I had a good friend by the name of Eugene P. McNeill who was a trucker in Chicago, owned a cartage company. We played a lot of handball together. He kept saying to me after the 1955 season, "Are you going back?" I was thinking the whole thing out at the time. I was well established in the corrugated box business at the time, and in all but my first year I made more money selling boxes than I did playing football. He asked me, "What are you going to accomplish out there on the field that you haven't already accomplished?" That kept running through my mind.

During the off-season I had some bone chips removed from my elbow, but I decided to go to training camp anyway in 1956. After about ten days, however, Halas and I could not agree on a contract. I think I was the first Bear ever to walk out of training camp, which I did for ten days. But I had an agreement with Halas that we would not try the case in the papers. So after ten days he called, and we got together, and he gave me the money I wanted.

And I said, "Coach, I quit." I had decided that if I couldn't be the best player out there, I didn't want to play. It was the best decision I ever made in my life. But it's the toughest decision any professional athlete has to make. A lot don't make the right decision and stay on too long, or go from club to club, and often people don't remember them at their peak.

I coached with the Bears for two years after retiring. I was an assistant coaching with Clark Shaughnessy at the time. I found out it was not easy. After a game in early 1956 in which the Lions annihilated us 42-10, I was running the projector, showing the game films, and commenting on who didn't do this and who didn't do that.

There were a lot of great defensive players on that team: Bill George, Doug Atkins, Fred Williams, Richie Petibon among them. There was a lot of grumbling coming from them in the back of the room. "Didn't you ever make a mistake?" "Who do you think you are?" Things like that. I found out there that the toughest thing is to go from a player to a coach and gain the players' respect as a coach.

With all the grumbling I heard, I finally kicked on the lights and said, "You know, you got the hell kicked out of you. I'm just trying to help. If you don't want to listen to me, I'll go out and sell my boxes; I make more money doing that than I do doing this, and I don't give a damn about you. You want to get beat again, or do you want to improve?" I was really fuming now. "I'll tell you what, I'm going to leave this room, I'm going outside, and if you want to come out, one by one, I'll take each one of you on."

Now I'm outside wondering what I've got myself into. I'm still in pretty good shape, but. . . . Then out walks Doug Atkins, all 6'8" of him, and I think, Boy, am I in trouble. He walks toward me, faking like he's going to swing at me, then stops, and instead holds out his hand, and said, "Coach, Coach George, we're going to listen to you." The next time we played the Lions that year we beat them 38–21, and went on to win the Western Division title.

After two years I got out of the coaching end of the game. It was too restrictive. All the coaches had been around for a long time: Halas, the assistants like Luke Johnsos, Paddy Driscoll, Phil Handler. I'd come up with an idea, and they would say, "Aw, we tried that twenty-five years ago, and it didn't work."

I kept my hand in the game, however, working as a commentator for CBS on its NFL telecasts. I enjoyed that more than coaching.

Connor's Initiation

I got my initiation into the street-fighting arena that is more commonly known as the pro football line of scrimmage as a rookie in 1948. In the preseason I was used as a backup tackle for Fred Davis. He told me, "When I raise my hand coming out of the huddle, that means I need a rest. You come in on the next play."

I watched. When I saw his arm go up, I grabbed my helmet from the bench and, when the play was over, raced out onto the field. As soon as the ball was snapped on the next play, my face ran smack into the fist of the lineman I was opposing. It was an especially unpleasant greeting in those days before face masks were routinely worn. I was startled but thought that maybe this was the typical welcome a rookie got to the brutal game I'd heard that the pros play.

Later in the same game Davis raised his hand again, and I replaced him on the next play. This time I was lined up opposite a different lineman. But the reaction was the same. When play began, this lineman smashed me square in the face too. After the game I tried to figure out why it was happening to me; perhaps they resented all the publicity I'd gotten for a rookie, or maybe it was because I came from Notre Dame—a lot of the pro players were less than fond of the Fighting Irish alumni in those days. I even asked a few other linemen about this so-called special greeting. They agreed that work in the line was violent as hell, but what was occurring to me did seem a bit extraordinary.

It went on for several weeks. Then one Sunday it all became crystal-clear. This time when Davis raised his hand, I for some reason kept my eyes on him rather than on the play itself. When the ball was snapped, I saw Davis lunge across the line, punch the opposing lineman in the face, and then trot off toward our bench.

For the rest of that year I announced myself to whoever the opposing lineman was when I lined up after coming into the game: "Connor in, Davis out!" It made my life a lot easier that rookie year.

A bevy of Bears is after Detroit Lion ball carrier Leon Hart in this early 1950s
game: George Connor (71), Joe Fortunato (31), Bill George (nearest Hart),
Doug Atkins (81), Fred Williams (75), and Ed Sprinkle (7). Connor, George,
and Atkins are members of the Pro Football Hall of Fame.

Michael McCaskey—
On Growing Up with
the Bears

Michael McCaskey, the Bears' current president and grand-son of George Halas, like Wellington Mara of the New York Giants and Dan Rooney of the Pittsburgh Steelers, had the unusual experience of virtually growing up with an NFL football team. Professional football played an intimate role in the lives of these men because they were a part of it practically from the time they took their first steps.

McCaskey, the son of Ed McCaskey, chairman of the board of the Bears, and Virginia McCaskey, the daughter of George Halas, took over as chief executive officer of the ball club in November 1983, but his ties to the team go back to infancy. Much of his youth was spent in the shadows of Wrigley Field and under the scorching sun at training camps in Rensselaer, Indiana.

A college football player himself, McCaskey was a two-year letterman as a wide receiver for Yale in the early 1960s. After graduation and a two-year teaching stint with the Peace Corps in Ethiopia, he earned a doctorate in business administration at Case Western Reserve University, then went on to teach at UCLA and Harvard Business School.

After taking over the reins of the Bears, he found he and his team triumphant in the Super Bowl (XX) two seasons later. He received the highest honor bestowed on an NFL executive after that 1985 season when *The Sporting News* named him NFL Executive of the Year.

I'm told my first encounter with the Bears was when I was less than a year old and my mother brought me to Wrigley Field; that was my first official attendance at a Bears game. I have no recollection of it obviously, but that would have been a pretty good team representing us then, the Bears of 1944, with players like Sid Luckman, Bulldog Turner, Gene Ronzani, and George Musso.

I do remember vividly, however, in the early 1950s as a young kid, going to Wrigley Field and sitting with a couple of my brothers on a blanket right next to the Bears' bench and watching the game from that rather unique vantage point. There were a couple of things you had to watch out for, though, when you were sitting that close to the field. One was that a team might run a sweep and bodies would come flying, and as close to the playing field as we were we had to be ready to sprint out of there at a moment's notice. The other thing was that my grandfather, George Halas, sold three rows of seats, green folding chairs to be exact, inside the wall, right down on the field, and if we stood up to watch a play on the other side of the field it would block the view of the folks sitting in those rows. And we would hear, not in the most mellow of tones, "Hey, you kids, sit down!"

When I was eight years old, I began to go to the Bears' training camp at St. Joseph's College down in Rensselaer, Indiana. That was my summer vacation in a sense. I would help out in the laundry room and try not to get into too much trouble. My grandfather was very busy with the team, but he would still try to keep an eye on my brothers and me. He also invested Ed Rozy, the Bears' trainer, with the additional duty to shortcut any significant trouble we might get ourselves into. After all, we were kids, and there were pranks, harmless ones, like jumping into the big ornamental pool in front of the school's administra-

Michael McCaskey—On Growing Up with the Bears   113

tion building and trying to catch the goldfish in it. We got a little heat about that, I remember. Nothing compared to some of the things the players would come up with.

It was an exciting adventure for us to be that close to the team and to get to know the players. I remember the first year I went down there, the room that was assigned to me was actually the room that Bulldog Turner had used the summer before. I felt like some great honor had been bestowed on me.

My first impressions of my grandfather were that George Halas had a special intensity and enthusiasm. He was so excited about the games themselves; he loved the contest, the competition. He engaged his whole self in the game.

I saw both sides of him from early on. Because I saw him off the field as well as on it as the owner and coach of the team, I knew why he was tough-minded in dealing with players and in salary negotiations. But I was also a young boy and friends with the players, and they would tell me their side of it. So I had a pretty good understanding of what was going on. I got the feeling that my grandfather was very demanding and tough to deal with when it came to contracts and discipline and things like that, but if there was ever a question of somebody needing help, he was a very soft touch.

It was pretty brutal at training camp back then. The hot sun down there in the cornfields, the humidity—it got to everybody, and this was in the days before the players conditioned very well in the off-season, much different from the training camp as we know it today. In fact training camp *itself* back then had as one of its major purposes to get you in condition, and believe me, just about everyone arrived in need of getting into condition.

One thing I remember is that everyone in those days thought it was better for getting into shape if you didn't drink water. Well, we know now that is wrong. We had a lot of very thirsty players on the practice field. These big football players down there—out of shape, overweight, sweating it out—were dying for something to drink, so we would slip them little chips of ice out of the ice bags that the trainers would keep on the sideline.

There was a lot of fun too; the players provided many fond memories. I remember the first political conventions ever to be broadcast on television occurred in the summer of 1952, and the players were very taken with this. They used to dress in the bleachers on opposite sides of the basketball court. And after having watched some of the convention on television, I don't remember which one, they held their own mock convention while they were getting dressed. It was mostly Fred Williams and Bill George that I remember. Fred Williams, who was from Arkansas and had played his college ball for the Razorbacks down there, would get up and give one of those grandiloquent speeches about how Arkansas is proud to cast its votes for whoever it was and go on with this long, convoluted statement about the great sun-drenched state of Arkansas.

The players used to play mumblety-peg, the game with the knife where you flip it and stick it in the ground, in front of the dorms at St. Joe's. They didn't have much else to do; they were in the middle of the cornfields. That's why my grandfather chose the place, so there wasn't much else to do but play and think about football. Pitching pennies for quarters was another pastime down there, and the players did that a lot. I would play mumblety-peg, but I wouldn't pitch for quarters with them, which is probably one of the smartest things I ever did down there.

I did have the opportunity to meet some remarkable individuals while hanging around the Bears. George Blanda, who was a great favorite of mine when I was a kid, taught me how to placekick. He was with the Bears for ten years and left after the 1958 season but of course didn't leave professional football until 1975—twenty-six seasons, an NFL record I'm sure will never be broken. At a Bears alumni party recently George was there, and I was sitting at the table with him, Fred Williams, and some others. We were sitting there telling stories on each other. Someone asked me to show how George had taught me to placekick. I got up and mimicked George down to a T, and everybody—guys like Bennie McRae, Bill Bishop, Ed Sprinkle, who were there—got a big kick out of it. Blanda was truly one of the great straight-ahead kickers and, needless to say, well deserves his niche in the Hall of Fame.

Later, when I was in college at Yale, I wanted to play either quarterback or wide receiver. I was fortunate to be able to work on both with the Bears. Bill Wade was a terrific help, and so was Sid Luckman, who was on the Bears' coaching staff at that time. They helped me get down the mechanics of setting up and throwing the ball correctly. And Johnny Morris was great on teaching me how to run the sideline pattern. He had a way of doing it that was especially effective, and later it really worked well for me in college ball.

Some of the games I most remember from the fifties were against the Chicago Cardinals, our traditional crosstown rivals. And it was some rivalry in those days; we always had a difficult time beating the Cardinals no matter how good we were or how poor a team they had. It was always a rock 'em, sock 'em, savage game. I especially remember Ollie Matson, their great running back, tearing through us in a game in 1955 in late December at Comiskey Park. It was a snowy, very cold day—so many of those games between the Bears and Cardinals over the years were played under those conditions. We were in first place in the NFL West and a solid favorite. The Cardinals had had a miserable season, won only a few games, and were far out of contention. But with Matson's running and the Cardinals fired up because they were playing us, we were destroyed that day, 53-14 [at the time, the most points ever scored against the Bears in their then-thirty-five-year history]. It, in fact, cost us the championship that year. We ended with a record of 8-4-0, and the Rams took it with a record of 8-3-1.

Two other great runners like Ollie Matson, who always gave us nightmares around that time, were Hugh McElhenny of the 49ers and Crazylegs Hirsch of the Rams. They were simply splendid runners. In my mind's eye I can still see the grace and quickness with which they moved. It was just spectacular when you were right on the sideline and got to see it up close, hear the noises from the field.

Lenny Moore of the Colts was always a scary player to us too, he was so good. And Frank Gifford of the Giants—he was always effective and a very versatile threat.

A little later came the Packers with all their great players— Paul Hornung, Jim Taylor, Bart Starr, Ray Nitschke, Willie

Davis, Herb Adderley—so many I can't name them all. The battles we've had over the years with the Packers are legendary.

I remember one time being on the sideline at a preseason game against Green Bay in County Stadium in Milwaukee. Vince Lombardi had his team moving the ball, but then there was a terrible call against the Packers. Bombastic Vince was ranting and raving at the officials, and then he looked over at my grandfather, who was still coaching then—both teams were on the same sideline that day—as if to say, "George, now you saw that, don't you agree that was the worst call you've ever seen?" And Halas just gave him one of those really sweet smiles, like he was saying, "Oh, Vince, come on." He was so good at that; didn't need to say a single word.

Surely the most memorable game of that time to me and a lot of others was the 1963 championship game against the New York Giants at Wrigley Field. The Bears of '63 were a team that I had practiced with in training camp at St. Joe's. That's when I was trying to get ready for my junior year in college football.

The week before the title game the Bears were practicing in Wrigley Field, and I got to practice with them there, which was a great thrill. As a wide receiver I ran some patterns against the defense, and I remember getting some hell from Bill George because I caught one pass that they didn't want me to catch.

I also got to watch the game from the bench. And it was quite a game. Everybody who was there remembers how bitterly cold it was, and those were the days before we had thermal underwear and thermal parkas and bench warmers—the kinds of things we have today. It was a long, frigid afternoon, but everyone who was there remembers it with great pride.

How can anyone forget it? I still recall clearly seeing a battered, frustrated Y. A. Tittle getting tackled, knocked around by our defense, who were magnificent that day. I can see those two crucial interceptions by Larry Morris and Ed O'Bradovich. I was really pleased to see them do so well, because at training camp I used to love to sit around with the defensive players because they were the most fun. There were guys like Joe Fortunato, Larry Morris, Fred Williams, Bill George, Bennie McRae, Rosey Taylor, Davey Whitsell, Ed O'Bradovich, Doug

Atkins, some of the best and most entertaining, each in his own way.

I remember sitting with them in the locker room while George Allen, our defensive coach, was trying to conduct a meeting. Now, George was an outstanding coach, and the players knew it, and he had their respect. But he was relatively new in that position, and they were the grizzled veterans. They just loved to kid him and find ways to put a little heat on him. He would still have the discipline when it was needed, but he would go along with their antics. There were times when he would just look at me during the meeting and shake his head, or after the meeting we would walk out together, and he would say, "Well, they're great players, and this is the *Chicago Bears defense.*"

That day in the cold of Wrigley Field the Bears wanted to use the quarterback draw, which Bill Wade ran to perfection. It was a perfect play that Halas came up with to attack the Giants' defense, which was a superb one. But it was so cold it was tough to hang on to the ball, and after Wade fumbled it on one draw early we sort of got scared away from it and didn't use it probably as much as we should have.

It went all the way down to the wire, as every Bear fan knows. And it was nothing short of exhilarating when Richie Petibon intercepted that Tittle pass in the end zone at the end of the game. It was 14-10 at that time, and the Giants were perfectly capable of scoring on that play—they had Del Shofner, one of the best receivers in the league, streaking toward the end zone. We were on pins and needles, but the ball ended up in Richie's hands, and that was the end for the Giants.

I admired the courage of the Giant players that day. They had some splendid ones: Tittle, Frank Gifford, Rosey Brown, Sam Huff, Andy Robustelli—a lot of Hall of Famers there. You have a lot of respect for an opponent that is as good as the Giants were. And the hallmark of that team was, for me anyway, their wonderfully courageous players.

After the game I went into the locker room and was surprised at how quiet it was. It was an extraordinary moment, one where it seemed people didn't know quite what to do. The players were stunned it was now over. And then my grandfather shouted something out. I don't remember the exact words, but it was a signal for all hell to break loose, and everybody just went crazy. Bottles of soda pop and champagne and beer were sprayed on people. Everybody yelling, slapping each other. It was a hectic scene.

In the locker room there they awarded the game ball to George Allen for the great defense he coached and inspired. Still the grizzled defenders were not about to let him off easy. They sang:

Hooray for George
Hooray for George
For he's a horse's ass

But they also knew that when you give someone a game ball, you are saying to the person he has made one major contribution. And those were the days when we gave only one or two game balls, not like the four or five we hand out today. It was one of George Allen's finest moments.

The next summer we started the season by playing the College All-Stars in the annual All-Star game at Soldier Field. That year they had Paul Warfield, the great flanker then from Ohio State, who was to go on to become a great wide receiver for the Browns and later the Dolphins. I remember I was focusing on him because I heard he was so good. This was before instant replay, and therefore you had to choose who you wanted to watch before a play began. Well, I was watching Warfield on this one play, and he started downfield, gave a fake to the outside, and Davey Whitsell bit on it; then Warfield broke over the middle. He caught a pass for a nice long gain. At halftime I said to Davey, "I was really surprised at Warfield's fake."

He looked at me incredulously and said, "*You* were surprised? How the hell surprised do you think I was?"

Some other games I especially remember were played in Memorial Stadium in Baltimore. That place was such a loud stadium, it was deafening. And the Colts were always dangerous in those days, what with players like Johnny Unitas, Lenny Moore, Raymond Berry, Jim Parker, Gino Marchetti—players of that stature. It was truly tough to win a game in that stadium, though we tried our darnedest.

One game in particular comes to mind. It was in October 1961. We were coming off a three-game winning streak. Willie Galimore was having one of this best seasons running for us. It was Bill Wade's first year with the Bears, and he was doing great throwing to Johnny Morris and Mike Ditka, who was a rookie that year. We really wanted that game in Baltimore. It also stands out in my mind because one of the sportswriters' lead-in to the game was "In the world's largest outdoor insane asylum. . . ." We quieted the inmates that day, though, by winning 21-20 when Galimore took a short screen pass from Ed Brown in the fourth quarter and ran 84 yards for a touchdown.

Without doubt one of the greatest football players of that era and—how should I put it?—most colorful was our enormous defensive end Doug Atkins. He was 6'8" and maybe 260 pounds. He was a crazy man, and true stories about his antics as a Bear abound. He shot a gun through the ceiling of the dorm at St. Joe's one training camp. The veterans were on the ground floor, and the rookies were on the second floor. There was no air-conditioning, and so it was uncomfortable, and when you got off your feet you really wanted to be able to relax. We came back from one of the practices, and a rookie upstairs turned his radio on loud. Doug pounded on the ceiling and shouted, "Turn down the damn radio!" The rookie ignored it and left the radio blaring away. So Doug took out a gun and shot it through the ceiling. I don't think the guy ever played his radio again the rest of camp.

Doug's run-ins with my grandfather were legendary. One story comes to mind. Halas made a real big deal about a player's weight, and he would fine a player for every pound he was overweight. He even instituted a "fat man's table" at camp to control the diet of those guys who needed to lose weight. Doug battled the weight thing all the time.

Different players had different ways of getting the weight off. Rick Casares, for example, would go into a sauna and sweat it off. Atkins, however, found a unique approach one year. Wednesday ordinarily was the weigh-in day, and Doug walked up to my grandfather on one Tuesday, and he had one of these big paper cups full of Ex-Lax. He said, "Coach, is there gonna be a weigh-in tomorrow?"

Halas looked at him and said, "Tomorrow's Wednesday, isn't it?"

Then Doug, right in front of him, downed this enormous cup of Ex-Lax.

My grandfather stared at him all the way through it, and when Doug finished chewing, Halas announced, "No weigh-in tomorrow."

Over the twelve years Doug was with the Bears, he and my grandfather had some pitched battles, but that was part of their kind of special relationship. Atkins was not at all afraid to pipe up with something, and it would almost always be funny, and my grandfather would either have to respond to it or laugh with everybody else.

How this crazy relationship got going I can only guess. The Bears acquired Atkins from Paul Brown of the Cleveland Browns, one of the great coaches of all time. Brown found it too big a battle or too disruptive to keep Doug, so he traded him to us. My grandfather, well aware of how great a coach Brown was, wanted to be able to show him that *he* could handle the problem. It was the old competition thing that was so much a part of my grandfather's nature.

All the great coaches, even Vince Lombardi, traded away some players who went on to very successful careers elsewhere. My grandfather did. Remember Bobby Layne?

Besides the competition, however, Halas also had a real good feel for Doug, appreciated what an outstanding football player he was, and, I think, even liked the irascible side of him. That was something Halas could deal with; he had been like that as a young man himself.

A later game that was also especially memorable was the last game of the 1977 season. If we won it, the Bears would earn a wild-card berth in the playoffs. The importance of it lay in the fact that the Bears had not made it to a postseason game since the championship of '63. The game was played at Giants Stadium in the New Jersey Meadowlands, and it was an awful day, with snow and slush coating the artificial turf. The two teams slipped and slid through four quarters, and at the end the score was 9-9. In overtime we had two chances, but Bob Thomas missed both field goals. But then in the last minute of the overtime, Walter Payton gained 15 yards on a little dump pass from Bob Avellini. With no time-outs left, the field goal team rushed out on the field with twelve seconds on the clock. My uncle Muggs [George Halas, Jr., then the Bears president] was there in the skybox next to me, and we were all just dying. If he missed it, we were out; if he made it, we were in. Well, he made it, a 27-yarder, and we went to the playoffs [the first overtime victory in Bears history]. No true Bears fan will ever forget that game.

The second part of my affiliation with the Bears came when I joined them officially. That was in November 1983.

Jim Finks, one of the NFL's great administrators, had been running the organization. He had been hired by Muggs Halas to do just that back in 1974, and he had done a lot to build the ball club and help speed the transition from a small, family-owned business to one that was professionally managed. His contributions were not only in the players he drafted—and he made some very good choices there—but also in the way in which the front office was run under his guidance. Everything was on a more businesslike basis.

When Muggs died unexpectedly in 1979, it set the stage for a kind of power struggle between my grandfather and Jim Finks. It was not necessarily over power as such; more a clash of the old and new in terms of ideas, areas of responsibility, things like that. Under Muggs it was clear that Jim Finks had been given the authority for the draft and the hiring of our head coach, but now with Muggs gone so was that agreement, and my grandfather came out of retirement and began to move into those areas. It became a difficult situation for everyone.

By 1982 and into 1983 my grandfather was too ill to watch over the day-by-day operations of the club; in fact he was confined first to a hospital bed and later to his apartment. Jim did a magnificent job carrying on as best he could under the circumstances.

Around that time my family began thinking about what would happen after my grandfather died. They approached me and asked if I would consider taking over the Bears, running the organization. I had never really given that kind of thing much thought, and my wife, Nancy, and I were very happy in our work, a business consulting company we owned and operated, and with our friends in Boston, where we were living at the time.

We spent a good deal of time thinking about it. We knew it would be a major change in our lives, but all things considered, it came down to a keen responsibility that I felt to my family and to the Bears, which had been so much a part of our lives. So I decided to come back to Chicago to see if I could help bring back some of the glory to the Bears that I felt had been so much a part of their heritage.

The goals to me at the onset were pretty evident. I wanted everybody, and I mean *everybody*, from the players to the front-office personnel, to be dedicated to turning the Bears into a championship team. I also wanted to see the Bears run in such a way as to make it a healthy, strong business with great prospects for the future. I wanted it to be a business that truly paid attention to its fans, those who supported the team and the game itself and therefore made it all possible. I was fortunate in that I had been a management professor on the college level and a business consultant, both of which helped me focus on my goals for the organization.

My biggest help came, however, from my father [Ed McCaskey, the Bears' chairman of the board] and Jim Finks, both of whom understood the NFL and the Bears so well. I respected their judgments, and I continue to gain from them to this day.

It all came together for the Bears, of course, in 1985—the team, Coach Mike Ditka; they brought us the Super Bowl trophy.

I sensed it coming in our first confrontation with the Dallas Cowboys. They had been the quality of the NFL for a long time, and it was a team you wanted to stand toe-to-toe with and

The trophy comes to Halas Hall. Bear president Michael McCaskey holds the Vince Lombardi Trophy, earned through the Bears' magnificent triumph in Super Bowl XX, where the Monsters of the Midway destroyed the New England Patriots, 46-10, in the most lopsided Super Bowl ever. Looking on is Bear chairman of the board Ed McCaskey.

beat them. It was always a major test. We went down there in the preseason, and I saw our team not only stand up to them, but stand out as the better team. Well, the real test of this came when we met them in the regular season, when it truly counts. We went down there again to Texas Stadium, this time with a 10-0-0 record. They were talking about being spoilers, all that kind of thing. We demolished them, 44-0.

I don't usually go down onto the field until the fourth quarter, but this game was such a milestone in our year, I felt, that I went down in the third quarter. At the time we were ahead something like 34-0, and the Cowboy fans were streaming for the exits. I saw Mike Singletary look at the fleeing crowd, then stand up from his middle linebacker position and shout at them, "Wait. I want witnesses!"

You could just feel the exuberance and excitement that were coursing through that Bears team that year. Otis Wilson, I believe it was, got the defense and the fans barking, and that carried on all the way to the Super Bowl. In Minnesota, a game we wanted very much to show we owned the NFC Central Division, we found behind our bench four guys dressed in Blues Brothers outfits—flip-brim hats, sunglasses, navy blue suits— and they had a sign: Blues Brothers on a Mission. The fans had picked up the momentum and the rich enjoyment of it all.

The entire week leading up to Super Bowl XX was like catching a wave and bodysurfing. It was just absolutely thrilling. I've seen other club presidents who, when they get to Super Bowl week, get wound up so tight that they can't enjoy it; they're deathly afraid of losing—it's all that is on their minds; it's a very tense situation with them. I did not find it that way. None of us did. We had our funny moments, we felt the exhilaration of being headed into the Super Bowl, and we were feeling very good about our chances of winning.

Then the game itself came, and when Walter Payton fumbled early, it sent a scare through us. The Patriots kicked a field goal and went ahead 3-0. Then on the video board at the Superdome down there in New Orleans they flashed the statistic that in the preceding 19 Super Bowls the team that scored first had won 17 of them.

But then, of course, everything changed. Our offense exploded. The defense was impenetrable. We were like a huge boa constrictor just squeezing down and squeezing down; there was no question we were going to win this game. It was just such a thrill, I didn't want to ever see it end.

Returning to it—that's our chief goal for the 1990s. To win several more Super Bowls: that's our number-one priority.

Off-the-field priorities: the list is headed by getting a new home for the Chicago Bears. For the long term that just has to happen.

We will also continue to look for new ways to market the ball club, new ways to provide a better connection between our fans and the team. We'll add new people and try to help them understand what the Bears are all about, what kind of football team we want to be, how we want to play the game with a special zest for winning.

We would like to have a Bears Hall of Fame here in Chicago as part of our way of conveying our tradition to the fans as well as the visitors to the city.

Here is a team that was a charter member of the NFL, begun in 1920, more than seventy years ago, one that has had some of the greatest players ever to play the game of pro football: Red Grange, Bronko Nagurski, Sid Luckman, George McAfee, Bulldog Turner, George Connor, Gale Sayers, Dick Butkus, Walter Payton—and that's just a few of them. And, of course, my grandfather, one of the founders of the game, sometimes called the "Father of Pro Football," who was instrumental in seeing the league through its tough times and developing it into the great sport it is.

The Bears have a noble tradition and a great future ahead, and I feel very fortunate to have been involved with it so long and so closely.

Marrying into the Family

Ed McCaskey, Bears chairman of the board, tells the story: "I was at the University of Pennsylvania, had a singing part in the *Mask and Wig* show, and a friend of mine brought a girl to the rehearsal. Her name was Virginia Halas. We didn't hit it off at the first meeting, but it wasn't too long after that I was pursuing her with great vigor.

"We had been dating for about a year and a day when, one day, I went into a little restaurant on campus and the owner said, 'The two men over there want to talk to you.'

"So I walked over to these two guys sitting there in their camel's hair coats and said, 'You want to see me?'

"One of them said, 'Are you McCaskey?'

"I said, 'Yes.'

" 'Well, I'm Bert Bell,' he said. 'And this is Art Rooney,' nodding to the guy with a big cigar stuck in his mouth. Bert Bell and Art Rooney at the time [the early 1940s] were co-owners of the Pittsburgh Steelers.

" 'Halas sent us here to check you out,' Bell said. 'And we already talked to Bill Lenox,' who was in charge of athletic tickets at Pennsylvania. 'He says you're OK. And if you're OK with Bill Lenox, you're OK with me.'

"With that, Art Rooney spoke for the first time: 'If you're OK with Bert here, you're OK with me.' Then he took the cigar out of his mouth and said, 'And whoever said Halas was an angel?'

"The following spring I met George Halas for the first time. My interests were in the big bands, the Dorsey brothers, Frank Sinatra, Bob Eberly . . . music . . . I didn't care about football that much. He wasn't very much impressed with me, but I didn't care; I was interested in his daughter, period.

"When we decided to get married in 1943, George Halas was in the navy, but we met with him in Washington, D.C., where he had flown in to watch the Bears play the Redskins. I remember we were sitting in the stands, and the Bears were losing to Washington, and all of a sudden Virginia was crying. I asked what was the matter.

" 'You don't think Daddy will let us get married if the Bears lose?' she said.

"Well, he did, reluctantly [the Bears lost 21–7 that day], and I became part of the family."

Mike Pyle

Mike Pyle came to the Chicago Bears in 1961 and immediately earned the starting position at center, which he held over nine seasons.

It was somewhat of a surprise, because he had apprenticed at Yale in the Ivy League, not noted for sending powerful and punishing linemen to the National Football League. Pyle had captained Yale's first unbeaten, untied team in thirty-seven years as a senior in 1960.

He was drafted by the Bears in the seventh round in 1961. After playing in the 1961 College All-Star game, which the former collegians lost to the Philadelphia Eagles 28–14, he suited up for the Bears and handled the center snaps for the rest of the decade. He was known as one of the best straight-ahead blockers of that era.

After the 1969 season Pyle retired from the game. Today he maintains touch with the Bears by hosting the "Mike Ditka Show" on WGN radio and the Tuesday Quarterback Club luncheons during the NFL season.

It came as a big surprise to me to be drafted by the Bears, because I had gone to Yale, and I chose that school certainly without the idea of eventually playing professional football. If I had ever entertained that thought, I would have chosen a school with a stronger football program.

We had a good team at Yale, however. We were in the Top 20 in both the AP and UPI polls my senior year and tied Navy for the Lambert Trophy, which is awarded each year to the number-one team in the East. And that was the Navy team that was ranked fifth in the nation and had the Heisman Trophy winner, Joe Bellino, in its backfield.

Well, after the season I got a call from George Allen. Besides being the Bears' defensive coach, he also handled personnel matters—recruiting, drafting, things like that. Today, of course, all those things are handled separately by specialists. We talked, and he told me the Bears might draft me. I said to myself, What a thought! The Bears might draft me. I'd been a Bear fan all my life, having grown up in the Chicago area. Then George told me to tell any other team that contacted me that I didn't want to play pro ball. "That way we'll get to draft you."

I was naive enough to think that was a neat idea. Later somebody tipped me off that if I did that the Bears would draft me in the last round, because they wouldn't have any pressure from anybody else in the league, or the AFL, to draft me before that. So I changed directions and told the other two or three teams who expressed an interest in me that I was interested in playing in the pros. The New York Giants were quite interested, and as a result the Bears ended up drafting me in the seventh round that year [1961].

I actually started playing football in sixth grade in Winnetka, Illinois. Then I played at New Trier High School in the same town. I also wrestled and was on the track team. In my senior year I made All-State in football; I was a tackle then on offense and defense. And I won the state in wrestling, and in track I won it in the shot put and the discus. Football was always my favorite sport, though.

At Yale I was a tackle my freshman and senior years and center my sophomore and junior. Our coach, Jordan Oliver, kept switching me around. Actually six of the starters on our undefeated team of 1960 were from the Chicago area.

With the Bears there was no question I was going to be a center, because that's what they needed then. In those days they held the draft in December, so by the time I got home for Christmas vacation I had already been selected by the Bears. Up to that time my only contact with the organization had been with George Allen.

George Halas thought it was wonderful I was coming home for Christmas, because he could save some money and not have to bring me into Chicago. So he set it up for me to come down to the Bear offices while I was home, to negotiate a contract. I didn't have an agent; I don't think anybody on the Bears had an agent in 1960 or '61. My father came down with me to give a little moral support.

It was an experience. Halas greeted us, ushered us in, and said he knew my father had season tickets for years and that he knew I was a great Bear fan and had gone to many, many games. On and on. He almost asked me to play just for the love of the Bears.

At any rate, I signed a contract. Teams today spend more money bringing in a first- or second-round draft pick to meet the media and the press and entertain him than they paid us for a year's worth of football.

The next summer I played in the All-Star game at Soldier Field. I was really pleased because my father was there, and I was announced as the starting center. Otto Graham was our coach, and he had an unusual way of picking starters. We had two centers: Greg Larson, who went on to have a great career with the New York Giants, and me. On the Friday afternoon before the game we were working out at Soldier Field, and Otto came up and said, "I gotta have a starting center, guys." Then he pulled out a quarter and said to Greg, "Call it." He did, and I won the toss. As it turned out, we each played a half. But I know it was a big thrill for my dad because he was such a good football fan.

On the Sunday morning we were to report to training camp, I was supposed to pick up Mike Ditka, who was a rookie too that year, and drive him down to Rensselaer. But my dad died of a heart attack the night before, and so my first training camp was not only abbreviated but a pretty stressful one as well.

Mike was one of my first good friends on the Bears. So was Bill Brown, a fullback from Illinois who played with us for a year and then about twelve with the Minnesota Vikings. There were a lot of players pretty well entrenched there when I first arrived, especially the defense—guys like Doug Atkins, Bill George, Fat Freddy Williams, Earl Leggett. They made fun of the fact that I'd gone to Yale. They gave me a little needling about being a "Yale boy." They'd give me a little extra shot in practice, then they'd kid me. One of the reasons, besides just being a rookie, is that they felt, I'm sure, that I had come out of a football program that was not as rugged as the ones they had come from, which was in fact true.

Eventually they kind of said, This guy's not a bad football player. He's standing up and taking it, so maybe he's not a Yale wimp or something. But they made me earn their respect.

Training was a lot different then. I think today's game reflects the much better methods they have. We did not lift weights. Actually one of us did, Stan Jones. He played guard, next to me, my first two years. Stan was one of the first weight lifters in the business, and he was kind of a unique attraction. He was so strong as a result. There used to be pictures of him in the newspapers doing push-ups with someone sitting on his shoulders.

The defensive linemen were big in those days, but most of them were fat guys. Today you've got guys equally tall and heavy, but they're solid and can run the forty in something like 4:6—much faster, more mobile.

We all had our own ways of training in those days. There weren't any specific step-by-step programs like they've got today. Earlier in my career I used wrestling and track as off-season training helps. When I joined the Bears, I did a lot of exercising. It was more to get you into shape and keep you there than strength training.

I got the starting job at center in the fourth preseason game. Larry Strickland, who was a great one, had retired in 1959. So, in '60, John Mellekas was converted to center. But John was a big tackle, maybe 260 pounds, and was not really mobile enough to play center. So John went back to being a tackle, and I became the Bear center.

It was just around that time when the teams in the league had adopted the four-man front line and three linebackers. So there was no longer a defensive player directly on the center. If anybody, it was the middle linebacker who was playing on the center, with the two defensive tackles playing on our guards. As a result the centers now had to be more mobile, quicker, and so for the most part they were smaller. It was around that time when Jim Ringo of the Packers and later the Eagles, who never weighed more than 235, revolutionized the position. He was All-Pro for about eight years. I was a little bigger, around 245, but the others were pretty small centers: Mick Tinglehoff of the Vikings, Bill Curry of the Packers and the Colts, Ken Bowman of Green Bay—guys like that.

We got pushed around some because we weren't as big as the other offensive linemen. Our job was to get in front of a defensive tackle and cut him off on running plays. On pass blocking we had to get back to cut off the middle linebacker from wherever he might be coming in. Sometimes we had the responsibility for an outside linebacker, so we had to snap the ball and come all the way out to the outside to get in front of him. So mobility was very important.

The most important thing for a center was technique in trying to block guys who were much bigger than us. We tried to do it with quickness.

From the start we had a great deal of togetherness as a team, both the offense and defense. Usually the team sort of split up, the offense hanging out together and the defense a separate group. But with a winning team everybody is together. And that's the way we were. We had only something like thirty-eight guys on the roster in those days.

After every game just about everybody went out. We'd have twenty-five or thirty guys going out on a Sunday night after a game. We'd go to The Cottage, which was on Belmont and Clark. After that we might go out to the bowling alley Mike Ditka owned in Willowbrook or the one Rick Casares owned in

Buffalo Grove. Sometimes we'd go to all three on the same Sunday night. We might end up driving ninety or a hundred miles.

In my second year with the Bears, 1962, the team decided to join the Players Association. We had a meeting with a representative from it, and then the team got together on a Tuesday before practice. Bill George and Stan Jones, who were the team captains at the time, conducted it. They said they would have to hold an election to see who would be the player rep. Then Doug Atkins stood up, all 6'8" of him, and said, "I nominate Mike Pyle because he went to Yale." Nobody else said anything, but Doug did not sit back down. Finally Bill George said, "Doug, you got anything else to say?"

"Yeah, I move the nominations be closed."

And that was it. No one challenged him, and I became the player rep, which I served as for the next seven years.

One game I remember especially from that year was against Baltimore. The Colts were a good team. Don Shula was coaching them then, and they, of course, had Johnny Unitas and Ray Berry and Lenny Moore. They also had Billy Ray Smith, one of the great characters of that era. He was a huge defensive tackle who hailed from Arkansas. My brother Palmer, who had played at Michigan State, also played for the Colts; he was an offensive guard. But we were killing them that day; the score ended up 57-0. Well, we were up 40 some points, and everybody knew the game was ours, and we just wanted to get it over with. But here was Billy Ray Smith playing like the score was tied and the title was on the line. He was coming across the line like a madman and just killing me. I finally said to him, "C'mon, Billy, we're going to win this game. It's all over. Why're you trying to kill me?"

"I'm doing it for your brother," he said.

The following year, of course, we won the title, and that was a great season. We didn't know we were a championship team going into the season, but each week we played better than the one before. We led it off by beating the Packers, which gave us a lot of impetus because they were the defending champions. They were [Vince] Lombardi's Packers. They didn't have Paul Hornung because he had been suspended for gambling, but all the others were there: Bart Starr, Jim Taylor, Boyd Dowler, Max McGee, Ray Nitschke, Forrest Gregg, Fuzzy Thurston, Jerry Kramer, Willie Davis, Jim Ringo, Herb Adderley, Willie Wood. . . . When we beat them, we felt we could beat anybody.

The second Packer game was one of the best I ever played in because we totally dominated them. We knew we had to win that game. We were both tied for first place in the NFL West. They came to Wrigley Field, and we were ready for them. Starr was hurt, which was a break for us. But even he couldn't have changed it that day. Our defense was fantastic. They didn't allow a single point until the fourth quarter, and by that time we had 26 points on the board. Our offense just pushed them all over the field that day, and we won, 26-7. After it the game ball was awarded to our offensive line coach, Phil Handler.

One of the other most unforgettable games I ever played in was another one against the Packers. It was in 1968. The division title was at stake. If we won, we would have it. We didn't, and the Vikings ended up the winner. Don Horn was playing quarterback for them that day, and he got them a couple of touchdowns early in the game.

At the beginning of the second half we were down by three touchdowns. It was the year that Gale Sayers got hurt and was out for the season. But we were still leading the league in rushing as a team, with the slack being picked up by Ronnie Bull and Brian Piccolo. Our offensive line was a disaster. Two guys went out with knee injuries, Bob Wetoska was playing with only one shoulder, a couple of other guys were out; we had only five offensive linemen on short yardage situations. I remember George Seals, one of our guards, a huge guy who the opposing teams had little liking for, going down out there. He was a marauder, a frightening guy. But he went down, his knee blown away, and I can still see Ray Nitschke, their middle linebacker, standing over him, yelling at him, taunting him. It angered the hell out of all of us.

We were forced to bring in Dick Evey, a defensive tackle, to play on the offensive line, and coming out of the huddle I had to tell him what to do on the play. Somehow we came back and scored 3 touchdowns and were within a point of the Pack. As the game was coming to an end, we reached their 25-yard line and had one last shot at bringing about one of the great comebacks in NFL history, but Jack Concannon's pass was picked off by Ray Nitschke, and we lost 28-27.

It was the most inspired football game I was ever in. Only five linemen, two on their way to the hospital as we were finishing it out, and we came back.

There were a lot of characters on the Bears during the years I played. Rick Casares, for example, was one of the funniest men who ever lived. He always had a weight problem—gained a little too much in the off-season. Coach Halas always wanted to keep him smaller than Rick wanted to be. It was tough for him, meeting Halas's weight rules. Finally he developed a formula. It was definitely his style. We had weigh-ins on Thursday mornings, so after practice on Wednesday Rick would get all dressed up and go out and cabaret on Rush Street all night long. He felt he would be so dehydrated the next morning he would make the weigh-in. Some of the times he did, but he could barely make it through the practice that day. But he did it for years.

He took a lot of punishment over the years. But Rick always came back. His legs were so banged up, his ankles a mess, but on Sunday he'd be there. Maybe he couldn't practice during the week, maybe he couldn't even run, but when the game started on Sunday you could not find a better competitor who ever lived.

And Rick Casares left a lot of people on opposite teams very well aware of the fact that they had played against him. He hit defenders with such intensity. Walter Payton was like that later—make them pay if they're going to tackle you. Rick sure did it.

Mike Ditka was probably the most intense competitor I've ever been around. I remember one game out in Los Angeles; we were playing the Rams on a Thursday night on national television. They were kind of testing out night television then. It was a very frustrating game because we weren't scoring and our defense was doing a great job of containing the Rams and getting the ball back for us.

After about the third time the defense got a turnover for us in Ram territory, this fan broke onto the field and was running down the middle of it with about four security cops chasing him. We were in a huddle and saw him coming from the other end. All of a sudden Ditka broke out of the huddle and decked the guy. Whacked him and knocked him right on his butt in the middle of the field. Everybody in the stands started booing Ditka. After the game, when he was asked why he decked the guy, Mike just shrugged and said, "The cops weren't gaining on him, so I just thought I'd give them a little help."

The real reason was because Mike was such an intense competitor and he was really feeling the frustration of our not being able to take advantage of what the defense was doing for us and score some points. He wanted the guy off the field so we could get the game going and do something.

Dick Butkus was another extraordinarily intense competitor. He came up my fifth year. I ended up spending a lot of money during training camps after Dick became a Bear. Dick would be just as intense in practice as he was in a game. His being a middle linebacker and me a center, we met rather frequently on the field in scrimmages at camp. I kept telling him he did not have to prove anything—not to us, not to Halas. We all knew he was the best in the game. So I'd spend all this money buying him dinner and beer and stuff like that so he wouldn't take it out on me in the scrimmages. He probably did shorten my career by a couple of years just in training camps.

Another outstanding player was Doug Buffone. He was always very underrated, playing in the shadow of Butkus. Doug was not a flashy player either. But he played pass defense very well, played against the run well, was always in the right place. He was very consistent, did everything very well, but just never got the recognition he deserved.

Probably the toughest guy I played against year in and year out was Alex Karras of the Lions. He didn't always make All-Pro, but he had some great moves. Alex had outstanding upper-body strength and very quick legs, and he was just a superb pass rusher. He used to give me fits.

Another one was Merlin Olsen of the Rams. He was awfully tough. Art Donovan of the Colts was always a handful too. And there were middle linebackers that no one who ever played against them could forget. There was Ray Nitschke of the Packers and Tommy Nobis of Atlanta.

It was playing against Nitschke that I hurt my ankle in 1964, and that was my worst football injury. It was the opening game of the '64 season up in Green Bay. On one play I was battling with Nitschke when Bob Wetoska, our right tackle, who was trying to block down on Hog Hanner, missed him but came down on me. I got a badly sprained ankle and was out for about five games. I came back, but the ankle was never the same. It just deteriorated from that point on. I was able to play despite it. Being a center, you just put more tape on it and go out and play, which I did for five more seasons. But finally it just gave out on me; there wasn't enough strength in it anymore to play, so I retired after the 1969 season.

I moved around a bit since. I was a stockbroker for five years. Then I spent a couple of years in the advertising business. I went back to Yale and worked for three years. Bart Giamatti, the late baseball commissioner who before that was president of Yale, asked me to come back to New Haven and help put together a corporate development program for Yale. Recently I've been in the banking business with First Illinois Bank.

Oops

The game was against the St. Louis Cardinals in 1969. Bear quarterback Jack Concannon, in the huddle, called the signal: center Mike Pyle was to snap the ball on the first word he heard from Concannon's mouth.

The Bears lined up, but Concannon did not like what he saw in the defense, so he turned and shouted "Time out!" to the referee. The well-trained Pyle, hearing the word *time*, snapped the ball before the referee could respond to Concannon's plea. The ball bounced off Concannon's buttocks and popped into the air, where Cardinal linebacker Larry Stallings grabbed it and ran 62 yards for a touchdown.

The Bears ended up losing that game 20–17, which was in keeping with the whole year—the Bears were 1–13–0 in 1969.

Doug Buffone

"One of the most underrated players I can remember" is the way Mike Ditka once described Doug Buffone. The reason, of course, was the awesome shadow struck by the middle linebacker playing next to him, Dick Butkus. It was a little like baseball's Dom DiMaggio of the Red Sox trying to get the recognition he deserved while playing in the outfield next to Ted Williams and while his brother gobbled up headlines with the Yankees.

Those who know football, however, are well aware that Buffone was one of the finest linebackers ever to play for the Chicago Bears.

Buffone came to the Bears in 1966, a fourth-round draft choice out of Louisville, and remained for fourteen seasons (only Bill George has played as many in Bear history). He played in a total of 186 games, four fewer than Walter Payton, who took the record from Buffone in 1987.

He was credited with 13 tackles in a game against the New Orleans Saints in 1974 and 11 solo tackles in the same game. Buffone had 22 career interceptions, a club record for a linebacker, which he shares with Dick Butkus.

Doug Buffone was the Bears' defensive captain from

1972 through 1979, the year he retired from the game.

Today Buffone still makes his home in Chicago, where he is often heard on WMAQ radio analyzing his former team, and is in the restaurant business.

I came to the Bears in the days of the bidding wars between the NFL and the AFL. A scout for the Bears contacted me after my last season at the University of Louisville [1965]. He said, "Joe Fortunato will probably be stepping down next year, and we would like you to play." I said, "I don't know about it. Call me back in the morning." I'd also gotten a call from the San Diego Chargers in the AFL. Regarding that, I thought, the San Diego Chargers, the AFL—this league will never make it. So I told the Chargers no, got back on the phone, and told the Bears yes. The scout came back over, and I signed a contract, more a letter of intent.

In negotiating my price, which came later with the formal contract, I can't even remember how I came up with some of my own numbers. George Halas said, "We will give you a one-year, no-cut contract." Well, I thought I was going to make it anyway, so I asked for a two-year contract: $15,000 for the first year, $17,000 for the second year, and a $20,000 signing bonus. That was my deal. And now I'm getting phone calls from a lot of my football buddies. They're saying, "Doug, are you nuts? You can go to the other league and get a lot more money." One guy I know called, and he said, "I know I can get you a $100,000 contract in the AFL." This was after I'd done pretty well in the Senior Bowl and the North-South game. But by that time I knew I wanted to play for the Bears in the NFL—it was history. Next thing I know I'm packing up and I'm going to Chicago to officially sign my contract and start playing pro football.

It was a good choice—look at all the Hall of Famers I played with there: Mike Ditka, Gale Sayers, Dick Butkus, Alan Page, Doug Atkins. And I was coached by Sid Luckman, who was a Hall of Famer, and Bill George, another Hall of Famer; George Halas was a Hall of Famer. And to move one step forward, I played with two guys who are also on their way to

Canton, Ohio, and the hall: Dan Hampton and Walter Payton.

I came from western Pennsylvania, a town called Yates-boro. Coal mining. My dad was a coal miner; his brothers were all coal miners. It was a true coal-mining town—company houses were built by the coal-mining company; you had the company store. When I was thirteen or fourteen, we moved to a house that had indoor plumbing and stuff like that. I went to a high school that served three or four coal-mining towns to-gether. In my graduating class there were thirty kids. And the football team—maybe we had twenty-five guys, and we all played. Nothing was really organized. We tramped from one little town to the next town to play the game. It is amazing when you think of the ballplayers that came out of that little area. Within a radius of about fifty miles there in western Pennsylva-nia, guys like Mike Ditka, Jack Ham, Jim Kelly, Dan Marino, Terry Hanratty, Johnny Unitas, and George Blanda grew up playing football.

At the time, though, what I really wanted to play was baseball. In that area we were always playing baseball, and I was scouted to play for the Los Angeles Dodgers. I had a cousin, Jerry Buffone, who was a great baseball player; both of us were touted as real good baseball players. So this scout came out and told us he really thought we could make it. His name was Tommy Lasorda, then the western Pennsylvania scout for the Dodgers. He said after he scouted us he was going to Pitts-burgh, because he wanted to sign this other guy who had a real good name, a helluva centerfielder by the name of Joe Namath.

When I first started playing football, I was an offensive tackle and a linebacker. I played both ways in high school, and it was expected of you in college back then too. If you're from Pennsylvania and thinking of playing college ball, you think Penn State, Pitt, Notre Dame. Well, I tried all those schools. Scholastically I could have gotten in—there was no problem—but I wasn't big. I was only 185 pounds, and they said, "You can't play tackle at 185," and all three said, "The kid is just too small." We had another ballplayer coming out of that area the same year, Bob Pellegrini. They told him the same thing. And look what he did. I kept looking, and finally I lucked out when the University of Louisville called. Louisville was not known at that time as a great powerhouse in football, but they said they'd give me and my brother scholarships, and so we bypassed baseball.

I played linebacker, and I also played offense for two or three years at center.

When I first came to Chicago, quite frankly, I was scared to death. I came into town, went to West Madison where the Bears' office was then, walked in the door, sat down, and did the contract. I never did have an agent after that either.

George Halas is sitting there, and I'm sitting across from the guy. It was in June 1966, and I was twenty years old. As I sat there, I thought, this is the guy that started all this—the Chicago Bears, the NFL. I was awed, you could say, and I probably lost some money as a result, but I don't think I'd ever change it. I was giving up the extra dollars to play for what I thought was the crème de la crème, the Chicago Bears in the National Football League.

When I joined the Bears in '66, there weren't many new guys who were going to make it with the Chicago Bears. The Bears had just come off a good season [1965: 9-5-0], and I was a fourth-round pick. As it turned out, there were only two guys, three guys maybe, who made it. There was a big kid who came up with me, Frank Cornish. He was about 300 pounds, and he stayed around four years [1966-69]. Another was Charlie Brown [1966-67].

The older guys you got to know right away because of the position you played. I got to know Mike Ditka pretty well because I played against him every day in practice. Which was a long day, believe me. With Mike, every day was *the* day. That's probably what helped me most, playing against Mike every day as a linebacker. Mike knew only one way to go, that was to give a hundred and some percent. And I was probably about the same way. So, every day at practice it was a battle. You'd go out to practice, and you'd play like it was a Sunday game. You went full speed ahead. Playing and talking to Ditka, you got to know the character of the man. I also had great immediate respect for Bill George, our linebacker coach, and Doug Atkins and Dick Butkus, who was one year ahead of me, and Joe Fortunato, whose spot I was eventually going to take.

When you arrived there, the veterans, they don't put a parade up for you, believe me. No roses thrown. Especially me. I walked in after the College All-Star game. They had already been in Rensselaer, Indiana, practicing, sweating, pounding each other in the wheat fields while I'd been up in Chicago. They're now ready to go play against the Washington Redskins. They want me to play. I don't even know what their system is. I ended up playing.

Another introduction to remember was meeting big Doug Atkins. I walked into training camp, and there he was, all 6'8", 260 pounds of him. He sort of snarled rather than said, "Who are you?"

I said, "Doug Buffone." I was kind of proud. I'd just come from the All-Star game and had done pretty well in it.

And he goes, "So what?"

"So I'm the new linebacker," I said. I had this Banlon shirt on, and Doug ambles over to me, and he took my sleeve and stretched it out of shape. I did the smartest thing you can do: I just turned around and walked out.

You weren't anything at training camp until you finally proved yourself. There was a real distinction between rookie and veteran. And the defense usually ran with the defense, and the offense ran with the offense. And you were impressed joining up as a rookie with guys you'd read about—Ed O'Bradovich and Mike Pyle and Gale Sayers and Johnny Morris. And, of course, Dick Butkus. He was a real quiet kind of guy at first, until we got to know each other playing alongside each other. But he was quiet during most of his career. He started loosening up toward the end of it. He would practice like a maniac. If you asked me who was the best middle linebacker who ever played the game, there would be no question in my mind. And I'm taking about everybody, yesterday and today. It was Dick Butkus. He had size, but he didn't have great speed. What he really had was a feeling for the ball, where the ball was going. He picked up a lot of fumbles; he himself ended up with 22 interceptions for his career. He had an uncanny knack for knowing where the ball was going.

It was always fun watching the battles between Doug

Atkins and George Halas. I always thought it was a game because those two were always fighting. There was no question
that Atkins would try to bug the Old Man. We used to have the
Halas mile, for example. They call it the Halas mile because he
timed everybody. He wanted to see if everybody was in shape. So
one year we ran it, and when it was time for the defensive
linemen to run it Doug ran one lap, and all of a sudden he ran
right off the track and headed toward the dressing room. The
Old Man, with his time watch in hand, yelled, "Where the hell
are you going, Atkins?"

Doug turned. "I'm no fucking track star," he said and
walked into the locker room.

Doug always brought his dog to training camp too. I think
it was a pit bull, to match his personality. He and Halas went at
it, but there was a mutual respect between them.

Brian Piccolo was there when I arrived, and he became a
good friend. We were in Rensselaer, Indiana, one day, and I got
sick, and so did Brian. So Brian and I were both quarantined to
the dorm. I had the flu. Brian had a slight cough and just
generally wasn't feeling good. I got better, but he still didn't
look too good even after we went up to Chicago for the regular
season. One day at Wrigley Field—my locker was right next to
his there—he was coughing, worse, it seemed, than when we
were quarantined together back in Rensselaer. So I said, "Pic,
you've got to get rid of that damn cough. Why don't you go see
a doctor or something?" He looks at me and says, "I think I got
cancer."

Now Pic was always a clown, loved to kid around. So I just
shook it off, because Pic was always that way. But then, down in
Atlanta, we're playing the Falcons, and it was very hot. Pic took
himself out of the game, and Pic would never come out of a
game on his own. He just couldn't breathe. They took him back
to Chicago and found out he had cancer.

We all went to visit him in the hospital. He had an operation and then got out. We had a basketball team when the
season was over, traveled all over. Pic couldn't play anymore, so
we made him our coach. Then, after one of the games, Pic said

to me that he thought he felt a lump or something in his chest. So back to the hospital he went. Then it was really all over. We all knew things weren't going well the second time he went back to the hospital. When we'd talk about it, Gale Sayers would say, "Well, give him a holler; it'll pick him up." And usually when you did call him he'd say, "Yeah, everything's fine."

I was in the National Guard on bivouac, and I called Pic the night before he died. But this time it was very different. Pic could hardly talk; he could hardly breathe. I was in a tent, and they hooked up this phone for me, and I got a call in to him and said, "Hang in there, Pic."

Pic was a great inspiration and a lot of fun. One of his best friends—one of my best friends too—was Ralph Kurek. Pic and Ralphie Boy used to drive me crazy. I would never go anywhere in Rensselaer, Indiana, during training camp. I would just stay in my room. Well, Pic and Ralph used to go everywhere. They'd drive around in their little Triumph sports car like two kids. They were just hilarious. And they were always on me: "Now, c'mon, let's go." I'd say, "Pic, leave me alone. My theory is this place does not exist; I'm not here." I would practice hard all day, and all I wanted after was to go back and rest. But they'd be out living it up—up as much as you could in Indiana farm country.

Another situation that was memorable in a sad way was when we were playing Detroit in 1971 and wide receiver Chuck Hughes died. We were on defense, and it was right before the half. They had to make a move, throw the ball, because there was not much time left. I saw them line up on the right side, and we called the defense, Butkus and me. Chuck Hughes ran a good pattern, and they threw the ball to him. He caught it, and he's going back to the huddle. I hear him breathing heavy, breathing louder than normal. They came back with the same play again with him running deep, and he comes across the middle. The ball was thrown short or whatever. I didn't notice him go down—I didn't even know what happened until all of a sudden Butkus and I look over and see he's lying there. We go over and know immediately something's wrong; the guy was turning blue.

Butkus started screaming for somebody to come out. They rushed out in the middle of the field and spent a long time working on him. When I saw them put him on a stretcher, I saw his arm go limp. It just sort of fell off the stretcher. And I think to myself, this guy's dead. You don't die on the football field; no one dies on the football field. They found out later that he had hardening of the arteries—arteriosclerosis, I think they call it. They said he had the heart of an eighty-year-old man. That was pretty devastating to all of us on the Bears as well as the Lions. Later Dick Butkus and I started getting hate letters, letters saying Butkus and I killed him.

The best game for me over the fourteen years I was with the Bears was the Giants game that we won in 1977 in overtime in the "Ice Bowl." That was a great game. After missing two field goals, Bob Thomas kicked one in the last minute of overtime, which got us into the playoffs. It was a miserable, rotten day, but it was perfect football weather for us. They had Larry Csonka at fullback that year. We had Walter Payton, but the halfbacks couldn't run well because it was too slippery. This was in New Jersey at the Meadowlands.

Jack Pardee was our coach then, and we're just going back and forth, back and forth with the Giants. They're running their fullback, Csonka; we're running our fullback, Robin Earl. So finally we get down close enough to kick a field goal that would win it for us. I'll never forget. Thomas came on the field. He had missed two earlier in the overtime. I played on the outside end with Bob Parsons to block for the field goal kick. Just before the snap Parsons turns around to Thomas and says, "You better not miss this fucking one." When he said that, I thought I'd die. You know kickers are a little strange anyway. And here Bobby's got all this pressure on him, and Parsons turns around and says that. Maybe it loosened Bobby up; maybe it scared the crap out of him. Anyway, we won the game and went to the playoffs. We lost to Dallas [37-7], but just to get to the playoffs was great.

Another great game that got us into the playoffs was down in St. Louis in 1979. I'll never forget that one. We had to beat St. Louis by at least 33 points, and the Redskins had to lose to the Cowboys—they played the late game that Sunday. Let me tell you something. We did something that day. We're punting, and on the punting team I was in the backfield, calling the signals. So I turned around to Bob Parsons—I had the right to call an audible on the punting team for a fake. I said to myself, Go for it. So I called, "Yellow," which meant "everybody alert." Yellow means we're not going to punt the ball; we're going to throw it. Now Parsons hears yellow, and he says, "Yellow?" The play was that the ball was supposed to be snapped to me by the center, but I saw there was a linebacker sitting right where I'd run with it, which meant that I couldn't get out of there. So I decided to call a screen pass—Parsons to get the snap and pass it to me. I'd let the Cardinal guy come in, bump him, and spin off. So I call "Yellow" again, which means we're going to throw it. The line sets up with no one going downfield. The guy comes in, I peel off, and Parsons rolls out—he had been a quarterback at Penn State—and he hits me with the ball. All of a sudden I'm wide open. I ran down the field maybe 35 or 40 yards. A Cardinal guy hits me and slams me out of bounds. We had to have all those points. We had to try everything. So next thing I'm calling audibles on field goals, punts, and on fourth downs. We went for it; we pulled out all the plays. And we did it. We beat St. Louis 42-6.

We also needed Dallas to beat Washington. After our game we all gathered in the parking lot underneath Soldier Field, but it looked like Washington was going to win. All of a sudden Staubach, Roger the Dodger, brings the Cowboys back, and finally we hear, "Touchdown!" Dallas won, and we were screaming, "We're in the playoffs!"

We went to Philadelphia to face the Eagles, but unfortunately, one bad call there, and we were out of the playoffs. We were winning the game, and Payton got the ball, broke loose, ran for 84 yards, all the way to the Philadelphia 1-yard line. It was the longest run he ever made from scrimmage, but there was a very late flag. Payton was halfway down the field when an official threw a flag and called Brian Baschnagel for being in motion. You couldn't figure it out six ways from Sunday. Then I somehow felt it wasn't meant to be. That was a big blow to us. We lost the momentum and eventually the game.

Then, of course, there were the games against the Green Bay Packers. I remember the first game I got into was against the Packers. Joe Fortunato started but went down. The coach called, "Buffone," so I go running in. Ed O'Bradovich, a very veteran defensive end, saw me come running in and said, "You know what the fuck you're doing?"

I said, "We'll find out." There's this old, grizzled player shaking his head, and you have a young kid running in, about to go up against Lombardi's Packers. Maybe he thought I was going to get killed out there.

In another game against Green Bay I ended Paul Hornung's career—not on purpose; it just happened. Anytime they got down near the goal line, Paul got the ball. He was the money ballplayer, the guy who would get the touchdown for you at the goal line. The first time he got the ball I hit him, bingo, and I stopped him. The second time I hit him again, but he got in there and scored. But he was hurt on the play, and after it he never played again. To this day we laugh when he sees me. I say, "Hey, I did you a favor; I put you out of your misery." He goes, "I let a second-rate, half-ass linebacker end my career."

The thing about the Chicago Bears and the Green Bay Packers was this intense rivalry. No one ever got too cute when we met. It was as if you took two guys and said, "Look, I'm going to stand you up in the middle of this ring, and I want you to just beat each other, and whoever's left standing at the end wins."

I started playing at Wrigley Field, and I played there until we moved to Soldier Field in 1971. I also went through five head coaches [George Halas, Jim Dooley, Abe Gibron, Jack Pardee, Neill Armstrong]. That was something when you think the Bears have had only nine head coaches in over seventy years. They were all different in their own way. Gibron and Dooley came out of the Halas mold because they were assistant coaches there under him. Pardee, who I have a lot of respect and admiration for, was from the University of Houston. He was a two-fisted, tough coach who also knew defense. He had played under George Allen in Los Angeles [Rams], who later coached the great Bear defense of 1963.

Abe Gibron was a true player's coach, the kind of guy you love. In Rensselaer, Indiana, under Abe we had Wednesday night cookouts. It was the greatest time in the world. He'd come up and say, "Wednesday night guys, this is it. Everybody out into the woods!" We'd build a bonfire; we'd bring in two kegs of beer; we'd bring in two lambs and put them on a spit. They'd get corn from the nearby farms. We would eat corn, lamb, drink beer, and sit around until about eleven o'clock at night. I saw Abe polish off twenty-some ears of corn one night. Abe loved to eat. There wasn't a place he didn't know in Indiana. You'd say, "I want fried fish," well, he'd take you over there. I'd say, "I like crab or steaks"; we'd go there. Abe had every restaurant pegged anywhere near Rensselaer. During the season, every Wednesday he would bring over a guy named Dick—I can't remember Dick's last name—who'd bring in Italian food, chicken, salami, and we would eat all this stuff, and then we had to go out and practice. It was called The Lunch.

He loved it. He was fun, but he still demanded a lot from you. Unfortunately he just didn't have enough material in the years he was head coach. Abe knew his football and had coached offense and defense. And in his day he was a helluva guard— played at Cleveland in the Browns' heyday. But our life under Abe kind of rotated around food.

I think the three guys who were the biggest help to me when I first came up were Joe Fortunato, Bill George, who was coaching linebackers at the time, and Jim Dooley, an assistant then who really knew the game, all aspects of it. Another big help was Sid Luckman, even though he was offense-oriented. Later Mike Pyle, one of the best Bear centers ever, was helpful. I used to learn the offense from him, get to understand what the guys I was going against were trying to do. I always believed if you know the offense, you can handle defense well. I wanted to know more about what the offense thought when they came out. How do they attack a game? If I got this defense, where does a quarterback go with a ball? What does he do with it? Everything on the field is a reaction to what you see, and the quarterback's generating it. I wanted to know all I could about offensive football. I got that information from guys like Sid Luckman and Mike Pyle.

There were also two others, behind-the-scenes guys who truly helped my career. One was Clyde Emrich, our weight coach, and the other was Fred Caito, our trainer. When I came up, I locked onto them. Freddy Caito was a great trainer. It was these two guys who kept me together for fourteen years.

Clyde used to tell me about working with weights all the time. I said, "Clyde, these guys, the older guys, they don't want to mess with these weights." Doug Atkins used to laugh at guys working with weights; he used to call them "milk muscles." But Clyde was right, and it helped me. It took Clyde until about 1968 to get weights into the regular mainstream of things with the Bears. The turning point, I think, was when we went down to play the Kansas City Chiefs in an exhibition game. All the way down Butkus and I are laughing. We think this is a joke, going down to play this AFC team—ha-ha, a big laugh. In fact they were roasting a bear in front of our hotel the day of the game, and we thought this was real bush league. We got out on the field that night at Arrowhead Stadium—I'll never forget— and we've got shoulder pads and helmets to warm up. They come out in their T-shirts. But you never saw a football team as big in your life. Butkus looks at me, and I look at him, and I say, "We're in big trouble." They had their offense towering over us. These guys are 6'6", 280 maybe, and they're all built up from weight training. They beat us really bad.

They had a horse with an Indian chief on it that raced up and down the sidelines every time they scored. I played the whole game, and I was so tired. But not as bad as that damn horse—his tongue was down by his hooves, he had to race up and down the sidelines so often. Finally he couldn't go anymore. They almost killed that horse. When the game was finally over, I said, "Thank God, we're out of here." Bobby Joe Green, our punter, was pushing me. "Let's get the hell out of here," he said. "They may want to play some more."

I truly learned the value of those two guys, Clyde and Freddy, when I got hurt in San Francisco in 1975. I tore my Achilles tendon. I'd never really gotten hurt before. I'd played like 150 games straight before that. What happened was, I went to make a move and go back, and my Achilles tendon totally snapped. No one hit me. Actually I thought I got hit, so I got up. Then I'm screaming, saying somebody kicked me. Well, no one had kicked me. I went back to the huddle because a lot of

Doug Buffone trots out for the last game of his fourteen-year Bear career (1966-79). Only Walter Payton has played in more Bear games than Buffone's 186, and only linebacker Bill George has played in as many seasons for the Bears as Buffone's fourteen.

times what happens when you get hurt is you go numb. So I'm calling the defense, and suddenly I realize my left foot won't work; it's just flopping. I'd never gone out of a football game. But I came running off and said, "Freddy, something's wrong here." He pulled up my pants and said, "Doug, you're finished today."

"What do you mean I'm finished?" I said.

He said, "Your Achilles tendon snapped; it's rolled up in the back of your leg." And with that I was sick, totally sick. So I went back to the showers. We won the football game, and I got a game ball. Freddy and Clyde came over to me and said, "We'll bring you back."

The next day I went and had the operation. Later I worked every day. Five, six hours a day. In fact they finally locked me out of the training room. When the season started the next year at training camp, I had to go in for another operation. I hadn't run a lick yet, but I'd been working. Clyde had me doing squats and benches and riding the bike. I worked with Clyde and Freddy until one day when I said, "I'm going full-speed today, Clyde." So I donned a pair of old hightops, wrapped up, and said, "This is it."

He said, "Well, we've done everything we can do. If it snaps, it snaps."

I buckled up and went out and went after it. And it didn't snap, and next thing you know I was starting—and I played another five years.

There were a lot of truly tough guys I met along the way. A lot of tight ends. Mike Ditka, who I went up against in practice. Jackie Smith, another great tight end from the Cardinals, was a helluva football player. Charlie Sanders from Detroit—he made a necklace out of my teeth, he hit me so hard. He was dropping a lot of people that year, and he sure dropped me. What happened was I took my eye off the block. He was coming across and got a forearm to the left side of my face. I played a whole game with the nerves of my teeth sticking out. And I don't remember the first half. That's the hardest I ever got rocked. He somehow got underneath my face mask. I finished the game, but I didn't play worth shit.

Another great combination was Larry Csonka and Mercury

Morris with the Dolphins. And there were the really elusive guys, who I hated—somebody like O. J. Simpson or Mercury Morris. Those guys were so tough to hit. Then there were the big guys: Csonka, Jimmy Taylor, Franco Harris. I liked the bigger guys because you could at least hit them.

I was fortunate to have such a long career in pro football—fourteen years, when the average life expectancy in the NFL is something like four years. I was thinking of getting out earlier. Buddy Ryan had instituted a new defense, and a linebacker like me was supposed to run with the wide receiver at times. A thirty-four-year-old linebacker running with a twenty-one-year-old receiver? I went to middle linebacker. The Bears talked me into staying. Buddy Ryan said, "Why don't you start against New England as a middle linebacker?"

I said, "I haven't played it, but I can play it." I'd played it years ago. In that game I had two interceptions. I felt good playing. I was tackling, doing everything pretty well. I said, "Hey, this is great," because in my mind I had been thinking of calling it quits.

The Bears said, "Stick around; take your time." They wanted me to help some of the young players, and I could still fill in, because I could play any of the linebacker positions.

Then we played Tampa Bay. They handed off to the fullback, a play I'd seen a hundred times before. I did the same thing I always did: hit the fullback—I mean hit him with everything I had—and he went down. But so did I. I was lying there, and all of a sudden I realized I couldn't move; nothing moved. I was scared to death. Automatically Freddy Caito came flying out on the field. He bent over me. I told him, "Nothing's working." Crazy things went through my mind. I'd seen the Darryl Stingley deal, and I said, "Fuck, not this late in my career. Not this shit."

Then, all of a sudden, I started to move—my feet, hands, my neck and head. I managed to finish the game. Afterwards I started to think about it. Here's what was happening. I wasn't changing my style of play. I knew that whoever got the ball, I was going to try to hit him as hard as I could hit him. I also knew that I wasn't twenty-one anymore, was now thirty-five, and I knew what those hits can do to you. I had lost weight because I wanted to be quicker, was down to 220. So it just didn't add up. And I knew I just wasn't going to try to finesse it. A lot of guys can end up finessing it, but I wouldn't do that. I *couldn't* do that, because I always played one way: you go out and hit. And so I said to myself, Maybe you pushed this thing as far as you can push it. You got fourteen years in; that's about it.

There is a time for every football player when he knows it's over. It's a shame in football that once you get to really know the game you've got to quit. My time had come. But what a fourteen years.

Ferocity Defined: Dick Butkus

Bill George on Butkus: "I've never seen anybody who was such a cinch. I'd been having trouble recovering from a knee operation, and from the day Dick showed up in camp I knew I was out of a job."

Jim Dooley on Butkus: Explaining the linebacker's ferocity on a given Sunday afternoon, Dooley said it was something Butkus worked himself up to days before a game. "He's very seldom happy during the week before a game. Maybe one day a week I'll see him smile. The rest of the time he goes around angry. He builds himself up mentally for the game, so by the end of the week he's really mad."

Butkus on Butkus: "Everybody gets the wrong impression of me. They think I hate everybody and that I eat raw meat. But I can talk and read and write like ordinary people do, and actually I like to have my meat cooked."

The master of crunch, linebacker Dick Butkus applies a little of it here to Green Bay Packer running back Dave Hampton in a 1969 game. Other Bears are Dick Evey (79) and Frank Cornish (73). Butkus, who was a perennial All-Pro in his nine years with the Bears (1965–73), was elected to the Pro Football Hall of Fame in 1979.

Joey Sternaman

Joey Sternaman joined the Bears in 1922, the same year that a coalition of eighteen football teams known as the American Professional Football Association, from cities as large as Chicago and as small as Marion, Ohio, officially adopted the name the National Football League. He won the starting job at quarterback immediately, joining in the backfield his brother Dutch, Pete Stinchcomb, and George Bolan.

In 1924 he accounted for 75 points running for touchdowns and kicking field goals and extra points, the most in the NFL that year and only 3 points shy of the record then held by Paddy Driscoll of the Chicago Cardinals.

Pint-size Joey (5'6", 150 pounds) was considered one of the finest quarterbacks and kickers in the NFL during the 1920s. He played for the Bears through the 1930 season—with the exception of the 1923 season, when he signed with the Duluth Kelleys, and the 1926 season, when he owned and played for the Chicago Bulls in the first American Football League.

Joey Sternaman gave this interview in 1983, when he was eighty-two years old. At the time of his death five years later, in 1988, Joey was believed to be the oldest living Chicago Bear.

Football I took to very early, and it became my favorite sport. We had a tree in our backyard with a big fork in it, and I'd go out there every day for hours and kick a ball through it. Drop-kicking was the thing in those days, and I'd practice it, getting farther and farther away. I also practiced my passing by throwing at the tree.

The person who got me most interested in football was my older brother Ed, who everybody called Dutch [co-owner and co-coach along with George Halas of the Decatur Staleys, which became the Chicago Bears]. He was very good at the game himself, a fine halfback and kicker, and was about four years older than I. He encouraged me all along. Well, Dutch took some time to explain to me a lot of things about running. The most important was that when you were running with the ball and you saw someone coming at you, you should take a step to the right or to the left and spin away. He taught me all kinds of twirls and side steps. I kept practicing them, at school and at home in the vacant lot next door, and they really helped me develop my open-field running. Over the years I got by many a player by racing up to them and sidestepping, twirling, spinning, and away I'd go.

I played football all through high school—started before the war and played right through it. In my senior year I was elected captain, and we had one of the best teams in the state that year. A lot of our players went on to be college stars at Illinois and Northwestern, and one or two even went to Michigan, I think.

It was no picnic, though. In those days we had no headgear and obviously therefore no nose guards. I recall one time in high school, playing down in Champaign, I'd carried the ball, and some guy swung around and totally flattened my nose. Another time in high school I played with a broken arm. I had my father, who was a pattern maker, fashion a couple of pieces of walnut to the shape of my arm. With those taped around my arm I was able to play in the last game of the season. I generally just used the other arm, but I don't recommend that anyone play with a broken arm.

Like my brother Dutch, I went to the University of Illinois.

Our coach, Bob Zuppke, decided to move me from halfback to quarterback and switch Laurie Walquist, who had been playing quarterback, to halfback [Walquist also later played for the Bears from 1922-31].

Zup was a fine coach. He had coached Dutch and George Halas earlier. He was also a fine man, and he never wanted you to get cocky. And, of course, he disliked the pros. He was very outspoken about that, just like old Amos Alonzo Stagg up at Chicago. Zup never wanted anybody to play the game for money.

[The] game I remember the most from my college days was that junior year against Ohio State [1921]. They were really something, supposed to be the best team in the country that year. We were really up for them. I ran about 80 yards with a punt return for a touchdown; it was called back, but then I scored on another run. And I kicked a couple of field goals that day, and, by golly, we won—knocked off the number-one team in the country. That day all eleven of our starting players played the entire sixty minutes. After the game Zuppke said, "A dead man would have been ashamed to be taken off that field."

That was also the year, though, that my friend Doug Simpson came up after the season and said, "How would you like to play in a game and make $50, maybe $100?" He said Carlinville was going to come over and play Taylorville—these were two football-crazy towns in central Illinois. A lot of money was being bet on the game, and therefore the towns could afford to pay the players some good money for playing in the game. He said that Laurie Walquist and Oscar Knop [another later Bear, 1923-28], who had been in the backfield with me at Illinois that year, were going down; so were a lot of other players. I didn't think there was any chance of the people at the university finding out, so I said OK.

Well, that day, lo and behold, there were all kinds of players there in Taylorville: college, pros, semipros. I didn't play in the first half; Charlie Dressen of the old Decatur Staleys did for Taylorville. He later went on to become a well-known baseball manager with the Brooklyn Dodgers. Anyway, he got messed up somehow, and so I went in for the second half at quarterback. We had some of the other Illinois boys in there too, and Carlinville had most of the Notre Dame team playing for them. They had Hunk Anderson [a Bear player, 1922-27, and an assistant coach for many years after] and Eddie Anderson and Chet Wynne—the whole doggone team. The score was 0-0 at half-time. I was able to move the ball down the field, and then I drop-kicked a field goal. I got two more later, and we won 9-0. And the story they told afterward was that they had to move the First National Bank of Carlinville over to Taylorville. [Officials at the University of Illinois did find out about Sternaman's involvement in the game and declared him ineligible for the 1922 season. So he joined the Bears.]

A while later, back at school one day, I got a call from George Huff [Illinois athletic director]. He wanted to see me. He said, "I understand you played down in that Taylorville game." He knew it, and that was that. So we all got kicked out of athletics at Illinois. So did the Notre Dame players. It didn't matter so much for most of them because they were seniors anyway, but I still had a year of eligibility left, and so it affected me a lot more. There's always been the story going around that I wore paint on my face and adhesive bandages to disguise who I was, but that wasn't really so. I don't see why I would have. We didn't think the schools would hear about it, and, hell, everybody at the game knew who we were, where we came from. But I guess it made for a better story. As it turned out, those of us from Illinois who were there ended up on the Bears the next year, and a lot of the Notre Dame boys were on the Chicago Cardinals.

The Bears team was the natural place for me to go. When the fellows came back from World War I, there was a lot of activity in pro and semipro football around the Midwest. My brother Dutch came back from the army and went into the Staleys, this team that was sponsored by a corn products company in Decatur. He and George Halas went there and ran the football team and worked for Staley in his plant there. The team didn't do all that well, I guess, or something went wrong down there, and [A. E.] Staley, the owner, washed his hands of it. So then they incorporated it, and Dutch and George brought it up to Chicago, and it became the Chicago Bears. My brother and

Halas shared everything then. They were co-owners, co-coaches, they both played, and they were always trying to recruit players from places like Illinois and Notre Dame.

A little while after, they brought in Chick Harley, an All-American from Ohio State, a big shot, one of the biggest names in the game then. Along with him was his brother Bill, a real egotistical fellow. Hell, he wanted to take over the whole thing, but Dutch and George were not about to let him to do that. "We're not going to take him in," Dutch told me. "That Bill is just too bossy."

So I went with the Bears when I couldn't play at Illinois anymore—that was in 1922. Dutch talked me into it. It worked out well. I was able to beat out Pard Pearce [1920-22] for the starting job at quarterback, which he'd had since the Decatur days. I had myself a pretty good year—scored maybe 4 or 5 touchdowns, which was a good amount in those days. That year Dutch did most of the kicking, field goals, and extra points.

The game was rougher than college football, I found out, but it didn't bother me. The players were bigger—hell, they were *all* bigger than me. I was only 5'6" and about 150 pounds. But I wasn't afraid of any of them.

And it was sure a simpler game than the one they play today. We didn't have a training camp or anything like that in 1922. We would just go out there maybe a week before the season and start practicing. We'd go over to a field at DePaul University in the early part of the season, because the Cubs would still be playing at Wrigley Field. Then, when the baseball season was over, we'd go to Wrigley Field for practice and our games. In the off-season I didn't work. Actually I went back to Illinois and took courses to finish my schooling.

During the season we would practice every day, but just in the afternoon. There was only sixteen of us on the team then. The only way we'd put in a substitute was if one of the fellows got hurt. Usually he had to be carried off the field before somebody would replace him. That's just the way we played the game in those days. I played quarterback on offense, called the plays and the signals, returned punts, and played safety on defense. I started out making about $150 a game, which was pretty high for a player back then, a little more than the others were making, except, of course, Halas and Dutch. The most I ever made playing football was $250 a game, a few years down the road. They'd pay you at practice on Tuesday, after the week's game, give you a check, and it had to be signed by both of them, Dutch and George.

I didn't stay in Chicago the next year. I got an offer to go up to Duluth and play, and I took it. The Kelleys was the name of the team. I'd signed only a one-year contract with the Bears, so I was free to go. They always tried to get you to sign a long-term contract in those days, lock you in, but I wouldn't do it. I was the coach up there for the Kelleys too; that's partly why I went. We had a fair team, played about seven games, some in Duluth, but we also traveled a little to places like Akron and Hammond, towns that also had pro teams then.

Their season ended before the Bears', and so, when it was through, I left Duluth and came down and played for the Bears a few games. And in 1924 I was again the Bears' starting quarterback. We were a good team. The whole backfield was from Illinois. Besides myself, there was Dutch and Laurie Walquist and Oscar Knop. We really won the championship that year, but there was some question about it, and I don't think we were recognized as winners. There were a lot of teams claiming it. You see, we all didn't play the same number of games then. One team might play twelve or thirteen games and another only seven or eight. Some teams that had far fewer wins had better winning percentages maybe. So it wasn't always that easy to figure who really won the championship. [Actually the Bears, with a record of 6-2-4, were in fifth place in the eighteen-team league that year behind the Cleveland Bulldogs, 7-1-1; Frankford Yellowjackets, 11-2-1; Duluth Kelleys, 5-1-0; and Rock Island Independents, 6-2-2.]

That was also a year when a play came off that I'll never forget. It was the time our fullback, Oscar Knop, intercepted a pass and took off for the goal line, only it was the wrong goal line he was racing toward. It was in a game against the Columbus Tigers. The ball bounced off the chest of the intended receiver and into the arms of Knop, who somehow got turned around on the play. The entire Tiger team just stood there and watched as he started running the wrong way. Most of them were laughing, I think. I took off after him, yelling, but I guess he couldn't hear me. Ed Healey [1922-27, a tackle who earned his way into the Pro Football Hall of Fame] was after him too, and he made a lunging tackle that stopped Knop just before he got to the goal. If it weren't for Healey, Knop would have had the distinction of being the first pro to score some points for the other team.

Before practice the next day our trainer, Andy Lotshaw, came up to me as we were getting ready and started wrapping my index finger in a big white bandage. I asked him what the heck he was doing and told him there wasn't anything wrong with my finger. He said loud enough for everyone in the locker room to hear that he wanted to make it conspicuous in case I had to point out the right goal line to some of the other players.

The next year Red Grange came with us. He was a great open-field runner. Red could sidestep anybody without losing speed; he had wonderful moves. He could wiggle and do this and that with his body and fake out most defenders, and he was very, very fast. I remember going over to Michigan to see him play in that famous game where Illinois whipped Michigan, who were supposed to be the best team in the country. I remember their coach, Fielding Yost, saying something about how he didn't think Red Grange was all that hot stuff. Then, on the kickoff, by golly, Red got the ball and started around toward the sideline. He had good interference and went all the way for a touchdown. A little later he went about 60 yards for another. Michigan players went for him, dived at him, grabbed air, and he just zipped around them or spun off them and raced on for a touchdown. I think he scored four or five that day. It was the greatest display of running I ever saw on a football field.

Well, when he came with the Bears, I was the play caller, and I said to him, "Are you interested in doing well for yourself, or are you interested in winning ball games?" After all, he'd been used to an offense down at Illinois that was built solely on opening a hole for him. Everything was geared to that. Well, we had a lot of different things, and we needed them in the pros. We had a quick opener that would work well with Red, but we also had a lot of deceptive plays that we used. We were not just going to blow open a hole for Red Grange. Well, Red was honestly interested in winning games, and, as I found out, he was one of the finest team players around. So what I did a lot after Red came with us was use him as a decoy. I'd fake handing the ball off to him, and they would swarm after Red. Why, they'd just clobber him, and, hell, I'd be bootlegging it around the other end or off on the other side passing it to one of our ends. We used a lot of deception, and it worked well. And Red took a real beating, especially that first year, but he never complained, just played his best.

It wasn't just Red that year either; we had a good team. In the line there was Ed Healey and George Trafton, Bill Fleckenstein and Jim McMillen. They were all fine ballplayers. Actually Red didn't come with us until after the college season. He played his last game and then quit school. That's the year we went on tour after the season. In one twelve-day period we played *eight* games, and they were in *eight* different cities too. And, of course, most of us played sixty minutes of each game, and we got pretty banged up, I might add.

It was just before the Thanksgiving Day game with the Cardinals, which was always a big one in Chicago, that Red came with us. We didn't have a chance to practice much with him in the lineup. But . . . he wasn't that big a factor that day anyway [the game was a scoreless tie]. Then, a week later, we got on the train to go to St. Louis, the first stop on our tour. We won there, got on another train, and went to Philadelphia and beat the Frankford Yellowjackets in a heckuva rainstorm on a Saturday afternoon. After the game we didn't even have time to change out of those wet, muddy uniforms. We went right to the train, the last one out to New York, and changed on it. There wasn't enough time to get them cleaned, much less dry, by the time we played the New York Giants the next day. We got a day's rest in New York and then went down to Washington, D.C., and from there up to Boston to play the Providence Steam Rollers. Then it was on to Pittsburgh, Detroit, and finally back to Chicago, where we played one last game against the New York Giants. Those were eight games we played, all within two weeks [December 2–13]. We had a full house in practically every place we played. Red really pulled them in. In New York, at the Polo

Grounds, we must have had seventy thousand people. There wasn't a square foot to be found in the standing room area. Red was the big attraction, but he played hard for us, never let up; but he got hurt somewhere along the line on the tour, and we couldn't use him all that much in the last few games.

We sure spent a lot of time on trains that year. The second tour took us all the way to California. We had a week or so of rest after the first tour, and then we got back on a train for Florida. We played some kind of an all-star team down in Coral Gables on Christmas Day. For that second tour we were pretty hot stuff. C. C. Pyle, Grange's manager and the guy who put it all together, got us our own Pullman car and personal porter for the whole tour. Very fancy. Then we went to Tampa and over to Jacksonville for two more games. After that we headed west, played a game in New Orleans, and then on to Los Angeles. That was the biggest crowd, at the Los Angeles Coliseum. They really pushed that game beforehand, and there must have been eighty thousand people out for it.

From there we went down to San Diego and then up to San Francisco, Portland, and finally Seattle. This second tour lasted five weeks—a lot easier than the first one of two weeks. I think through it all I got $200 a game. Red, of course, got much more—thousands, I believe—but he was the drawing card. It was quite something, and we all enjoyed it—the second tour, that is. We saw all the nightlife of New Orleans and a lot of the stars in Hollywood, and there was always something going on. Pyle saw to that. I had my first airplane ride while I was on it. Up in Portland, Oregon, there was this fellow, Oakley Kelley, I believe his name was, and he took me up in an open-cockpit plane. I was sitting on a parachute while we flew over the city. That was really something in 1925. That Kelley was the first man to fly across the country, coast to coast, from dawn to dusk.

In 1926 I left the Bears again to start the Chicago Bulls. Red Grange and Pyle went out to New York; Pyle had started a new league when he couldn't work things out with the Bears or the NFL for Grange. It was called the American Football League, and Grange went with the Yankees, which was the name of the AFL franchise in New York, and I started up a team in Chicago.

There were a number of teams in other cities. Well, I owned the Bulls, coached them, and played quarterback. It was a big gamble, and I got talked into making it. It seemed like a real good thing at the time.

We actually had a pretty good team, though, and as I recall we even beat Red and his New York Yankees. But we didn't get the crowds. We played out at Comiskey Park on the South Side—not the best of neighborhoods in those days—and we just couldn't make it go. We sure tried. But everywhere in that league it was tough. We had plenty of big names and fellows who tried to make it work. Besides Red Grange and me in the AFL, there was Eddie Tryon, Harry Stuhldreher of the old Four Horsemen of Notre Dame, Wildcat Wilson, Century Milstead—people like that. But it went under at the end of the year. I came out broke after it; it was a bum gamble.

I went back to the Bears again after that and played with them through the 1930 season. Grange came too after his knee injury, and we had Paddy Driscoll [1926-30, another Pro Football Hall of Fame honoree], but we didn't do as well as we should have in those years.

. As I think back on it, it sure was a lot different in those days, not just in the fact that we made maybe $150 a game and some of the boys today may make a million a season. Take the quarterback, for example, because he sure is different today than when I played. I'd call each play, set the signals. We'd talk in the huddle. Somebody would tell me who was pulling out on defense or who might be hurt a little bit and maybe slowed down some or who he felt he could move out or beat. We'd talk things over, and often I'd just call a play like "left halfback around right end." No numbers, no code, just that, and everybody had the sense to know what to do. Today the quarterback is just there, hands the ball off, and that's it. Sure, he's a good passer. But somebody runs out onto the field and tells him what play to call. And they've got coaches in the press box and radios and headsets and a dozen coaches on the sideline. Hell, our coaches, guys like Halas and Dutch, were on the field playing in the game, in the huddle with us. Today the quarterback wouldn't think of blocking somebody. And today a team loses 10 percent of its interference because a quarterback doesn't block. That was natural to me; one of the best parts of the game, running interference.

I played against all kinds in those days—mean and nasty ones, those who didn't care what happened to you or to them. And there were some great ones to be sure. I never played against George Gipp, although he played in some of those games for money while he was at Notre Dame, like the rest of us did, like the Taylorville-Carlinville game. But I ran up against many who you can never forget. There was Red Grange, of course, maybe the greatest runner ever, and then there was Harry Stuhldreher and Johnny Mohardt of Notre Dame, and Jimmy Conzelman and Ernie Nevers. I especially remember playing against Jim Thorpe and Pete Calac and Little Twig who played for the Indian team (the Oorang Indians). Thorpe was a marvelous athlete, could do anything: run, pass, kick, tackle like a steamroller. You had to be careful when you ran up against him because he was so powerful and big—around 6'2" and over 200 pounds—especially if you were 150 pounds like I was. I wouldn't even try to run head-to-head with him. I'd just go as low as I could, tumble, and try to trip him up. Another really good one was Benny Friedman, a fine quarterback. And there were some truly tough fellows. We had a bunch on the Bears: George Trafton and Hunk Anderson and Jim McMillen. And Ed Healey was one of the greatest linemen I ever saw.

I quit after the 1930 season. I was over thirty, and some new people had come along. It wasn't the way it had been anymore, and I knew it was time to get out. But it was great to be there then, to play the game like it was in those days. What a game it was.

Creative Refereeing

Referees were a little looser in the 1920s and early thirties than they are today. Some were, one might say, more open to improvisation. Two examples feature none other than Papa Bear himself.

They had a referee in the 1920s, Jim Durfee, who was a character. He and George Halas were pretty good friends. Durfee, however, took special pleasure in penalizing the Bears. When Halas was riding him pretty hard in a game one day, Durfee began marching off a 5-yard penalty.

Halas got really hot. "What's that for?" he hollered.

"Coaching from the sidelines," Durfee yelled back. (It was in fact illegal in those days.)

"Well," said Halas, "that just proves how dumb you are. That's a 15-yard penalty, not 5 yards."

"Yeah," said Durfee, "but the penalty for your kind of coaching is only 5 yards."

Another day Durfee was penalizing the Bears 15 yards, and Halas cupped his hands and shouted, "You stink!" Durfee just marched off another 15 yards, then turned and yelled back to Halas, "How do I smell from here?"

Unruffled Loser

Jimmy Conzelman, Hall of Fame tailback in the 1920s for a variety of early teams and coach of the Chicago Cardinals in their heyday of the 1940s, never took the crosstown rivalry with the Bears lightly, as he once explained:

"Don't get the idea," Jimmy said after a 1941 contest at Wrigley Field, "that being beaten by the Bears 53–7 bothered me a bit. Oh, not in the least. I went home after the game, had a good night's rest and a very hearty breakfast. I said good-bye to the missus and strolled down the hall to the elevator, whistling a light tune. I pushed the elevator button and took in my profile in the hall mirror. I was a picture of elegance in my Cavenaugh hat, tweed sport jacket, and well-shined tan shoes. Then I went back to my apartment and put on my trousers."

Joey Sternaman (1922–25, 1927–30) takes off around right end in a 1924 game against the Chicago Cardinals at Cubs Park (Wrigley Field). "Little Joey," as he was known, was 5'6" and 150 pounds during the eight years he quarterbacked the Bears.

The Power of Prayer

Ken Strong, Hall of Fame tailback for the New York Giants in the 1930s, always liked to tell this story about one of his encounters with the Chicago Bears:

It was a regular-season game in 1933 at the Polo Grounds, one that eventually enabled the Giants to win their division and meet the Bears for the NFL title that year.

The score was 0–0. Late in the game the Giants were within field goal range. Strong kicked it, but New York was offsides. Strong kicked it again from 5 yards back. It was good again. But as Strong trotted off the field, he saw his head coach, Steve Owen, fuming on the sideline.

As Strong told it, Steve wasn't mad because of the offside penalty. He was furious because he had observed his brother, Bill, one of the Giant tackles, on both kicks. Bill had made no effort to pulverize the Bear across the line from him, guard Joe Kopcha.

"Why didn't you destroy that Kopcha?" Steve shouted at his brother on the sideline. "He was just kneeling there at the line of scrimmage on both kicks, and you didn't do anything!"

"I couldn't," Bill said, shaking his head in dismay. "On each kick Kopcha raised his eyes toward the heavens and said, 'Please, God, don't let him make it.' Gosh, Steve, I couldn't belt a guy when he was praying."

That's the way Ken Strong told it, anyway.

Ed Sprinkle

"The Meanest Man in Football" was the title of the *Colliers* magazine article about him in 1950. After one game Chicago Cardinal coach Buddy Parker pointed out to the press five cleat marks on the chest of his halfback Elmer Angsman, shouting, "He's the dirtiest football player in America," and he was not referring to Angsman. His coach, George Halas, said, "He's the greatest pass rusher I've ever seen." Ed Sprinkle garnered a lot of notice in the twelve years he played end for the Bears (1944–55).

Sprinkle swears to this day that he was not a dirty player, just a rugged one—there is a clear line of distinction, he declares. There is little question, however, that the 6'1", 210-pound end was one of the roughest, toughest, most intimidating players ever to don a Bear uniform, and he evoked more than a little wariness in all opposing players.

While opponents feared him and other outsiders often wailed about his alleged overzealousness, his teammates and Coach Halas had an abiding affection for him. Halas called him "a fine, clean-cut young man." His teammate Bulldog Turner, who took a backseat to no one in terms of toughness, said Sprinkle was "as fine a gentleman as you could meet."

Sprinkle played both defensive and offensive end, but he is remembered most for the punishment he doled out tackling runners and rushing passers. He made it to the Bears on the recommendation of Turner, who had earlier gone to the same small, unheralded Texas university named Hardin-Simmons. He was not even among the thirty draft choices the Bears made in 1944, but he was the only newcomer to win a starting berth and survive into postwar pro football from that year's large crop of rookies.

Ed Sprinkle started with the Bears as a guard, but in 1946 he was switched to end when Halas, it is said, observed, "The big boys are coming back [from the war]. We'd better move this kid out to end before he gets killed." As an end Sprinkle went to six Pro Bowls before he retired after the 1955 season.

After football Sprinkle went into sales in the automobile and recreational vehicle field, where he is still active today in the Chicago area.

I went to high school in Texas, eighteen miles south of Abilene, in a little town called Tuscola, and that's where I first played football. Our total enrollment at that school was no more than a hundred, but they started a six-man football team league with schools in four or five of the small towns around there.

In six-man football we just had a center, two ends, two halfbacks, and a quarterback. We were so ignorant about the game we didn't even know how to put on the equipment. We had hip pads with the big flap that's supposed to protect your tailbone; we thought that went in front and were all trying to put the hip pads on that way. It was a rural community, and if there ever were a hundred fans at a game, it was a lot. Anyway, we got to the championship game and got to play under the lights at Hardin-Simmons.

I didn't get a football scholarship to go to college, not to start anyway. My parents were sharecroppers, and there was no way they would have been able to send me to college either. But in the state of Texas then, the highest-ranking boy and girl in the senior class of their high school got a one-year college scholarship. I was the highest-ranking boy in Tuscola High, so I got it, and I chose Hardin-Simmons.

I went out for football there that freshman year, and the coach told me to line up at tackle. Well, I didn't even know what tackle was; there wasn't a tackle on our six-man team. He lined me up there and said he wanted to see what I could do on defense. I guess maybe I didn't know any better, but I did just what we tried to do in six-man football—get off the line quick as you can and go right for the ball. It kind of surprised the blockers I was coming across the line so quick, sometimes even before the snap of the ball. I guess I was making those older guys at Hardin-Simmons a little aggravated. So one play they just snapped the ball, and all of the blockers came after me. They didn't care about the play, they just wanted to teach me a lesson.

After my freshman year I got a football scholarship and was able then to stay in school. I was about 200 pounds then, 6'1", and played two years for Hardin-Simmons [1941-42] at tackle and made All-Conference down there. My last year we went to the Sun Bowl in El Paso and played the Second Air Force team, who had a bunch of pros on their team, and it was a helluva game, but we lost 13-7.

And then the war caught up with us, or we caught up with it. I really wanted to be a Navy Air Corps pilot. So I joined, passed the examination, and was brought into the Navy Air Corps Reserve. Through the efforts of a teacher I had at Hardin-Simmons I then got an appointment to the U.S. Naval Academy in Annapolis, Maryland.

I played football for Navy in 1943—still a tackle, but a lot of times they would line up with a five-man line and I would move out to defensive end, where I got my first experience at playing that position. We had a very good team and even beat Army that year, 13-0. That was just before [Doc] Blanchard and [Glenn] Davis came along, and then nobody could beat Army. I didn't do as well in the classroom at Navy, though, and at the end of the year I flunked out.

Back in Texas I talked with Bulldog Turner. He had gone to Hardin-Simmons and was about four years ahead of me. By 1944 he was a star with the Bears. I'd gotten to know him when he used to come back down to Hardin-Simmons; he even used to help coach us in the spring. He said to me, "You know, you don't get a lot of notoriety or publicity playin' for a small school down here in Texas, so the pros aren't goin' to notice you." I didn't know much of anything about pro football in the first place and wasn't up on the Bears except knowing that Bulldog played up there. He said he was going back up there for the '44 season, and why didn't I just come along with him and give it a try.

I had a lot of respect for Bulldog, so I said, "Sure, I'll go with you."

When I got up there, they took a look at me, and Ralph Brizzolara—he was the business manager running things then, with Halas in the navy over the Pacific—offered me a contract to play: $200 a game. I was happy as could be and signed it. To show how dumb or country I was, I didn't even know that I still had to make the team. I thought when I signed the contract I was on the team.

After I signed, the coaches [Paddy Driscoll, Hunk Anderson, and Luke Johnsos] asked me what position I played. I told them tackle. They looked at me kind of funny and said, "We don't need any 200-pound tackles in the pros." So I switched to guard. It wasn't all that difficult making the team in 1944, what with so many of the regulars gone off to the war. It would have been a different thing if I'd come up in 1946. I don't think I ever would have made the team, being a lineman as small as I was and with all the veterans coming back from the service.

I played ten games that year and earned $2,000. I had pretty good years in both '44 and '45, and therefore I was kind of established by 1946 and could hold my own.

I remember when I first made the team, I saw George Musso out there, a big guy, 6'2", probably weighed over 260. He was maybe in his middle thirties. I thought he was one of the coaches. I had no idea he was a notorious All-Pro guard.

That was at training camp. It was the first year the Bears held camp in Rensselaer, Indiana. We were on the campus of St. Joseph's College. I think the reason they were there at that particular time was because during the war in 1944 it was hard to get all the good kinds of food. Everything was rationed, and you had to get it with stamps. Down there, however, in farm country, the college was more or less self-sustaining in that they raised their own beef and pork and grew corn and vegetables and had their own cows.

It was a pretty tranquil neighborhood. But then I was pretty far from a city boy in those days. I enjoyed going down there, getting away from everything. It was really a kind of getaway from everyday life.

I always worked very hard in training camp. I ran a lot, and I never loafed out there. But I never worked out in the off-season, nor did anybody else in those days. To make a go of it, you had to have another job in the off-season. So, for about the first two weeks of training camp, you'd be so stiff and sore you didn't want to do much of anything. We worked out twice a day. Actually the first couple of days I felt great, but then the stiffness and soreness would set in, and it would be a real drag to get out there and go through all the misery. I think I would have loved the situation, like the guys have it today, where you could work out and stay in shape twelve months out of the year, make enough money so you didn't have to work in the off-season.

They didn't haze the rookies at camp, like maybe the older guys would do to a freshman in college, but you didn't get into the inner sanctum without having a friend already on the team. Most of the guys who I would call old-timers down there would go out for a beer after practice. So Bulldog would take me along. We'd go out with guys like George Wilson, Scooter McLean, and some others, but it still took quite a while before I got accepted in the group other than as a friend of Bulldog's.

Bulldog was my best friend with the Bears. We roomed together for eight years. George Wilson, who played end for us, was another terrific guy. He'd been there eight years by the time I arrived. And George Musso, who I finally discovered was a player and not a coach, had been there twelve years. Ray Nolting, a real good halfback, was another who had been around for a while, since 1936, and was a fine guy. Sid Luckman was there, and he had built quite a name for himself by that time. Luckman was kind of aloof, never associated all that much with most of the other players. But meeting all those guys and seeing how they played football, you could easily see why they had such great teams just before the war.

We got $400 total for exhibition games, and that money was supposed to cover you for the whole time you were at training camp until you started the regular season. Halas always told us that was a bonus.

I'll never forget my first meeting with George Halas. It was after the war, and he was back from the navy. He called a meeting for everybody, veterans and rookies. He was telling us all about the history and tradition of the Bears, the great teams they had in the past. And then he said, "And you All-Americans among the rookies, you've got an equal chance of making this team." He didn't want those who had All-America credentials to feel they were special.

Halas was a great leader, a motivator, and an excellent football tactician. He demanded respect just by being there, and he got it. I always had a lot of admiration for George, and we got along fine. I think there was a mutual respect there. I also think in the later years, after I left the game, pro football passed George Halas by; I think he stayed in it too long. But he'd probably never admit that. If he was still alive today, I doubt he'd admit that.

I have nothing but fond memories of the years I played with the Bears. I made some good friends: George Blanda, Fred Williams, George Connor, Bill Bishop, Bill George.

I think we should have won more titles than we did. We won only one, in 1946. But we had only three seasons worth forgetting [1945, 1952, 1953] during my twelve years; all the others we had winning seasons. I can't put a finger on why we didn't. We had some great ballplayers: Luckman, McAfee, Stydahar, Turner, Connor, Blanda, George—they're all in the Hall of Fame. And other great ones too, like Kavanaugh, Osmanski, Hugh Gallarneau, Lujack, Bray, Fred Davis, Wash Serini, Williams, Bill Wightkin, Harlon Hill; that's just some of them.

Of all of them, Bulldog influenced me more than anybody. He always tried to impress me that we were "The World Champion Chicago Bears." "Let the other team fear you," he would say. "Walk tall. Walk proud." And when we went out onto the field, that's just the attitude I had. I never feared an individual on a football field.

A lot said I played dirty. That's just not true. Mean maybe, but not dirty. Once in a while there might be an isolated case of a guy pulling a dirty stunt, but a guy wouldn't have lasted very long in the league if he played dirty regularly. The others would have taken care of him. We were meaner, I think, in the 1940s and fifties. There were fewer positions, and we fought harder to keep them. Some of us could be characterized, I guess, as a little overaggressive maybe. I know I was as aggressive as any football player who walked on the field. If I had the opportunity to hit someone, I hit him, and I hit him just as hard as I could. That's the nature of the game.

Nobody was really making much money playing football, but Halas always wanted us to go first-class. We always traveled dressed up—no jeans or anything like that. But we weren't dandies when we took the field.

We had some real tough games with the Cardinals in those years, especially in the 1940s. They had some great teams then with Charley Trippi, Paul Christman, Elmer Angsman, Pat Harder, Mal Kutner, Billy Dewell, Chet Bulger, Buster Ramsey. They knocked us out of the division title a couple of times, beat us the last game of the regular season [1947, 1948].

I don't think we ever thought of the Cardinals as a bitter rival, though. We kind of just considered them the South Siders. I don't believe we ever really psyched ourselves up to play the Cardinals like we would for the Green Bay Packers. Now, there was a rivalry. We'd go up to Green Bay knowing we were in for one helluva battle. Beating Green Bay was like winning a division championship. But the Cardinals looked at it a little differently. If they could beat the Bears, it made their season.

I never had any particular dislike for the Cardinals, but I had some pretty good run-ins with some of their players. Charley Trippi and I had quite a thing going. We went back and forth at each other all the time. I admired Charley Trippi. He was a great competitor and a great runner, passer, receiver, defensive player. My job was to stop him, and his was to beat me. I really labeled him a few times. One time at Wrigley Field they started an end run around my side, and I went under a pile of blockers, and I must have caught a knee in the head. I was down on all fours, dazed, and Trippi was running back to the huddle, stopped, punched me, and then ran off the field. It was probably out of exasperation, maybe a little getting back for some of the hits I put on him. Who knows? Still, I have a lot of respect for Trippi, always had, and today we're friends.

Another guy on the Cardinals I always hit hard was their quarterback, Paul Christman. He was a fine one. But I'd kill him out there if I got the chance, and he knew it. He used to get so mad at me. One time he threw the football right at my face when I was rushing him. I'd had a particular run-in with him earlier in the game. I was harassing him the whole game in fact. I was getting to him pretty good, and he was hurting, I think. Finally, he said to me, "We're going to get you."

I said, "I'm wearing number 7, and I'm playing right end, and I'll be here all day. You know where to find me." So, instead of trying to complete the pass this one time, he just hauled off and aimed it right at my face, throwing it just as hard as he could. Fortunately it didn't hit me because he could throw it pretty damn hard.

The Eagles were another terrific team around that time. They had a back who was at least as big as I was, Steve Van Buren, and he was a great running back. Green Bay had Tony Canadeo, another wonderful runner. They were a couple of the best I ran up against. Hugh McElhenny of the 49ers was another—fast, great moves, and he was tough. They had a specially tough backfield; Joe Perry was the fullback, and he was powerful. I played against Bill Dudley; he was a memorable one too. I personally think he was overrated, but he was a good, tough football player on both offense and defense. I played against him when he was with Pittsburgh, Detroit, and Washington. I also played against Jim Finks when he was the quarterback for the Steelers. I remember he came up to me after one game and said, "You are a mean son of a gun."

And Cleveland—we could never beat the Browns in those days. What a great team they had in the fifties. It used to get Halas so mad because we couldn't beat them.

End Ed Sprinkle (7), who gave meaning to the word *mean* during his twelve years with the Bears (1944-55), gives a little head slap to Detroit Lion quarterback Frank Tripucka, whose pass is about to be gathered in by Bullet Bill Dudley in the end zone. Other Bears in the picture include Bill DeCorrevont (36) and Ed Cody (16).

The guy on Cleveland I had the most run-ins with was their fullback, Marion Motley. He was a big, powerful guy [6'1", 238 pounds], and he was damn fast for his size. He would go up against me blocking a lot, and that's where we had our run-ins. On those sweeps they would run to the left, Motley was often out front to block. So I had to get by the offensive lineman and then Motley to get at the ball carrier. Plus Motley was there to block when I tried to rush [Otto] Graham, their quarterback. We had some real battles, Marion and me—nothing dirty, but we sure went at it.

Abe Gibron was one of the Browns' guards then, and he used to block on me a lot. He was so quick off the ball, about as quick a guard off the ball as I ever played against. I had a lot of trouble getting by him. One game I was having all kinds of trouble getting around him, so finally I just jumped over him, and it surprised the hell out of him to see me going over the top of him. I got to Graham on that play and sacked him. I was ecstatic because that was a big deal. They really set their whole offense to protect Graham, and that was maybe the only time I ever got to him for a sack.

The Rams had some huge guys, like Motley, in their backfield too. They had Dan Towler [6'2", 225 pounds], Dick Hoerner [6'4", 220 pounds], and Tank Younger [6'3", 228 pounds]; we called them the "Elephant Backfield." Hoerner was tough, and Younger was a guy who'd dance every dance with you out there on the field, but Towler was scared. Towler wouldn't block on me. He'd come out of the huddle, and he'd hide, look the other way when I was coming at him. But I loved it when he was out there; he was a lot bigger than me, but sometimes I'd just come looking for him to do a little battling.

One of the games I liked the best was the championship we played for against the Giants in 1946. A lot of the boys from the championship teams of 1940 and '41 were back with us after military that year—guys like George McAfee, Bill Osmanski, Kenny Kavanaugh, Joe Stydahar, Ed Kolman, Hugh Gallarneau, Chuck Drulis, Ray Bray. Needless to say, we had a heckuva team.

We played the Giants in the Polo Grounds, and I had one of my best days ever on defense. The night before the game their quarterback, Frank Filchock, and their fullback, Merle Hapes, were suspended for not having reported a bribe attempt. For one reason or another they let Filchock play. We were all over him. I got him in the first quarter. He dropped back to pass, and I got in and really whacked him. I broke his nose. I came up over a blocker and hit him just when he was letting the ball go. It just kind of fluttered out there, and our defensive back, Dante Magnani, grabbed and ran it in for a touchdown.

That helped us, but we won the game on a play Sid Luckman called in the fourth quarter. The game was tied at that point, 14-14. The play was called "Bingo keep it." It was a bootleg play. Luckman faked a handoff to George McAfee on what looked like an end run around left end. But Luckman kept the ball and rolled out around right end. I led the interference for him, although most of the defenders were on the other side of the field going after McAfee. Luckman went 19 yards in for the touchdown. We won the game 24-14; we kicked a field goal after that for a little icing on the cake.

On that play I was split out wide to the right. They sometimes played me that way when they ran the ball to the left, like the way McAfee went on the fake. I was out there to do what they called a "comeback block." It was used to shake up a linebacker or get the attention of somebody out there who was a little too aggressive. I'd come back across the field and hit a guy from the blind side. He'd be out there, and he wouldn't be looking at you; he'd have his eyes on the ball carrier going to the left, and I'd just clobber him. I was devastating on that block. They wouldn't let me use it a lot because I hit too many guys too hard.

It wasn't dirty. It was just part of the game. All the teams had a play like that. Some guys were just better than others at it. I never had an animosity for any particular guy in a game. I just tried to win the game no matter what I had to do to accomplish that. I wanted to do as much damage as I could to the other team because they were the opposition. When the game was over, everything was forgotten. I remember playing against Detroit, and they had this enormous lineman, Les Bingaman. He was 6'3" and about 300 pounds in the 1950s, and he was blocking on me. I did everything I could think of to him that day. I had to. He weighed almost a hundred pounds more than me. I knocked his tooth out. And I knocked him out of the game. Afterwards, I walked into this bar, and he was there. He came over, laughing, and said something about "You really gave me a shot. All I saw was two feet—mine," he said. "I was on my back, and all I remember seeing was my two feet down at the other end of me." And we had a beer together and laughed about it.

I wish they had recorded sacks in those days. If they did, I think I would have been right up there at the top, because I used to get to the quarterback a lot. When I first came into the league, you could chase the quarterback and hit him until the whistle blew the play dead. It didn't necessarily matter if he had the ball or not. That's why Luckman would throw the ball and then take off running—he'd run the other way so as not to get clobbered. Two guys I especially loved to chase down were Bob Waterfield and Norm Van Brocklin. They were both with the Rams then, and I know they remembered me long after they got out of football.

There were always some pranksters around. But George Halas was not an advocate of playing practical jokes. In fact he was dead set against it. He tried to maintain a pretty civil organization. He ran a tight ship. An example of that: In the early 1950s we had this little halfback from Tulsa by the name of J. R. Boone. He was quick and a good pass receiver. We'd played an exhibition game in Mishawaka, Indiana, and we lost it. We were taking a shower afterward, and J.R. was singing in the shower. Halas came by and said, "What the hell are you singing about?"

J.R. said, "What do you want me to do, cry?"

That week Halas traded J.R. to the 49ers.

After twelve years I decided it was time to retire. My last year was 1955, and physically, after each game, I could really feel it. I wasn't all that old, thirty-one, but it was getting to me. Even at the end of my career I was still playing on punt return teams, kickoff teams, kickoff return teams. After a Sunday game it would be like Thursday before I was 100 percent again.

Another factor was that the Bears were in the process of switching to a four-man line on defense, and they didn't really need a 210-pound end in there trying to handle a 275-pound tackle. And I didn't want to sit on the bench.

I remember that last year, going in to see Halas about my contract. We were $200 apart. So I asked George, "Mr. Halas, why don't you just give me the $200? It's my last year. I can take it and say for once I got paid what I asked for."

He shook his head. "I can't do it, my boy, just can't do it."

I look at the players today, and I see they're a lot different than we were. They're bigger and better conditioned than we were, but they aren't any tougher. Today their whole concept of the game is different, and being mean is not a part of it.

The Bronk

Bronko Nagurski was a legend in his time. A fullback on offense and tackle on defense for the Chicago Bears, he was known as the most battering, bruising ballplayer of the 1930s. Stories of his ferocious exploits abounded.

Johnny Dell Isola, a linebacker for the New York Giants in the last half of the thirties, recalled his first encounter with the Bronk:

"I had heard a lot about him, but I thought most of it was exaggerated. We were at the Polo Grounds when I first ran up against him. It was first and ten and they gave the ball to Nagurski, up the middle. Well, a huge hole opened and I saw him coming. I put my head down and charged into the hole. We met at the line of scrimmage, and you could hear the thud all over the Polo Grounds. I had my arms around his legs and my shoulder dug into him. It was the hardest tackle I ever made, but I made it and said to myself, well, I guess that will show you, Nagurski! Then as I was getting up I heard the referee shout, 'Second down and two!' "

Dick Richards, owner of the Detroit Lions, it was told, once approached the Bronk before a game and said, "Here's a check for $10,000, Nagurski. Not for playing with the Lions,

The mighty Bronko Nagurski, chewing up some yardage here in the early 1930s, was the Bear fullback from 1930 through 1937 and then came back in 1943, to help the Bears win that year's NFL championship. Nagurski is a charter member of the Pro Football Hall of Fame.

because you belong to the Bears, but just to quit and get the hell out of the league. You're ruining my team."

George Halas, Nagurski's coach in Chicago, often told another story about a game at Wrigley Field during the Bronk's rookie season. Because the stadium was designed for baseball, at one end of the field the outfield wall was not very far from the end line. The Bears were on about the 2-yard line. Nagurski got the handoff; with head down and legs churning, he plunged into the line. He blasted through two would-be tacklers as though they were a pair of old saloon doors and kept on going right through the end zone. His head still down, Nagurski ran full-speed into the brick outfield wall, went down, then got up and trotted off the field. As he approached an ashen-faced Halas on the sideline, Nagurski shook his head and said, "That last guy really gave me a good lick, Coach."

Irv Kupcinet—
On George Halas

Irv Kupcinet, also known as "Mr. Chicago," has been an institution in Chicago journalism—columnist, television personality, pulse-keeper of the city, and onetime sportswriter—for more than five decades.

Kup, a quarterback, was also an outstanding college football player at North Dakota, good enough to make the College All-Star team of 1935, a squad that boasted such memorable players as Don Hutson and future president of the United States Gerald Ford but still succumbed 5–0 to the Chicago Bears in the annual classic at Soldier Field. Kup was also a professional football referee in the 1940s. In fact he was the head linesman in the unforgettable 73–0 annihilation the Bears wreaked on the Washington Redskins in the NFL championship game of 1940. And, of course, Kup, along with Jack Brickhouse, announced the Bear games on radio from 1959 through 1982.

Through his legendary column in the *Chicago Sun-Times* and his "At Random" television talk show and current TV commentaries, Kup has been host to practically every show business celebrity and major political and sports figure of the past fifty years. One who appeared quite often was his longtime and extremely close friend George Halas.

183

One word best sums up George Halas: tough. George was in fact the toughest man I ever knew, both physically and mentally. He feared no man at any level. He bore great pain without ever a single complaint. He seldom knew a day without pain, going back all the way to the time when he suffered a hip injury playing for the New York Yankees baseball team in 1919. He got a hit off the famous pitcher Rube Marquard of the [then New York] Giants in spring training and tried to stretch it into a triple and injured the hip sliding into third. Halas always used to say, with that wry smile of his, that his having to leave the Yankees opened up the left field spot for a guy by the name of Babe Ruth [Ruth was in fact acquired by the Yankees from the Boston Red Sox after the 1919 season].

George was a tough man to deal with across the desk, but he was always fair. He was a tough guy on the field—tough on his players because he demanded discipline, which is so necessary in handling a football team.

He saw the great possibilities of pro football, and he was there at the very beginning to get it launched. He saw it through the Depression—I remember one year in the thirties he was ecstatic because the Bears turned a $300 profit at year's end. He said, "We just turned the corner." And he contributed so much to professional football over the years. He was not just Papa Bear; he was the Grand Old Man of the game itself.

I first met him in 1935 when I joined the old *Chicago Times* as a sportswriter. Because of my football background, I was assigned to cover the Bears, which meant dealing with George Halas himself. He was the team's best publicity man. Every night before I'd write a story about the Bears for the next day's paper I'd call George at his office and talk to him. He would give me slants or ideas, who looked good and who didn't. He was amazing. He would coach all day, run a business on the side—because those were very lean years during the Depression and the Bears were certainly not much of a profit-making organization then—and still have time to serve happily as the team's press agent at night.

I remember when he first brought Sid Luckman to Chicago in 1939. Sid had been a great tailback for Columbia, and George wanted him to quarterback the Bears. I was still covering the Bears as a sportswriter in those days, and George called me up on the telephone. "I've got a young kid coming from New York who's never been west of the Hudson River. He thinks we're all Indians out here." He asked me to take him around town and introduce him to some of my friends so he'd get to know some people and be able to find his way around the city.

I took Sid around. There were all kinds of different people I knew, and I introduced Sid to them. A short time later I got word that Sid was being investigated by the league for associating with various unsavory characters. Some of my friends in those days were bookies and bettors and not considered the most savory of characters, I guess, in the office of the NFL.

Nothing came of it. It turned out it was mostly at the instigation of Fred Mandel, who was a department store heir in Chicago who at the time also owned the Detroit Lions. He was kind of envious about Luckman going to the Bears and was trying to stir up a little trouble. He had reason to be envious. Sid, of course, went on to become one of the game's greatest quarterbacks and finest gentlemen.

I got to know George Halas on the field too. I was an official for the NFL in those earlier days, and I handled some of the Bear games. We were pretty good friends by that time. In fact we had a group that used to get together for dinner every Monday night at the Tavern Club, which included George, Henry Crown, the multimillionaire industrialist; Don Maxwell, the editor of the *Chicago Tribune*; and some others. We would have a lot of laughs, great time, but once you got on the field all bars were down as far as George was concerned. He treated me with no more consideration or respect than any other official on the field, which means none at all. If you were wearing those stripes, you were the enemy—if you were calling something against his team, that is; against the other team, well, that was a different story. I can remember going by him on the sideline, and he was calling me every name in the book. George, as everyone who was ever on the field with him during a game knows, had the foulest language out there I ever heard.

On the other hand, George loved to rib me about my

officiating. He told this story several times at functions when I was present—and let me preface it by saying it is a purely apocryphal story: "We were playing our bitterest rival, the Packers, at Green Bay, and Kup was working as the head linesman. It was the usual ferocious game between the Bears and the Packers. Late in the game we were marching for the winning touchdown and reached the Packers' 10-yard line. It was fourth and one when Luckman sent Bill Osmanski off tackle. It was a close spot. Kup had to call for a measurement to see if we made the first down. When he brought the chains out and saw we made it, Kup jumped up and down, clapping his hands and shouting, 'We made it! We made it!' "

The game I remember most from my officiating days was that incredible championship game in Washington in 1940. The Bears went down there with savagery on their minds. I was the head linesman that day, and I, like everybody else, thought the game was a toss-up. Both teams were superb, and they had played a close game earlier in the season, which the Redskins won by only a couple of points. It was anything but a toss-up. At the half the Bears were winning by four touchdowns. In the fourth quarter, I remember, there was a lull in the game, and at this point the Bears were winning 60-0. I heard the stadium announcer on the public address system there at Griffith Stadium say, "Your attention is directed to a very important announcement regarding the sale of seats for the 1941 Redskin season." That's all I could hear because it was greeted by thunderous boos. It was the only thing Washington fans had to make noise about all day. It was certainly the most ill-timed announcement in NFL history. The Bears, of course, ended up winning the game 73-0, the most points scored in a game in NFL history.

I talked to Halas after the game, and, needless to say, he was jubilant. But he was pretty calm and quiet about it. He was a good friend—friendly rival—with George Preston Marshall, the Washington owner, and Ray Flaherty, their coach. He did not want to rub it in; he knew how awful they must have been feeling. I think what he said was that the Bears had a great "on-day" and the Redskins had a great "off-day."

George was accused of being a little tightfisted with the dollar at different times, like when Mike Ditka said that Halas threw nickels around like they were manhole covers. But things were tough for the Bears over the years. George had to borrow $25,000 in the early thirties when he split with Dutch Sternaman to keep control of the Bears, and that was a fortune in those days. He wasn't making any money from the team. Nobody was. Bronko Nagurski, that fabulous fullback, made maybe $5,000 a year, tops, when he was with the Bears. That's all they could afford to pay him.

They always liked to tell the story about George and Sid Luckman, after the 1940 season, just after the Bears had annihilated the Redskins 73-0 in the championship game. Luckman came in to see Halas about a bonus. "How much are you thinking of?" George asked.

"How about $1,000?" Sid said.

"That's outrageous," George said and pulled an old white envelope from a desk drawer. On it he had some notes, which was a custom of his, always writing notes to himself. He pointed to the scribbling on the back of the envelope. "Here, Sid, you threw an interception against Green Bay. You fumbled against Detroit. You called the wrong play against the Giants. You missed a tackle against the Lions." Then, shaking his head in dismay, he said, "The best I can do is $250."

About a week later Luckman got a letter from George requesting that he report a few weeks early for the 1941 training camp to learn some new plays Papa Bear was planning to install. For that he would pay Sid an extra $750. Sid got the $1,000 bonus he'd asked for, but in George's way.

Halas paid Luckman more than any other Bear up to that time, except for the special deal he had with Red Grange for the barnstorming tour in 1925. I believe it was $20,000 at his peak. The reason: Halas heard from George Preston Marshall, the owner of the Washington Redskins, that that was what he was paying his great quarterback, Sammy Baugh. When Sid came in to discuss salary, Halas told him he was getting $20,000, very big money in those days, because "I don't want any quarterback in this league to get more money than you."

Over the years Halas helped many of his former players financially when they were troubled with health or business failures. He looked after many people and many different charities, but he always did it quietly and shunned any publicity related to those things he did.

The Bears, of course, were George's life. He saw them born; he raised them, looked after them. Henry Crown once offered him a number of millions of dollars for the team, but he turned it down. Later, after he had retired from coaching, Sid Luckman, who had become eminently successful in business after his football career ended, and A. N. Pritzker, one of the wealthiest men in the country, made George quite an offer. They said they would buy the team and Halas could set the price—whatever it was, they would meet it. And he could run the organization for as long as he wished at whatever salary he wanted. But he turned that offer down as well.

They once tried to persuade George to run for mayor of Chicago. It was Don Maxwell of the *Tribune*. He was convinced that George, with his great following in the city, could be the savior of the Republican party. Chicago had not had a Republican mayor since Big Bill Thompson left office in 1931. Maxwell got all the bigwig Republicans in town to talk Halas into running. But George would have none of it. As he told me, "If I did run, the first thing that would happen to me is the Bears would lose all their Democratic fans. I don't want to split my following." But it shows the feelings and respect many of the major people in Chicago held for George Halas.

Outside Chicago as well. One of his great friends was Bob Hope. They had been close ever since World War II. During the war George was serving in the navy in the Pacific, a lieutenant commander who was handling special events for the troops— sports, entertainment, those kinds of diversions. One day he heard that Hope was to be in the area, on his way home with his group after a long, grueling junket entertaining troops over there. George wanted desperately to get Bob to entertain the boys on his ship. He got hold of him by telephone and pleaded his case.

Hope explained that he was exhausted, that he and his entertainers had given a dozen shows in the last five days alone

Even after he retired, there was no keeping Papa Bear away from where Bear action was. Here he is pictured with Bear trainer Fred Caito at training camp outside Halas Hall in Lake Forest. Halas, a charter member of the Pro Football Hall of Fame, along with partner Dutch Sternaman, founded the Bears in 1920 and was the organization's guiding spirit until his death in 1983. As head coach of the Bears he won more regular season football games (326) than any other coach in NFL history.

and they were headed home. As everybody who ever played football knew, George did not give up easily. He begged Hope to squeeze in just one more performance. As Bob later told me, "I could tell by the sound of his voice how much he wanted us to come over to his ship and entertain his boys. Over the telephone

I could see the tears in his eyes." So Hope changed his schedule to include one last performance before going home, and he and George remained good friends from that time on.

Both George Halas and Bob Hope were at a dinner that commemorated the twenty-fifth anniversary of "Kup's Column." Bob was the headline speaker that night, but George preceded him to the podium and told some wonderful, funny stories. He had that blue-ribbon audience in stitches. When he finished, Hope leaned over and whispered to me, "Don't ever invite me to follow that son of a bitch again."

In professional football, however, George Halas had no peer. He saw the game growing into what it is today, and he worked so hard to make it happen. For the good of the league he and his buddy, George Marshall, were responsible for making the game what it is today. George understood in the 1930s that certain teams were dominating the NFL—his team, the Packers, the Giants—and that if the league was to survive it had to have some kind of parity. If they didn't even up the play in the league, the competition would suffer, and eventually everything would collapse. So they came up with the draft—he and Marshall, they were the ones who propagated it. It was, in fact, one of the lifesavers of the league.

There were, in fact, a number of times that George Halas saved the league from demise. When he brought Red Grange into the game, when he nursed it through the Depression, when he brought in the T formation . . .

His contributions to the game of pro football were enormous. He personally guided so many rule changes through the NFL in the earlier years of the game, and they helped make it the exciting game it is today.

We had a birthday party for George every year. On his eightieth birthday he addressed us beginning with "I'm eighty years old today. . . . Now that the first half of my life is over. . . ." That was the way he was—an optimist and a wit. He packed more into a lifetime than a dozen men, and he contributed more to professional football and sports entertainment in general than anybody I ever met. The National Football League is his monument.

The Guarantee

Barry Gottehrer wrote in his book *The Giants of New York* of this benevolent confrontation between Tim Mara, owner of the New York Giants, and George Halas, player/coach/owner of the Chicago Bears. Their two teams were scheduled to meet at the Polo Grounds in December 1926:

By game time the temperature was 18 degrees, the wind was blowing 25 miles an hour, and two-foot snowbanks covered the entire field . . . except for a few photographers, reporters, and members of Mara's family, the stands were deserted. . . . Mara crossed over from the Giants' dressing room to tell the Bears the field was in unplayable condition. Halas, who with the rest to his players was still dressed in street clothes, listened while Mara talked and then nodded his head. "That's fine with us," he said, "but where's our $3,000 guarantee?"

"What guarantee?" shouted Mara. "There aren't a dozen paying customers in the house."

"That's your problem, Tim," said Halas. "We've got a $3,000 guarantee, rain or shine, and we're not leaving without it."

"Okay, if that's the way you want it," said Mara. "You boys better get into your uniforms. If you think you're going to get that $3,000, you're going to play that game even if there are only two people in the stands." Mara slammed the door and stormed out.

The Bears cursed, grumbled, started undressing, and cursed again. Ten minutes later, someone opened the Bear dressing room door a few inches and, without coming into view, said, "How about $2,000?" Halas looked at his players, who wanted to play even less than Mara, and answered, "We'll take the two."

Never Sneak Up on an Indian

George Halas told this story many times. In 1927 an aging
Joe Guyon, then thirty-four years old, was in the backfield
for the New York Giants. Guyon, a full-blooded Indian who
had played at Carlisle and on various pro teams with Jim
Thorpe, was a great player, destined for the Pro Football
Hall of Fame.

As Guyon faded back for a pass, Halas, the Bears' right
defensive end, burst through. Guyon's back was to Halas, a
perfect setup for a blind-side hit, maybe a fumble, but if
nothing else a reminder that the pro game was indeed a
rough one. At the last second, however, Guyon unloaded
the pass and wheeled around to greet the charging Halas
with his knee. It broke several of Halas's ribs. Guyon shook
his head at the grimacing Chicago Bear on the ground.

"Come on, Halas," he said. "You should know better
than to try to sneak up on an Indian."

Stan Jones

Stan Jones was considered one of the finest offensive guards ever to play the game of professional football, a position he performed at nobly for the Bears during the 1950s and early sixties before making the transition to defensive tackle, which he played his last three seasons in Chicago.

As a guard Jones went to seven consecutive Pro Bowl games (1955–61) and earned All-Pro honors four times. As a defensive tackle he was an integral part of the Bears' front four in 1963—along with tackle Fred Williams and ends Doug Atkins and Ed O'Bradovich—which was one of the key elements in bringing the NFL championship to Chicago that year.

Jones learned to play both sides of the line of scrimmage at the University of Maryland, where he played tackle on both offense and defense. He was a consensus All-American his senior year and was honored with the Knute Rockne Memorial Trophy as the nation's outstanding college lineman.

The Bears thought so highly of his prospects that they drafted Jones while he still had a year to go at Maryland. The following year, 1954, he joined the Bears and instantly won a starting berth at offensive tackle. Because of his quickness and the fact that there was now a need for larger, mobile guards in the pro game, he was switched to guard the following year.

Jones served as the Bears' offensive captain for a number of years, and according to teammate Fred Williams, "He was a natural leader, somebody you looked up to. And I'll tell you one thing: he could lift the side of a house, he was such a strong son of a gun."

Jones was strong partly because he was one of the first and foremost advocates of weight lifting as a part of conditioning for pro football. And he was durable, never having missed a game of pro, college, or high school football because of an injury.

Stan Jones received the ultimate recognition for his work in 1991 when he was elected to the Pro Football Hall of Fame, one of only four offensive guards in the history of the game to be so honored.

Jones played his last year of football with the Redskins and then retired from the game after the 1966 season but remained active in it on the coaching staffs of the Denver Broncos, Buffalo Bills, Cleveland Browns, and New England Patriots, where he is presently employed.

I got started playing organized football as a freshman in high school in Lemoyne, Pennsylvania, just after World War II. After three years on the varsity I won a football scholarship to the University of Maryland. I wasn't really familiar with the school; in fact all I knew about it was they had played Delaware and a couple of teams in Pennsylvania.

Jim Tatum was the coach there then, and he was a fine one. And we had some very good football players on those Maryland teams: Dick Modzelewski, a tackle who went on to star for the Giants and a couple other teams; Jack Scarbath, an All-American quarterback, almost won the Heisman Trophy but didn't do all that well in the pros; Chet Hanulak, who played halfback for Cleveland; and Dick Nolan, a defensive back for the Giants who went on to become head coach of the 49ers and New Orleans Saints. In the three years I played there we had, I think it was, twenty-two boys go on to play pro football. In my last year, 1953, we won the national championship. We were undefeated [10-0-0], but when we went to the Orange Bowl, we lost to Oklahoma.

I'd been drafted the year before, in '53, by the Bears in the fifth round. I wasn't looking all that forward to pro ball— actually I was hoping that I would pass my flight physical and be playing football for Bolling Air Force Base in Washington, D.C. But I flunked the physical, and so I started looking for alternative things to do and then figured I might just as well play pro football.

The first person from the Bears I had contact with was Phil Handler, the line coach at the time. They were having the '54 draft in Philadelphia that year, and even though I was drafted the year before, I was told to come up there to sign my contract. So I took the train up from Washington, met coach Handler, and signed a contract.

I came to Chicago that summer to play in the College All-Star game. We got whipped by the Detroit Lions [31-6] at Soldier Field. I remember they had Doak Walker. Bobby Layne didn't play—I believe he was hurt—but they didn't seem to miss him that night anyway.

When I met George Halas, he was fifty-nine years old, already a legend. My first impression was that he was more like a businessman than anything else; he was not very warm or friendly. He was the type of person, I found out, who you had to get to know for a while before he became friendly with you.

Once I'd made up my mind to play in the pros, I got very excited about it. I'd seen only a couple of pro games up to that time. The U. of Maryland was not too far from Washington, D.C., and so a few times we went over and saw the Redskins play, but that was about all.

What I think impressed me the most at first in Chicago was the feeling of the fans. They seemed so enthusiastic, loyal; I hadn't really expected that in the pro game. I thought they'd just come out like they were going to see an exhibition or something. I didn't think they'd have the spirit. I was surprised, but I felt good about it, glad I'd made the decision to play.

The game was rougher than college ball. The players were

all talented, each one a high caliber. We had some very good teams at Maryland, and we were accustomed to good coaching, so it didn't come as a huge surprise to find myself playing with really talented individuals.

My first roommate with the Bears was Harlon Hill; we roomed together during that first training camp in '54. He was a rookie too, from a place called Florence State Teachers College, and he was destined to be one of the great receivers for the Bears. During the season I roomed with Zeke Bratkowski. We were both bachelors and had some great times going around together and have been good friends ever since.

We had played against each other in college. Zeke had gone to Georgia, and he used to claim he was the one who made me an All-American. It went back to a game my last year at Maryland against them. He dropped back to pass, and I broke through and hit him solid just as he was releasing the ball, knocking him on his can. The ball kind of fluttered down the field, and we intercepted it. I saw our guy coming with the ball, and the next thing I saw was Zeke getting up, so I knocked him down again. George Halas was in the stands that day, his Bears were playing the Redskins the next day. Halas kind of liked that.

After the All-Star game I reported to training camp in Rensselaer, Indiana. It was awful, just awful. I've never had the slightest interest in ever going back to look at the place. It wasn't a bad town, in all fairness. It was the idea of the training camp in those days; one purpose—get the guys in shape.

The college there, St. Joseph's, didn't have a summer program, so you didn't see many people other than the priests and nuns. We couldn't have any family there. We were isolated. It was sort of like a state penitentiary somewhere. Halas put a mile radius limit as to how far we could go from the camp—I forget exactly how far that was, but the next closest town of any size, Remington, was one mile outside the radius. We still used to go to Remington, though, drink a couple of beers and eat a braunschweiger and onion sandwich, or we'd go over to Indiana Beach on a lake, and that was always a real test to see if we could get there and still get back in time for curfew.

The old building we were in wasn't air-conditioned. And

Halas had a security guy, a policeman type we called Dick Tracy, who would go around and check on us, and if you weren't there he'd get a bonus when he turned you in. They actually chained the doors at night after curfew.

Rick Casares had his dog down there, a little Yorkshire terrier. I think he trained the dog to take a crap in front of Halas's door every morning, because often there was a little pile there in the morning.

I developed my own form of conditioning. I had been working on a carefully planned weight-lifting program since my high school days. No one was lifting weights with the Bears when I got there. It was not in vogue in the 1950s; in fact I was warned that I might be risking my career working with weights. They thought I'd become muscle-bound and lose my speed and agility.

Actually, if I hadn't started lifting weights early, I would never have become a pro football player. And I know it helped me as a pro—I never missed a game because of an injury. It never slowed me down or hampered me in any way. Just the opposite: it made me stronger and more durable. Now it's an integral part of every NFL team's training program.

I started out playing offensive tackle, like I had in college. Actually I played guard from time to time as well. Kline Gilbert, who was a starting Bear guard then, and I interchanged a little bit that year. The next year I moved solely to guard. One of the reasons was that the defenses had begun to move their tackles in and the nose guard out. So the offensive guards had to regularly go up against the defensive tackles. The guards in those days were usually around 230 pounds, and now they were going up against guys weighing maybe 265 or 275, huge guys like Leo Nomellini and Art Donovan. I was playing at 255 then, so I was bigger and stronger and could handle the tackles better. I also had good quickness to pull out when I had to. So what Halas did was shift me and Herman Clark—he was about 255 too—to the guard positions. We were probably the two heaviest guards in football at the time.

We had a really fine team in 1956, especially the offense. We averaged 30 points a game and 206 yards rushing in each game. I like to believe our line contributed strongly to those statistics. Rick Casares led the league in rushing that year [1,126 yards and 12 touchdowns in a twelve-game season, both Bear records at the time]; he just had a wonderful year. Ed Brown and George Blanda kind of split up the quarterbacking, and Harlon Hill had a great year, caught passes for more than a thousand yards [1,128, another Bear record]. Besides Herman Clark and me, we had guys like Bill Wightkin [tackle], Larry Strickland [center], and Bill McColl [end] on the line, and they were very good blockers. On defense we had Bill George, Joe Fortunato, Fred Williams, Doug Atkins, J. C. Caroline. It was an impressive team.

We folded up in the championship game, however. We had tied the Giants in the regular season [17-17], but when we went out to New York for the title, it did not turn out to be a very memorable game for me. The field was frozen; it was only about twenty degrees above zero. We wore rubber-soled sneakers that day, but it didn't help. We really got beat up [47-6].

I enjoyed playing on the offensive line in those days, but someone said, and I think it's probably true, that offensive guard is the most obscure position on a football team. No one seems to know what the guards are doing out there. They don't keep records of your blocks. I did have one advantage, though. In those days we used to do a lot of pulling. People could see more of what we were doing then.

I played with some really memorable players. When I first came up, there was George Connor. He had been a hero to me. I'd read about him in *Football Illustrated* magazine and *Sport* magazine. He'd been All-America at two schools [Holy Cross and Notre Dame] and an All-Pro in the NFL I don't know how many times.

Another guy around that time that I looked up to was Don Kindt, one of our halfbacks.

These guys were not just great football players, but off the field they were gentlemen. Just class acts. They were the kind of guys who, if you got out of line on one hand or had a problem on the other, either way, they would take care of it.

And, of course, there was Doug Atkins. He was some character but just a natural football player. He was so strong. I never really had to play against him, but I remember going against

Chick Jagade (30) carries the ball through a snowstorm for the Bears against the crosstown rival Cardinals in this mid-1950s game. Blocking for him is guard Stan Jones (78), who played for the Bears from 1954 through 1965 and was enshrined in the Pro Football Hall of Fame in 1991.

him in intrasquad scrimmages. He was the toughest and strong-est—really one of the great ones.

He always had these things going with Coach Halas. There was this back-and-forth kind of thing, and Doug was the Peck's bad-boy type. Halas would always be saying, "Atkins is question-ing my leadership," and they would go at it. Halas, of course, always won out, but Doug gave everybody a lot of laughs along the way.

I remember one instance between the two at training camp that was really something. How Doug got away with it, I'll never know. We lived in a dormitory, and it was a really cloistered life. Well, this one camp some wallets turned up missing—not all at once, but every so often. So we got to referring to whoever was taking them as the "phantom."

Well, Halas himself was making bed checks around that time. And one night he steps into the room where Doug and his roommate were, shining his flashlight. Doug was behind the door with a blanket and throws it over Halas, shouting as loud as he could, "I got the phantom, I got the phantom." Doug, of course, knows it's Halas, but everybody comes running out of the other rooms and sees Doug holding this guy wriggling like hell under a blanket. Then they heard Halas's voice from under the blanket saying, "Doug, let me the hell out of here." When Doug did, he said real innocently something like "How was I to know, Coach?"

George Blanda is another one that's hard to forget. George would bet on anything. You'd go to a bowling alley, and he'd bet he could beat you. You'd play a pinball machine, and he'd be there with a bet.

Blanda was a nervous kind of guy. One of the funniest things I remember from those days was when we were breaking the huddle and lining up one game, and all of a sudden I feel George behind me. I was the right guard, and he's there behind me, his hands under me, and he starts calling the signals. Larry Strickland, the center, who's got the ball, looked over at me with this strange expression on his face, trying to figure out what the hell George was doing with his hands under the guard instead of the center.

Another time George damn near got me fired. It was near-
ing the end of the half, and he was a little frantic with time
running out, and he told me to fake an injury—you know, to
buy some time, which you were sometimes able to get away with
in those days. Well, I did, and I was lying there. But they didn't
stop the clock, and George is now yelling, "Get up. Get up. We
got time." So I started to get back up, but by the time I did the
gun went off. Halas met me about 20 yards from the sideline and
kicked me all the way to the dugout there in Wrigley Field.

Bill George was another one—a really great football player.
Somebody once said he had the cross-build between a pelican
and a gorilla. He had these enormous shoulders and long arms.
He was a wrestler-type player and had great quickness and
reaction time, and he was one helluva tough guy out there on
the field.

The toughest players I ever went up against? Well, as an
offensive guard, I'd have to say certainly Art Donovan of the
Colts. He was always the toughest defensive tackle for me to
block. Donovan was not only big; he was quick. He was like a
matador. He'd move one way and go the other. Art was the
smartest tackle I ever faced. He was the man who covered the
inside, handled the run, which opened up Gino Marchetti to
rush the passer.

There was also Leo Nomellini of the 49ers. He was big and
durable and fast. Anybody who went up against him knew he
was in for a real battle. Another who gave me a lot of grief was
Bud McFadin of the Rams.

When I switched to defensive tackle, the best I ran up
against was Forrest Gregg, a tackle who also played guard for
Green Bay when Jerry Kramer was hurt.

I actually retired after the 1962 season. I was thirty-one
years old, and it frankly had gotten to the point where I was
moving back and forth so much between Chicago and Washington, where I was teaching in the public school system in the off-
season, that it was becoming a real hardship. I also wasn't
making all that much money playing football, so I told Halas I
was retiring.

Halas hired George Allen to take over the defense for the

1963 season, and Allen hired Joe Stydahar to coach the defensive line. Well, they had some gaps to fill, they felt, and one of them was at defensive tackle. They'd looked at some film where I'd played a little defensive tackle the year before due to some of the regulars having gotten hurt. I guess they liked what they saw, because they contacted me and asked if I would come back and play another year or so as a defensive tackle. Well, the thought of that intrigued me a bit, and so I went back with them.

The switch back to defense on a regular basis, after all those years since college, was not all that easy. It was a little strange, in fact. I never saw so many guys coming at me at once. Once in the beginning I went in and nobody touched me. I was so surprised I didn't know what to do there in the backfield.

But I adjusted, and I found I liked it. On offense you are somewhat limited. You have more freedom on defense. You can dish it out for a change. In Coach Allen's scheme my primary responsibility was run control. I was expected to guard against the rush while the defensive ends—Atkins and Ed O'Bradovich—rushed in to harass the quarterback.

I especially remember the first regular-season game in '63 against the Packers up in Green Bay. Bob Kilcullen was slated to play defensive end alongside me because O'Bradovich was injured. We were kind of last-minute entries into a pretty heralded defense.

Before the game Bill Gleason, a Chicago sportswriter, looked at the roster and said something to the effect that the Bears had an impressive-looking defense except for a pair of real question marks at left tackle and left end, me and Kilcullen. He mentioned that Kilcullen was an artist in the off-season and I was a schoolteacher—these two are *questionable*, he said. Well, the night before the game Kilcullen and I were in this restaurant having dinner, and we saw Gleason there. Bob shouted over to him, "Hey, Gleason, regardless of what you think, we're showing up out there tomorrow." Not knowing how this whole transition was going to turn out, I said to Kilcullen, "Hey, don't call any more attention to us."

The next day it was no surprise to the Packers that we were new to the defense. They ran practically every play over our side of the line. But we stopped them, and they scored only 3 points all day, and we won the opener [10-3].

That was a wonderful season. And as it turned out, we had the best defense in the NFL that year. In fact the championship game they said pitted the game's best defense, ours, versus the league's best offense, the Giants—they had Y. A. Tittle, who had had a great year, and they were averaging better than 30 points a game. We forced them into a lot of turnovers and held them to 10 points. Our defense also set up the Bears' 2 touchdowns, and we won the championship [14-10]—it was probably my greatest pro football thrill.

I retired again after the 1965 season and went back to Washington to take up teaching full-time. Well, the Redskins had a number of injuries on their defensive unit, and they needed some help. So Otto Graham, who was their head coach, talked to me about playing for them. Just one more season, he said.

They had to talk to George Halas, though, because the Bears still had the rights to me. He knew they were offering me a good deal and that if I played I only wanted to play near my home, so he agreed to trade me to Washington for John Paluck, a defensive end. I ended up getting $19,000 for the year; the most I ever got with the Bears was $14,000.

After that season I really did retire . . . from playing anyway. I've been in it ever since as a coach and weight trainer.

1963 Championship Game

At Chicago, Wrigley Field, December 29, 1963

OFFENSE

New York Giants		Chicago Bears
Del Shofner	WR	Bo Farrington
Rosey Brown	LT	Herman Lee
Darrell Dess	LG	Ted Karras
Greg Larson	C	Mike Pyle
Bookie Bolin	RG	Roger Davis
Jack Stroud	RT	Bob Wetoska
Joe Walton	TE	Mike Ditka
Frank Gifford	FL	Johnny Morris
Y. A. Tittle	QB	Bill Wade
Phil King	RB	Willie Galimore
Joe Morrison	FB	Joe Marconi

DEFENSE

Jim Katcavage	LE	Ed O'Bradovich
Dick Modzelewski	LT	Stan Jones
John LoVetere	RT	Fred Williams
Andy Robustelli	RE	Doug Atkins
Jerry Hillebrand	LLB	Joe Fortunato
Sam Huff	MLB	Bill George
Tom Scott	RLB	Larry Morris
Erich Barnes	LCB	Bennie McRae
Dick Lynch	RCB	Dave Whitsell
Dick Pesonen	LS	Richie Petibon
Jim Patton	RS	Rosey Taylor
Allie Sherman	Coach	George Halas

Giants	7	3	0	0	—	10
Bears	7	0	7	0	—	14

Touchdowns—Giants: Frank Gifford; **Bears:** Bill Wade (2)
Field Goals—Giants: Don Chandler
PATs—Giants: Don Chandler; **Bears:** Bob Jencks (2)

The way it was when Wrigley Field was home to the Chicago Bears (1921–70). This 1963 game against Green Bay was one of two the Bears needed to win from Vince Lombardi's Packers to capture the Western Conference title, which they did 26-7 and 10-3 earlier in the season. The Bears went on, of course, to claim the NFL championship that year.

Ted Albrecht

Tackle Ted Albrecht was the Bears' first-round pick in the 1977 draft and the fifth offensive lineman selected that year. Jim Finks was in the stated process of building a young Bear offense—he had drafted Walter Payton two years earlier in the first round and offensive tackle Dennis Lick the year before in the opening round.

Albrecht earned a starting berth his rookie year, joining Lick, guards Noah Jackson and Revie Sorey, and center Dan Neal in the Bears' offensive front line.

Albrecht, an AP All-American his senior year and a two-time All-Pac-8 tackle with the University of California, Berkeley, won NFL All-Rookie Team honors in 1977 and was also the recipient of the Bears' prestigious Brian Piccolo Award that year. He became a mainstay in the Bears' offensive line for five years before a back injury cut short his fine career.

Retiring after the 1981 season, Albrecht has stayed with the game in the broadcast booth for both television and radio. He also founded his own travel service business, which he runs out of Arlington Heights, Illinois.

I think the biggest thrill in my entire football life was being drafted by the Chicago Bears. When you're really serious about sports, and I certainly was, you always want to reach the pinnacle; you want to be the best at your position.

Up to that time I'd played in so many sports in high school and college on an amateur level, and I never felt I reached that pinnacle until the Bears selected me in the first round of the 1977 draft. It was like they were saying to me, "We believe you're the best around at your level now, and we think you've got the stuff to be the best in the pros." It was a great honor, I felt, to know all your work had paid off and your dream had come true—you were drafted by a team like the Bears with all its great tradition.

It came as a surprise, in a way. I had never been contacted by anyone in the Bears organization. Jim Parmer, their great scout, had been around Cal in the spring and the fall of my senior year, but we never talked. Four teams did talk to me, and I visited the four before the draft—the New Orleans Saints, Green Bay Packers, Cincinnati Bengals, and New England Patriots. Those teams actually spent a lot of time with me. Three of them were drafting before the Bears, and so I thought I might end up with one of them. But all three passed on me.

The first contact I had with the Bears was when Bill McGrane, who was Jim Finks's assistant at the time, called just after they picked me. The Bears flew my dad and me out to Chicago that day. My dad had met George Halas in the 1950s, and so on the airplane he gave me all kinds of insights about the man and about the Bears and their heritage. Bill McGrane met us at the airport along with Jeannie Morris and her CBS video people and took us directly over to meet Mr. Halas.

It was amazing: Mr. Halas remembered my father and was very nice with him and me. My father had grown up on the South Side of Chicago, where he lived for a good part of his life. We moved to California when I was three. Halas was just what you always heard about him: tough, ornery, pleasant, personable, penetrating eyes that could look straight through you, a wonderful smile—all those things.

After that we went over to the press conference, and that's

where I met Jim Finks. I was very impressed with Mr. Finks from the very outset. I had heard he was one of the great executives in the league, and I learned that was true during my career in Chicago. He was a very shrewd businessman and a genuine gentleman.

I got my start playing football in the Pop Warner League in Vallejo, California, around thirteen years old. But that was just a passing thing. The first real opportunity for organized football that I had was in high school in the Bay Area out near San Francisco. In those days I played defensive tackle. We had this drill at Vallejo High School, and it almost drove me out of football. They put down this plank, which was twelve inches wide and eight feet long. There was a line drawn in the middle, at the four-foot mark. Well, you put your hand down at one end of the plank, and the opposing lineman did the same at the other end, the idea being that you meet full-speed at the four-foot mark and see who would drive the other guy off the plank.

I was a sophomore when I first did that, up against a senior who was an inch or two taller than me and maybe forty pounds heavier, and he just creamed me. We had a terrific fullback, and he grabbed me by the back of the helmet and dragged me up. He said, "Do you see that fence down there?" It was about fifty yards away. "Well, that's what you run down the plank for, the fence; forget the plank, forget the guy in between. Just pure power, you going for that fence." Well, the next time I did it I didn't stop, and I knocked the guy right off the board. I got the idea. I said to myself, just be violent as hell; just kick ass. It was my first real football lesson.

I was recruited by maybe a hundred schools. They didn't have All-State rankings in California, but I had a good reputation as a major lineman, and I had the size. I even got some letters from Big Ten schools, but I concentrated my ten visits on schools in the Pac-8 and other western state schools. I visited Arizona, Arizona State, Washington, Oregon, UCLA, Stanford—all of them. But I selected Cal/Berkeley because I knew it was a great institution, I thought Mike White was a wonderful coach, and I knew I really had a chance to play. UCLA recruited me, and they swore they weren't recruiting any junior college

transfers. Pepper Rodgers was their coach, and they had something like 180 guys out for football the year I went to Cal/
Berkeley, counting all the transfers and everybody else.

The offensive line coach at Cal my first year was Howard
Mudd. He had been a wonderful offensive guard for the San
Francisco 49ers in the 1960s and had played his last two years
in the NFL with the Bears [1969-70]. When I first met him, he
said, "What I'm going to try to teach you in the next four years
is that an offensive lineman is basically a bag of tricks. Inside
that bag are all the tools you'll need to be the best in the
business. Develop them. Use them. Set your ultimate football
goal on becoming a professional when these four years are
over."

The bag of tricks he was talking about included such
things as concentrating on being mentally tough, how to position yourself, how to use leverage, and how to handle yourself so
that you're never off balance. And if you have to hold: how to
hold and when to hold. Of course I *never* held.

Unfortunately I had Howard Mudd as a coach for only one
year at Cal before he moved on to coach in the NFL. But it was
from him that I got my first real desire to set a goal of playing
in professional football.

I had no recollections of the city of Chicago when I went
out there to meet with the Bears because I was so young when
we left the city, but when I came back in '77 I thought it was the
greatest city I'd ever seen. You'd look at that skyline, meet the
people; they were proud and had reason to be.

Gene Upshaw, one of the game's greatest offensive linemen,
was the first to tip me off to Chicago. He was playing for
Oakland then, and he and a lot of the Raiders used to come over
to Berkeley and get involved with our program. After I was
drafted by the Bears, he called me and said, "You've just been
drafted by one of the greatest sports cities in the United States."
He said, "It's the hub of the country. You'll love it there. Just
keep your nose clean and show respect, and they'll love you in
Chicago."

That's the attitude I came to Chicago with.

My first training camp was in Lake Forest. Jim Finks had

just moved it up there from Indiana where, I guess, it had been for years. There were some veterans around—guys like Doug Buffone, Mike Phipps—but most were young guys, part of Finks's new regime.

I tried to low-profile it because I did not want people thinking here was a number-one draft choice who thought he was something special. My thought was, Try to be a normal guy, try to gain some respect from my teammates. Still, I took a lot of heat because the veterans would call me "Number One," and they were going to put me through the paces. The harassment was over money; they knew coming in as a top draft choice you were going to get decent dollars. They were there to see you earned it.

It was the longest training camp ever that particular year. We had six preseason games and the Hall of Fame game on top of that. I was in training camp for ten weeks—actually eleven because rookies came in a week early. It was right after July 4th that I went to camp. It was unbelievable. Halfway through it I said, If this is pro football, I don't want it. This is murder. But once we got into the season, it was something else, one helluva lot better. It was what we all came for.

There were some very impressive guys there that year. I think I was most impressed with Walter Payton in terms of a pure football player. From the standpoint of dedication in practice as well as games, there was no one quite like him. He did everything that was asked of him and was always in perfect shape.

Roland Harper was another one. He was such an unselfish guy. He spent most of his time blocking for his buddy in the backfield, Walter. I think that's an important part of the reason the Bears have done so well in recent years running from the tailback position—besides great runners like Payton and Neal Anderson, they had terrific blockers there with them like Roland and later Matt Suhey and Brad Muster.

Doug Buffone was the salty veteran. He'd been with the Bears twelve years when I got there. I remember once we were out there on the field doing stretching exercises before practice. I was in this group with Bob Thomas, our kicker, and Bob

Parsons, our punter, and Doug. We were just talking back and forth while we were doing the stretching exercises, and I said something about buying a condominium. Doug said, "No, no, don't do that. Buy a house. Buy one every year. Don't live in it, though; rent an apartment and rent out the houses. You'll probably stay around about eight years, so when you're done with football you'll have eight houses. Real estate, that's the investment." Six weeks later I closed on my first house. Well, I stayed around for only five years, but at one time I owned four different houses. We'd talk about crap like that all the time when we were warming up.

I actually started out playing offensive guard. I was fighting for the starting job with Noah Jackson and Revie Sorey, and I lost out. But in our second game of the season down in St. Louis against the Cardinals, our left tackle, Jeff Sevy, was having a bad game. And to top it off, with a couple of minutes to go and us down 3 points, we had a third-down-and-three situation, and he jumped offsides. So it was third and eight, and we didn't make it, and we ended up losing 16-13.

Our offensive coordinator at the time was Sid Gillman, and he was fuming. Things didn't get better. So a few weeks later he came up to me and said, "All-bright"—he called me that when I did things well; when I did things poorly, he called me "Seldom-bright"—"Next week you're going to start at left tackle. You've got four days to get ready, so take your playbook home, study the position, and know it perfectly by Sunday."

I started to walk away, and I was favoring my leg a little because I'd hurt my knee in the game the day before, and he shouted after me, "Study it! And quit limping."

A day or two later Jack Pardee, our head coach that year, came up to me and said, "You know who you're going to be playing against next week?"

I said, "I know I'm playing left tackle, and we're playing the Vikings."

"Do you know who *you* are going up against?"

I didn't. I hadn't had time to even get into that.

He said, "Try Jim Marshall."

I knew him as one of the famous "Purple People-Eaters."

Coach Pardee just looked at me, shaking his head a little. "You know how old you were when he was a rookie in the NFL?"

I said, "No, sir."

"You were one," he said. [Actually Albrecht was five when Marshall joined the NFL in 1960.] "You think he doesn't know every trick in the game? You think he doesn't know you're a raw-ass rookie? So you better be ready to play your ass off out there Sunday."

I went home and said, "Oh, God." But I did do my homework, and it worked out, and from that point on I was our left tackle.

During those five years I had a lot of great times. We got to the playoffs twice, in 1977 and 1979, and I got to meet and get to know a lot of wonderful guys. The offensive line was a group that stuck together. We would go out together, confide in each other, have a good time together. We used to get together every Friday night at Dan Neal's house [Bear center, 1975-83] for a few laughs, some beers, maybe play some cards. We usually got out on Fridays and went over there right after practice. It was just the offensive linemen and the tight ends. Then some of the other guys wanted to come, but we said no. You are the "skilled athletes," we told them; we are the "pig bodies." We don't mix.

Revie Sorey was a very funny guy—our flashy right guard, we used to call him. The first time I met him was in training camp my rookie year, 1977. Revie had been there a couple of years by then. He had this long, old Cadillac with license plates that read "Rock Hollywood." He also had a car phone. In those days I'd never even heard of a car phone. But I would always see him in that big car, talking on his phone. After practice, on our way to the mess hall or coming back from it, Revie was always talking to somebody. I thought it would be nice to have one of those but had no idea where you got one. So I asked a couple of the other veterans one day who were standing around where to get one like Revie's and how you get it installed. They just laughed and told me it was an old phone he'd dismantled from his house with a cord dangling down from it that he kept between the bucket seats and pretended he was talking to someone.

I played next to Noah Jackson, our left guard, for five years. Noah was always worried about himself on each play; he was always conscious of everything going on around him. I remember when we played against Tampa Bay and I had to block on their All-Pro end Lee Roy Selmon, and he was surely one of the best defensive linemen in the game. I wanted to keep him as far away from the quarterback as possible. So I would line up, leaving a pretty sizable gap between myself and Noah. The farther I moved out, the more I reduced his angle from the end spot to the quarterback. This would force him to rush the quarterback from farther outside.

When I did this, Noah would look over at me just as we were setting up and say, "Ted, shit, get in here. You're too far out, man." He'd shake his head. "Too big a gap, Ted, too big. Lee Roy's gonna kick your ass anyway."

Well, on third and long everybody knew we were going to pass, and my only thought was to contain Selmon. But when we came to the line of scrimmage, Selmon would line up in tight, right near the guard. So I'd line up a little distance away from him, thinking I was a little away from him, but I really wasn't. He was six inches from the guard when he was supposed to be three feet from him. So he had pulled me in, and when I put my hand down to go from a two-point to three-point stance he would move out. Well, I couldn't move once I was set.

Lee Roy was also the best against the run I ever went up against. He would play 2 yards off the ball on first down, looking like a linebacker in a three-point stance. He'd play a yard and a half off the ball on second down. And depending on the down and distance on third, and sometimes second, he'd play you 4 yards wide, set up in a sprinter's stance, looking like a wide receiver like Willie Gault getting ready to take off full-speed. It would be like he was out there getting set to rush the passer. But what he did was, after the snap, play you head up, and he was so quick that if you overreached him, got out in front too fast, he'd just run right by you. And if you were a little short on your reach, he'd go right around the other side of you and snag the ball carrier. You had to be perfect with your technique if you were going to block Lee Roy Selmon.

Another thing Selmon did that made our lives difficult was that he was always looking at the guard, at Noah, not me, and eyeing backfield formations. He played tendencies. If he saw the guard come straight out, he'd come straight on. If he saw the guard pull left, he'd pull left, and I'd be chasing him on a pursuit angle across the field. If the guard went right, he'd go with the flow right. But he didn't always do that; he always kept you guessing, kept his game of mental tendencies. Besides having to play tough and be quick against Selmon, you had to play a mental game with him too, because you really didn't know just what he was going to do next.

Bob Thomas got us into the playoffs my rookie year when he kicked that field goal in overtime against the Giants the last game of the season. There was about four inches of slush on the field when he did it, but he made it, and we won 12-9 and got a wild-card ticket to the playoffs.

That enabled us to play the Dallas Cowboys, a team I'd always dreamed of playing against. They had a great team, with Roger Staubach, Tony Dorsett, Drew Pearson, and the Doomsday Defense. They were easy winners of the NFC East. And the defense was awesome, the Doomsdayers; up front they had Harvey Martin, Randy White, Jethro Pugh, Too Tall Jones. I had to handle Harvey Martin, who had twenty-some sacks that season and was named All-Pro. Every time he had a sack, he said the quarterback was "Martinized." Well, as a team we had a terrible day and lost [37-7]. The only good thing I can remember about it was that Bob Avellini was Martinized only once, and that was on the last play of the game.

We got into the 1979 playoffs on a shoestring too. That was again the last game of the season, and this time we had to defeat the St. Louis Cardinals by 33 points for the point differential to get in as the wild card. It was also the day that Muggs Halas, the team president, died suddenly that morning of a heart attack. We wore black armbands on our sleeves that day to honor Muggs Halas. And it was also the game Walter Payton had to outrush Ottis Anderson by more than 100 yards if he was to win the NFC rushing title that year.

I'll never forget it. We won the toss, and on our opening

drive we ran a play into the middle. There was a big pileup. I was sealing off the back side and was somewhere inside the pile. I heard the referee saying something about somebody was fooling around with him, and he was kind of kicking a foot around. He'd had it down to spot the ball, and he thought someone was grabbing at it trying to trip him. I didn't think much of it until about three or four plays later. We were down inside the 25-yard line, and it was a similar situation, big pileup. We were trying for a first down. The same official is there with his foot down in the pile, trying to mark the spot of the ball. I was right at the bottom of it this time, and I saw his foot, and I saw these two wristbands there, each marked 34, and I knew it was Walter [Payton]. He was untying the shoelace of the official. Well, back in the huddle while they're bringing out the chains to measure, we saw the official down tying his shoe. We all knew it was Walter. Who else would do something like that? So I said something about it, and Walter just smiled and said something about him [the referee] being lucky because he was trying to tie one lace to the one on the other shoe.

Anyway, we won the game 42-6, and Walter rushed for 157 yards, and we held Ottis Anderson to something like 25 yards. We went to the playoffs, and Walter had the NFC rushing crown.

Walter was a notorious prankster. He used to say, "I don't get mad; I just get even." Well, that certainly was true. I can personally vouch for it.

Down in Tampa during my rookie season, Walter was lying in a lawn chair under the sun. I took the ice bucket from my room, put some ice and water in it, and dumped it on him. And I said laughingly, "How's a black guy going to get a tan? It just doesn't work." That night, when the dessert cart came by about eleven o'clock, I went out in the hall to get something. While I was there, Walter snuck in the room I shared with Vince Evans, who purposely kept me preoccupied at the dessert cart, and threw a couple of buckets of ice and water under my sheet and blanket. When I climbed into bed, it was nothing but a sheet of ice water in there. I had to call the maid, and she came up. It took a while to set it up again, and in the meantime the coaches came in yelling about what was going on and why was I up so late and what did I do in my bed. I said, "I didn't do anything. Walter did it." They just kind of looked at me funny and said, "Walter's not here." And Vince said, "Yeah, I haven't seen Walter all night."

The playoff game that year, the last one I was a part of, was a really memorable one too. It was in Philadelphia against the Eagles, and we should have won that one. We were leading by 7 points at the half [17-10]. Then in the third quarter, Walter Payton broke away on an 84-yard run from scrimmage all the way to Philadelphia's 1-foot line. It seemed for sure we were going to be up by 17 points, but there was a very late flag on the play, and the run was called back. One of the refs said Brian Baschnagel had been in motion on the play. It was an absolutely brutal call, an absolute joke, and the films later proved that.

What we did was call a 21-Toss, wide to the right, and what we did on that was bring the wide receiver [Baschnagel] in motion toward where we would run the ball. We used him as either a block-first force to crack back on the point of attack, or he would go to the second level and hit the first linebacker that would show. Well, he [Baschnagel] ran it perfectly, and just as the ball was snapped he turned and blocked into the point of attack. We pulled the tight end [Greg Latta] around that block, and the fullback [Roland Harper] chopped down a linebacker. Both our guards, Jackson and Sorey, had pulled and took care of the other two linebackers. Dan Neal and I had the inside sealed up. Walter [Payton] just turned the corner and, whoosh, was gone—84 yards.

But it was called back. And we never got over it and ended up losing [27-17].

The next year we cornered the head of officials and asked him about that call. The head and a couple of other officials would come each year to the different teams' training camps to talk about new rule changes and things like that. Well, we asked him about it. We said we wanted to know about that call on Brian. He avoided the question. We said, no, we wanted an answer. What was the final feeling by the league officials on that motion call after they watched the films? He said the call was blown.

I was glad Sid Gillman switched me to offensive tackle back in '77. I got to play against some really great defensive players. Besides those I already mentioned, like Lee Roy Selmon, Jim Marshall, Harvey Martin, there were guys like Fred Dean when he was with San Diego and A. J. Duhe of the Dolphins, but the toughest to play against the pass was Al Baker of the Lions. He was nicknamed Bubba. Baker had only one assignment: get the quarterback. And antagonize and verbally abuse anybody that's between you and the quarterback. I mean he talked an awful lot out there. I won't say he was a dirty player, but he didn't play within the way most defensive players did. He played within the rules, but he was a talker, always hyped with emotion, always talking at everybody on the field. I guess that bothered me because I'm not a talker. At the same time he was quick, tall, and powerful.

Playing on the offensive line doesn't garner any glamour on the football field. It's the only position on the team where you don't tote up any statistics—you don't throw the ball, run with it, kick it, catch it, tackle somebody who has the ball. No one even notices you until you do something wrong. It's sort of like a catcher in baseball. You're in on every play, but nobody really pays attention to you until you get a passed ball. No one knows you're on the offensive line in football until a referee flags you for holding or offsides and then announces your number to the crowd. In the offensive line no news is good news.

I had my bumps and bruises along the way, but I never really got hurt in a game, enough to sideline me, that is. My career-ending injury came in August 1981, when I hurt my back in the weight room, not on the football field. The Bears placed me on injured reserve before the start of the regular season that year, but my back got progressively worse. I went with the spinal injections, which were common then, rather than the surgery like Joe Montana had later. Nothing worked for me, and I never got off injured/disabled. So, in 1982, I left football as a player.

I thought I would have been around longer, but in professional football you never know. I remember some wonderful advice my attorney gave me just before I signed with the Bears.

He said, "Don't ever forget, your first football game in this league could be your last." In effect: Don't forget there is life after football, and you never know just when you'll have to face it.

Running for His Life

George Trafton, center for the Chicago Bears, future Hall of Famer, and notorious on-the-field ruffian, was less than popular in Rock Island, Illinois, when that city fielded an NFL team, the Independents, in the early 1920s. During one matchup in 1920 a number of the Rock Island players had to leave the game with assorted injuries after encounters with Trafton. The crowd, already angry, became enraged when Independent fullback Fred Chicken joined the casualty list as he tried to race around end and out of Trafton's reach.

"I tackled him right on the sideline," Trafton said. "There was a fence close to the field, and after I hit Chicken he spun up against a fence post and broke his leg. After that the fans were really on me." An understatement to say the least. At the end of the game they chased him out of the stadium and down the street under a shower of rocks, empty bottles, and other lethal projectiles at hand. Dutch Sternaman, a halfback and half-owner of the Bears then, tried to pick him up in a taxicab, but the pursuers were too close. Trafton finally managed to escape with the help of a passing motorist.

The next time the Bears appeared in Rock Island, the game was again an especially physical one, and the crowd grew almost as ornery as it had the time before. When at the end of the game George Halas was handed $7,000 in cash—the Bears' share of the gate receipts—he handed the money over to Trafton for safekeeping.

"I knew that if trouble came," Halas said, "I'd be running only for the $7,000. Trafton would be running for his life."

George McAfee

When he first carried the ball for the Bears back in 1940, George McAfee instantly stirred memories of Red Grange with his dazzling moves and breakaway speed. And after seeing him play that year, Grange himself remarked, "He's the most dangerous man with a football in the game today." As a result of his spectacular runs from scrimmage and on punt and kickoff returns, he was soon dubbed "One-Play McAfee," a moniker that stayed with him throughout his pro career in Chicago.

McAfee, slight by today's standards, played running back at about 175 pounds on a 6' frame, but he was truly the complete football player. He not only could run but also was a fine left-handed passer and left-footed punter. He was also an excellent blocker and on defense was considered one of the best safeties of his era.

His debut as a Bear was in the season opener of 1940 against the Packers up in Green Bay. He fielded his first kickoff in NFL competition that afternoon and ran it back 93 yards for a touchdown. A short while later he tossed a touchdown pass to fellow rookie Ken Kavanaugh and still later raced 9 yards around end for another touchdown to help the Bears rout the Pack 41–0.

McAfee's best season was 1941, when he led the team in rushing with 474 yards, an average of 7.3 yards per carry; punt returns, with an average of 31.6 yards per; kickoff returns, averaging 31.9 yards; and interceptions with 6, then a club record.

McAfee left pro football at the peak of his career after the 1941 season and spent the next three years in military service, but he returned for six more Bear seasons in 1945.

He still owns the Bear record for the most yards gained returning punts (1,431) and his career average of 12.8 yards per punt return remains today the best ever in NFL history.

George McAfee was inducted into the Pro Football Hall of Fame in 1966, and his jersey number, 5, is one of only eleven the Bears have retired.

After a postfootball career in the oil business, McAfee has retired and lives in North Carolina, not far from where he once starred in the backfield for Duke University.

W hen I was asked to be interviewed about my days as a pro football player with the Chicago Bears, I thought suddenly of my first encounter with the pros. That was back in Ironton, Ohio, a mill town at the south end of the state on the Ohio River. They had a team there in the 1930s, not an NFL team but still a pro team, called the Ironton Tanks.

The Tanks had a triple-threat tailback by the name of Glenn Presnell who was my idol in those days. What he could do on a football field! Presnell went on to play in the NFL for the Portsmouth Spartans and then the Detroit Lions and was a player who should be in the Hall of Fame today. In 1930 the Tanks played both the New York Giants and the Chicago Bears over in Cincinnati and beat both of them, and the Bears had Red Grange and Bronko Nagurski playing for them that year.

Well, I grew up in Ironton, came from a family of nine boys and three girls. I was number ten in the family. All the boys in the family played football for Ironton High School. One of my older brothers, John, went on to play for Ohio State. I kind of just followed along with the rest of them in the football thing.

The biggest influences on my football life were my brothers; Presnell, my idol; and our high school coach, Dick Gallagher, who later became director of the Pro Football Hall of Fame in Canton, Ohio, for several years. I was a quarterback on Gallagher's team, but it was not the T formation; we played the single wing and the double wing, and therefore it was a different kind of quarterbacking than we're used to today.

I weighed only about 150 pounds in high school, but we had a very good team; in fact we were undefeated my senior year. I was originally planning to go to Ohio State, but there was a fellow named Bob O'Meara from Ashland, Kentucky, which was right across the river from Ironton, and he had gone to Duke down in Durham, North Carolina. Well, he got the people from Duke interested in me, and their end coach, Dick Boyle, came to Ironton to talk to me. He invited me down to visit Duke, and I just fell in love with the place. The campus was spectacular, everything you dreamed of in a college. The visit changed my mind about Ohio State, and I enrolled at Duke.

In those days Duke had a great football coach, Wallace Wade, one of the most respected coaches in the country in the 1920s and thirties. When I visited down there, I met him, and he simply said he'd like to have me come play for Duke—no pressure, nothing like that. And I know now I certainly made the right decision then.

I didn't play much at all at Duke until my junior year, which was 1938. That was the year Duke was undefeated, untied, and unscored on in the regular season. We went to the Rose Bowl that year to play Southern Cal, and it was quite an experience. It took us five days to get from North Carolina to southern California by train and five days to come back. I remember we were staying at the Huntington Hotel in Pasadena—palm trees all around, which was certainly something new to me. Coach Wade took us over to the Rose Bowl one day before the game, and, looking around from inside it, it was awesome. It had seats for 104,091 people. We were all standing around kind of overwhelmed, and I remember I had this two-inch firecracker that I lit and threw. It landed just behind Coach Wade and went off, and in that empty stadium it sounded like a forty-millimeter gun going off. When he came back down to earth, Coach Wade announced rather breathlessly that if he found out who did that he was shipping him back home on the train immediately. Later he did find out, but he didn't send me home.

We were winning 3-0 going into the last minute of the game at the Rose Bowl, but our unscored-on and undefeated season ended there when Doyle Nave threw a touchdown pass to Al Krueger with forty seconds left in the game and Southern Cal beat us 7-3.

After my last year at Duke I was drafted in 1940 by the Philadelphia Eagles in the first round, but the Bears traded a couple of players to them for the rights to me, so I ended up coming to Chicago. I was very happy to join the Bears and play for George Halas. I had seen the team play down in Ironton and several times over in Portsmouth when they came down to play the Spartans—Portsmouth is only about twenty-five miles west of Ironton. I had seen Red Grange play for them and all the others on those fine teams they had in the thirties. When I watched them in those days, I never dreamed I might someday be playing for them myself.

I was late in signing with the Bears that first year, and they were already into training camp when I arrived. We had a great crop of rookies that year: Bulldog Turner, Ken Kavanaugh, Lee Artoe, Ed Kolman, Harry Clark, and Scooter McLean.

I will never forget my first impression. I walked into camp—it was on a Sunday morning, and the Bears were having a scrimmage. The first thing I saw was Harry Clark catching a punt and running it back. Bill Osmanski came flying in and hit him and knocked Clark out cold. I said, Lord of mercy, what am I getting myself into? I made up my mind there and then that I would do everything in my power to run as fast as I could and be as elusive as I could.

I got along with Mr. Halas real well right from the start. I had no disagreements with him, and during my entire career he was never anything but just fine with me. We didn't have agents in those days; we just sat down and worked out a contract. I always felt he was fair with me as far as pay went. I was satisfied, and I think he was satisfied with what he was getting too.

The first friends I made on the Bears were Joe Stydahar, a very rugged tackle who's in the Hall of Fame, and Al Baisi, a guard who was also a rookie that year. And, of course, Sid Luckman. He looked out for everyone, helped them fit in, adjust to the pros. He was a terrific fellow as well as a great quarterback.

I got a good amount of publicity at the beginning because I was the one everybody saw carrying the ball. I think most of the time people give too much credit to the guy with the ball. They don't give near enough credit to the guys up front, who make all those runs possible. Look who I had up front blocking for me then: Bulldog Turner, Danny Fortmann, George Musso, Joe Stydahar, Lee Artoe, Ken Kavanaugh, George Wilson. Four of them [Turner, Fortmann, Musso, and Stydahar] are in the Hall of Fame. It was a pleasure to run behind them.

In the 1940s we had to play both ways. If you started a ball game, you couldn't go out and come back in during the same quarter. But I didn't mind it; it was just the way things were in those days. I did a little punting too. Halas had everybody do as much as he could.

The first season was, of course, a very memorable one. Our first game of the regular season was up in Green Bay. That Packer team had Don Hutson, Clarke Hinkle, Cecil Isbell, and Arnie Herber on it. On the train going up there some of the veterans told me that if we beat the Packers we could have a beer on the train ride back. Well, we walloped them up there that day [41-0]. So, on the way back, we were on the train sitting in the dining car, and I had a beer in front of me. I saw Mr. Halas coming down the aisle, and he stopped at our table. I was the only one with a beer in front of him. He stopped, and suddenly I thought maybe those guys had been pulling my leg on the way up. Mr. Halas looked at me, looked at the beer, then back at me rather sternly, and said, "Are you going to drink that?"

I didn't know what to say. So I looked him right in the eye
and said, "You're damn right." Well, he just laughed and went
on his way. And then I found out that's the way it really was; if
we won, he'd let us have a beer.

We had an excellent team that year and won the NFL West,
but we lost three games—one to the Chicago Cardinals, one to
the Lions, and, of course, that one to the Redskins late in the
season. They beat us 7-3, and the game ended on a controversial
call—or should I say noncall? Bill Osmanski was interfered with
in the end zone on what should have been a touchdown for us at
the end of that game, but there was no call and we lost.

Their owner, George Preston Marshall, called us all kinds of
names afterwards: "crybabies," "quitters," things like that.
Well, after it we were a mad bunch of Bears. We told each other,
"Don't worry, we'll be back." And, of course, we were, because
we won the NFL East.

It was real quiet on the train going down to Washington for
the championship game that year. We were all very intense,
remembering the loss three weeks earlier there and all of Marshall's remarks. We all had our playbooks out on the train,
studying the plays and talking among each other about things
we could do. We were really getting ourselves ready for them
mentally. And I can say that will win a lot of ball games for you.
If you go in with the right frame of mind and you're mentally
ready to play, you will ordinarily do just fine.

Still, we were all very nervous before the game. A lot of the
players threw up. Joe Stydahar, he always got sick to his stomach before a game. We'd be in the locker room, and we'd hear
from the bathroom someone in there heaving. And we'd say,
"Well, Joe's ready." I always got so keyed up during the ball
game that it was after it was over when I would get sick. It used
to make me so darn mad because all the other guys would go
out together after a game and have a big meal and a good time,
and I couldn't even think of eating anything until maybe midnight.

We could sense something right from the start that day,
however. It was on the second play of the game when Bill
Osmanski ran 68 yards for a touchdown. And it wasn't just him,
although it was a great run. Our end George Wilson threw a

block that blew away the last *two* Washington defenders. One of them, I think, ended up in about the fifth row of the stands.

It turned out to be one of those games where we couldn't do anything wrong and the Redskins couldn't do anything right. We intercepted three of their passes that day and ran them back for touchdowns, and a team seldom does that. That's how I got my one touchdown that day—on an interception. We scored eleven touchdowns in all that game. And it wasn't because we were trying to run up the score. We weren't that kind of team. It just happened that way. We played everybody, and it seemed everybody who got his hands on the football scored with it. Mr. Halas, of course, loved it. He always had this competition thing going with Marshall, and they'd go at each other all the time, but they were good friends at the same time. I think I read somewhere later that Halas was viewing films of the game and turned to whoever was watching them with him and said, "Hmm, I think I see where we should have scored another touchdown."

I believe the team we had in 1941 was better than the one that beat the Redskins 73-0. We had a lot of rookies playing for us in 1940, and they were all back and better, more experienced, in 1941. We lost only one game that year, and that was to the Packers, 16-14. It was a real flat day for us. After all, we averaged 36 points a game that year. But we avenged ourselves in the playoff game against them that year, 33-14, which enabled us to go to the championship game, where we beat the Giants [37-9].

Then World War II came along. I enlisted in the navy in 1942, and a lot of the other fellows left too. I remember asking Mr. Halas sometime later how many championships he thought that team of '41 might have gone on to win if the war had not come along. He just smiled, shook his head, and said, "There's just no telling, kid."

I spent my time in the navy in the physical education end of it. I started out as a chief petty officer and was discharged a lieutenant JG. In 1945 I was stationed in Hawaii. During that time Mr. Halas was in Hawaii too; I think he was a lieutenant commander or full commander. Well, the war was over now, and we were both going back to the States. I was over in his office one day, and he told me he was flying to San Francisco and that he would be there for a while. He gave me the name of a certain hotel there and told me to call him if I came through San Francisco on my way back. I thought I would be coming back by ship, but I got lucky and ended up on an airplane myself.

I remember I got in about seven at night, and I called Mr. Halas, but they said he'd checked out. At about midnight I thought, What the heck, and I tried him again and got him. He hadn't checked out. He said he was leaving by plane in the morning for Chicago. He tried to get me on the same plane but couldn't. I was able, however, to get one an hour or two after his. When I told him, he said, "Good, I'll meet you in Chicago. And, by the way, we're playing in Washington on Sunday."

I was in lousy shape. So I started exercising there in the hotel room, anything to try to get myself into a little better shape.

I got to Chicago, met up with Mr. Halas, and the same day we were on the train for Washington. I was in Honolulu on Tuesday, San Francisco on Wednesday, Chicago on Friday, and in Washington playing on Sunday, a game we lost, by the way, 28-21. It certainly was a lot different in those days in the NFL.

The team I joined up with in 1945 was not doing too well. The loss to the Redskins was their seventh of the year, and they had won only one game so far. Some of the other guys had been filtering back from the service, and we won the last two games of the year, beating the Steelers and the Chicago Cardinals. [Out of shape perhaps, but McAfee scored 4 touchdowns and averaged 8.7 yards on 16 carries during those three games.]

It didn't really take all that long to get back in condition. And it was a great thrill to be reunited with those boys from the 1940 and '41 championship teams, most of whom were back for the 1946 season. Right away we got things back to the way they were when we left, went right out and won the NFL West, and then trounced the Giants at the Polo Grounds 24-14 for another NFL championship.

That was the last championship team I played on. I stayed with the Bears for four more seasons after that, and they were all winning seasons, but we never got to another title game. We came close in '47, lost out on the last game of the season when we were beat by the Chicago Cardinals [30-21], who had their dream backfield then [Paul Christman, Charley Trippi, Elmer Angsman, and Pat Harder]. The Cardinals knocked us out of the running for the NFL West in '48 again in the last game of the season. We were both 10-1-0 going into it, and they won the game 24-21.

We came in second to the Los Angeles Rams in 1949. They had Bob Waterfield, Norm Van Brocklin, and Crazylegs Hirsch then, and they beat us both times we played that year. We lost out to the Rams again in 1950, my last year. We had identical records of 9-3-0 at the end of the regular season, and that year we had beaten the Rams both times we met. But they were better in the playoff game, and we lost 24-14.

During the 1950 season I'd gotten my nose broken running back a punt. I just got tackled and my face pushed into the ground, and the nose broke. I was thirty-two years old then, and I thought I'd had just about enough. So I retired. Later I officiated in the NFL for six or seven years, but that was the only real touch I had with football after retiring.

We had some wonderful teams during those years, and if we weren't winning the championship, we were taking the fight for it right down to the wire every year. They were a great bunch of guys, and I sure enjoyed playing football with them.

The Morning After

The 1940 NFL championship game pitted the newly T formationed Chicago Bears, 8-3-0 that year, against the dated single wing of the Washington Redskins, 9-2-0—quarterback Sid Luckman vs. tailback Sammy Baugh. The Bears, the T formation, and Luckman prevailed that historic afternoon at Griffith Stadium in Washington, running up the largest margin of victory in the history of NFL postseason or regular-season games, 73-0.

After the carnage these were some of the thoughts and comments recorded for posterity:

Sammy Baugh, when asked if the outcome might have been different had end Charley Malone caught what appeared to be a touchdown pass in the first quarter with the score a mere 7-0, Bears: "Hell, yes, the score would have been 73-6."

Bob Considine, in his syndicated newspaper column "On the Line": "The Chicago Bears massacred the Washington Redskins 73-0 yesterday. . . . The unluckiest guy in the crowd was the five-buck better who took the Redskins and 70 points."

Bill Stern, famous radio broadcaster of the day: "It got so bad that, toward the end, the Bears had to give up place-kicking the extra points and try passes instead because all the footballs booted into the stands were being kept by the spectators as souvenirs. And they were down to their last football."

Red Smith, in his column "Sports of the Times" for the *New York Times*: "George Preston Marshall, the mettlesome laundryman who owned the Redskins, looked on from the stands—except when he turned his back to charge up the aisle and throw a punch at a dissatisfied customer—and when his ordeal was over, every hair in his raccoon coat had turned white."

And a wag in the pressbox, when the final gun signaled a merciful end to the slaughter, with a look of horror on his face turned to the reporter sitting next to him: "My God, Marshall just shot himself."

1940 Championship Game

At Washington, Griffith Stadium, December 8, 1940

Chicago Bears		Washington Redskins
Bob Nowaskey	LE	Bob Masters
Joe Stydahar	LT	Wee Willie Wilkin
Danny Fortmann	LG	Dick Farman
Bulldog Turner	C	Bob Titchenal
George Musso	RG	Steve Slivinski
Lee Artoe	RT	Jim Barber
George Wilson	RE	Charley Malone
Sid Luckman	QB	Max Krause
Ray Nolting	LH	Sammy Baugh
George McAfee	RH	Ed Justice
Bill Osmanski	FB	Jim Johnston
George Halas	Coach	Ray Flaherty

Bears	21	7	26	19	—	73
Redskins	0	0	0	0	—	0

Touchdowns—Bears: Harry Clark (2), Bill Osmanski, Sid Luckman, Joe Maniaci, Ken Kavanaugh, Hampton Pool, Ray Nolting, George McAfee, Bulldog Turner, Gary Famiglietti

PATs—Bears: Bob Snyder (2), Jack Manders, Phil Matinovich, Dick Plasman, Joe Stydahar, Joe Maniaci

Johnny Morris

Johnny Morris came to Chicago in 1958 to join a Bears team that two seasons before had worn the NFL West crown and then roller-coasted down to just one story above the cellar of that conference the next year. With Morris now on the roller coaster as a rookie halfback, the Bears roared back up to a second-place finish in '58, only a game behind the Johnny Unitas–led Baltimore Colts.

Morris was a twelfth-round draft choice out of the University of California, Santa Barbara, but he quickly proved to be the key selection of that year's draft. His speed was documented: he was coholder of the world record for the 50-yard dash (5:2) when he arrived in Bear camp. And he put it to good use that rookie season of 1958, leading the team in both kickoff and punt returns and ranking third in rushing behind Rick Casares and Willie Galimore.

Morris was, however, destined to leave his indelible mark in Bear lore as a pass receiver. In 1961 the Bear passing game took on a new and much healthier look when the fleet Morris was switched to flanker, a rookie tight end by the name of Mike Ditka was added to the roster, and Bill Wade took over the quarterbacking. Morris quickly proved with his great speed that he could get loose for the long pass and at the same time pose a constant threat snatching short passes out of the most congested of areas.

By the time Johnny Morris retired from the Bears ten years later, he owned a slew of Bear all-time pass reception records. In 1964, his finest season, Morris led the NFL and set two Bear standards when he caught 93 passes for 1,200 yards—both records still stand today. His most memorable game was in 1962 against the Dallas Cowboys, when he caught 10 passes for 201 yards. The only player in Bear history to exceed that yardage was Harlon Hill, who gained 214 yards on 7 catches in 1954.

Morris holds the Bear career record for yardage gained on pass receptions (5,059), and only Walter Payton caught more than the 356 Morris hauled in between 1958 and 1967.

After his pro career ended, Johnny Morris forged a full-time career in television broadcasting and has become a familiar face on CBS television, talking sports and handling the color on NFL broadcasts.

I've been involved with professional football since 1958, playing it for ten years and covering it on television since 1964, when I started as a part-time broadcaster.

I played a little bit in junior high school out in Long Beach, California, and some in high school, but I didn't really blossom until I got into college. I played halfback on offense and defensive back for the University of California, Santa Barbara.

It was, in a way, a stroke of fate that I got into pro football. In my senior year out there, 1957, our coach got sick, and he was replaced by Ed Cody, who had played fullback for the Bears back around 1950 and for Green Bay before that. Well, I had had a good season and the year before that had tied the record for the 50-yard dash.

In those days they did not have the scouting combines like they have now, nor was scouting nearly as organized within the club organization. Halas had gotten many of his players by word of mouth from Bear alumni or other football friends around the country. That's what happened with me. Ed Cody called Halas and said, "Hey, I've got a little guy out here who I think can make it in the pros."

If Cody had not called him, I'm sure I would never had played professional football. Nobody scouted Santa Barbara in those days. And I was quite small—weighed about 170 pounds and was 5'10".

The Bears, I learned, originally planned to pick me up after the draft as a free agent, figuring nobody else would have heard anything about me. But then Ed Cody said, "Son, we ought to try to get you a little bargaining power." So he called the Packers, where he knew a lot of people as well, and told them about me. Then Ed called Halas and told him the Packers had sent me a telegram inquiring if I would be interested in playing for them in the NFL. So the Bears didn't wait around for free agency and drafted me in the twelfth round, afraid that otherwise Green Bay might take me. Ed Cody paved the way for me into pro football and into a Chicago Bears uniform.

After the Bears drafted me, George Halas called me on the telephone and said, "Kid, we like you. We think you've got potential. We're going to send you out our standard rookie contract, $6,000 a year." It sounded like pretty good money, but it was also the minimum wage the Bears paid. He said if I did a good job, he'd take care of me.

I flew into Chicago in the summer of '58, and we all met at Soldier Field to get on a bus to go to camp down at Rensselaer, Indiana. Halas was there and came over and shook everybody's hand and said welcome to the Bears and all that kind of stuff. And off we went.

Well, I had a pretty good first season. I started about half the time at halfback—I kind of alternated starting with Willie Galimore—and I ran back most of the kickoffs and punts.

After the season I was called in to see Halas. I felt good; I really proved myself, I thought. I knew our talk was to be about the next year's contract. With memories of "You do a good job, I'll take care of you" still in my head, I was thinking maybe $10,000, $12,000, something like that. I was excited.

Halas gave me that smile of his when I sat down. "You had

a good year. I'm going to give you a $500 raise." I played for
$6,500 in '59.

Training camp was something else in those days. We would
report in the first or second week of July, and we would go seven
days a week for a solid month. And when we went to play
exhibition games, we would fly out that morning and fly back
that night. The guys today don't know how good they've got it.
We'd go two-a-days every day except Sunday, when we just had
one session so the guys who wanted to go to church could go.
Of course there was an off-season then, and a lot of times during
that period no one did anything about staying in shape, not like
they do today. That's why our training camps were so different;
we needed them to get back into shape. Today the players are
paid enough that they don't need to do anything in the off-
season except work at staying in shape.

I stayed in pretty good shape, and so I wasn't hurting as
bad as a lot of the others when we showed up in Rensselaer. I
played halfback for three years. My most productive year was the
last, 1960, when I averaged 5.7 yards a carry and gained more
than 400 yards rushing. I also continued to return kickoffs and
punts during those three years as well.

By 1961 Halas decided he wanted to have Galimore and me
in the lineup at the same time, not alternating as we had been.
So he switched me to flanker. It was also around that time that
teams in the NFL began putting little, fast guys out at receiver.
Before that the ends were mostly big, lanky, slower guys, like
Bill McColl and Jim Dooley.

Bobby Mitchell of the Cleveland Browns and later of the
Redskins was the first fast halfback that was moved out to
flanker. Tommy McDonald, who was with the Eagles around
that time, was the next to move out to flanker. I was the third.
After that there was a rash of them, and pretty soon the only
wide receivers in the game were the smaller, fast, quick guys.

The move to flanker also lengthened my career consider-
ably—I'm sure of that. I used to be so sore after games when I
was a running back I could hardly get out of bed on Monday
mornings, and I wasn't even playing all the time—maybe carry-

ing the ball eight or ten times a game, nowhere near like Walter
Payton, who carried twenty-five or thirty times a game every
week, which tells you what kind of incredible athlete he was. As
soon as I switched to flanker, became a receiver instead of a
running back, I was never sore after a game. The difference was
amazing.

It was a natural move. We needed a passing attack. We had
a terrific running attack with Willie Galimore and Rick Casares
in the backfield. Casares was great, powerful, quick, and a guy
everybody respected. He was always getting into trouble with
Halas, though—late for team meetings, breaking curfew. He
was a single guy and a ladies' man. And Halas was onto him. I'll
never forget the time we got on an airplane to go to one of the
games. Casares walked onto the plane with three suits slung
over his shoulder. Halas took one look at him and fined him
$500. "What the hell are you fining me for?" Casares said.

"Because this is a one-day trip," Halas said, "and anybody
who takes three suits on a one-day trip is up to no good."

I kind of spanned two or three generations in the ten years
I was with the Bears. When I first came up, there were guys like
George Blanda, Harlon Hill, and Bill George, who had been
around for a while. I remember when I came up as a rookie
everyone saying that Blanda was all washed up, over the hill. He
was our third-string quarterback then and our field goal kicker.
Then he retired, sat out a year, then came back and starred for
sixteen more seasons in the AFL. Shows how much the doom-
sayers in Chicago knew back in 1958.

Then I went through the Gale Sayers-Dick Butkus era. I
had never seen anyone who could run and cut like Sayers. And
Butkus—I'd never seen anyone as mean as him. I was still there
when they had guys coming up like Jack Concannon and Dick
Gordon.

There were a lot of unique characters too. There were
always guys trying to put one over on Halas, but it was pretty
hard to put one over on him. I remember we had a guy by the
name of Dick Klein, a tackle in the later 1950s. He snuck out
one night and left this elaborate dummy in his bed—not just
pillows under the covers but a real mannequin dummy with a

head and hair and everything. When he came back late that night, he found the dummy lying there with a note on it. It said: "Dick, please see me tomorrow, George Halas." And beneath it: "Remember you can fool some of the people all the time, and all the people some of the time, but you can't fool George Halas any time."

And then there was Mike Ditka. Ditka got in more trouble with Halas than anybody. He called the Old Man tight, cheap, and everybody remembers that famous quote of Ditka's about Halas throwing nickels around like manhole covers. He was a guy who really defied Halas, one that I saw publicly do it anyway. He kind of stood up and talked back to him, and people just didn't ordinarily do that to George Halas in those days. I think, in the long run, however, that Halas actually respected Mike for doing that.

I'll never forget the time out in San Francisco that we really got beat up by the 49ers. It was in 1964, and we were walloped 52-24 the opening game of that season. In the meeting the next week we were watching films of the game, and Halas was really railing at us. We were all together, offense and defense. At one point Willie Galimore missed a block, and Halas said, "You guys, I don't know what the hell's the matter with you. You hit 'em low, if you're going to hit 'em. We had a guy named George McAfee. He didn't weigh 160 pounds wringing wet, and he could cut those guys down like they were nothing." All of a sudden from the back of the room somebody said, "Fuck George McAfee."

Halas was startled. He shouted, "Who said that?"

And Ditka stood up and said, "I said it. This is 1964. This isn't 1940. Who cares about George McAfee?"

Well, it was the first time I ever saw George Halas flustered. He just said, "I'll see you after the meeting."

Another time Mike and I went to a banquet. This was in 1964. At that time there was a quarterback controversy about who should be starting—Bill Wade or Rudy Bukich. We didn't think there was anybody from the press at this banquet. It turned out that Ray Sons of the *Chicago Sun-Times* was there. If I'm not mistaken, I think it was maybe his first assignment covering the Bears. Anyway, we didn't know him from Adam. We were just out there making a little speech to pick up some extra money on the side.

One of the guys in the audience stood up and asked us who we thought should be starting at quarterback. Wade was the starting quarterback, but we said we thought it ought to be Bukich. We gave our reasons, not knowing, of course, that it would be quoted in the newspaper the next day. The headline was something like "Morris and Ditka Say Bukich Should Be Quarterback." Well, Halas went through the roof.

Ditka got a call early, before he was even awake. I got one fifteen minutes later. He told us to be down in his office in an hour or something like that. When we got there, he was all over us. "You betrayed the team," he said—all kinds of stuff like that. He told us he wanted us to apologize to the whole team before practice that day.

So later he called everybody into the locker room and said, "Morris and Ditka said some things last night that they say were taken out of context. I believe that they want to make an apology to all of you." And then he said, "Mike," gesturing to Ditka.

Mike said, "I don't have any apology. Forget it."

Then Halas turned to me and said, "Johnny, do you have anything to say?"

I stood up and said, "Well, we were just at a banquet; we didn't really mean it the way it came out." I tried to make it sound like an apology. But here was Mike, with all these guys in front of Halas, and Halas puts him on the spot, and he says, no, no apology.

That's Mike Ditka, and it was a combination of all those things that got him traded [to the Eagles in 1967]. It was also the things that I believe got him the head coaching job fifteen years later. Halas, maybe begrudgingly, respected him for the way he stood up for things, saw the strength in him, and respected him. And that's why he brought him back to coach the Bears in 1982.

Ditka was the epitome of the rough, tough, talented football player. He left many bruises on opposing players, and he could never conceive of giving less than 100 percent; it just wasn't in his nature. Who can forget that run he made in 1963 against the Steelers? If we lost that game, we would never have gotten to the championship that year. It was right at the end of the game. It looked like we were beat at the time, but Mike took this short pass and knocked over everybody in sight, went 63 yards, which set up a field goal that salvaged a tie for us. I was on the field at the time, blocking somebody, but I saw him going down the field, and it was incredible. I remember feeling terribly disappointed when that last guy tackled him. If anybody deserved to go all the way, it was Mike on that play.

Mike and I both had memorable years in 1964, although the team had a miserable one. Because we were behind in most of the games we played that season, we had to throw the ball a lot. Wade started out at quarterback that year, but later he was benched and Bukich took over. It also helped because Mike and I complemented each other. With him at tight end and me at flanker it made it difficult for the opponents to double-team either one of us. At any rate, we had a lot of success with the passing game that year. I caught 93 passes, which was an NFL record then, and Mike caught 75. We lost most of the games that year because our defense wasn't near what it used to be, like it was the year before. We ended up 5-7-0.

The greatest individual moment I can remember, however, was the 1963 championship game. That was such a battle. The feeling I had after that game, I experienced only once in my entire career. And it was the defense that year that got us to the title game against the Giants, and it was the defense who won that game for us.

They were awesome in '63: Doug Atkins, Ed O'Bradovich, Stan Jones, Fred Williams, Bill George, Joe Fortunato, Larry Morris, Richie Petibon, Rosey Taylor, Bennie McRae, Davey Whitsell.

And then there was J. C. Caroline. Nobody was better on special teams than he was. We had to beat Lombardi's Packers twice that year and we did, and we ended up just a half a game ahead of them at the end of the season. In our second game with them that year, an absolutely crucial one, in mid-November,

J. C. had a just spectacular day. He made the first tackle of the game and virtually destroyed whoever was trying to return the kickoff. He had the greatest game I've ever seen of a guy on special teams that day. When we watched the films of the game, watched him making tackle after tackle, everybody was overwhelmed. When the film was finally turned off, somebody said his name, and everybody in the room gave him a spontaneous ovation. Here were forty hard-nosed guys just wrapped up in their emotions watching what he did in that game and just breaking into an ovation. That was really something.

I played against a lot of great ballplayers too. The toughest cornerback I went up against had to be Herb Adderley of the Packers. He was so difficult to beat. Jimmy Johnson of the 49ers was another. I had a little better success against him than I did against Adderley, but Jimmy was darn tough to beat too. The best offensive back I saw, aside from some of those on our team, was Lenny Moore of the Colts. What a great football player he was. He played running back, and he played wide receiver. They moved him back and forth, and he was a deadly threat at either position.

We played against some very good teams during those years. The most notable had to be the Packers under Vince Lombardi and the Baltimore Colts with Unitas, and the Detroit Lions were usually pretty damn tough in those years. Most of the years I was with the Bears we were in serious contention. We had only three disappointing seasons in the ten years I played.

There was something about playing professional football that is unlike anything else I ever experienced. There was this incredible buildup each week before a game. I was always good for nothing the entire week before a game, the tension of the game we were going to play building all the time. I was nervous all week. I wouldn't feel good until the game started. There's something about the sport—I don't know if it's because you are young and impressionable when you're playing it, just learning about life, or if there was a Halas syndrome because he was so dedicated to it, or maybe just the overall drama of the game being played out before sixty thousand screaming fans.

The pressure is enormous. You're so visible out there; everything you do is so public. When you drop a punt or a pass bounces off your chest or you fumble the ball away or fail in some other way, you feel the whole world has seen it. There are few jobs in the world where you are under such close scrutiny and subject yourself so openly to criticism.

Your sole purpose out there is to win, and when you do it's wonderful, and when you don't it's awful.

In 1966 I hurt my knee and was out for most of the season. I tried to come back the following year, but the knee was not the same. So I got to thinking, I don't want to tear the knee up again. I don't want to be traded. The better playing days are over. So I retired.

I had been working in television since 1964, part-time, doing sports and news for CBS. When I left the game, NBC offered me a contract, and I worked for them about six years and then came back to CBS, where I've been ever since.

I did color on TV for the Bears games for CBS for about fifteen years, mostly regional coverage. When the Bears became real hot in 1985 and thereafter, they started putting their New York people on the Bear games, and I was traveling to other games in Green Bay, Pittsburgh, all over. It got to be quite a hassle, covering a game and then getting back to do a Sunday show with Mike Ditka. So I got out of that end of the broadcasting business.

My life with the Bears was a great one. And being a Bear is the reason I got a career in television afterwards. A lot in my life came about as a result of that telephone call Ed Cody made to George Halas back in 1957.

In a 1962 game against the Baltimore Colts, flanker Johnny Morris grabs the pass, pops it up, then finally gathers it in. Morris, one of the NFL's finest receivers in the late 1950s and 1960s, still holds a number of Bear pass reception records. On this particular day the Bears handed the Colts the worst defeat in their history (57–0).

Notable Quotes

George Preston Marshall, owner of the Washington Redskins in 1940, prior to the NFL title game between his team and the Bears: "The Bears are front-runners, quitters. They're not a second-half team, just a bunch of crybabies! They fold up when the going gets tough." (Just prior to the Bears 73–0 annihilation of the Redskins in the NFL's most lopsided game ever.)

Rosey Grier, All-Pro defensive tackle with the Rams in 1965, after rookie Gale Sayers had run with a screen pass for a touchdown against them out in Los Angeles: "I hit him so hard, I thought my shoulder must have busted him in two. I heard a roar from the crowd and figured he had fumbled. Then there he was 15 yards downfield and heading for the end zone."

Lawrence Taylor, the New York Giants' great linebacker when asked before their NFC playoff game of 1985 about the prospect of perhaps having to tackle a 320-pound ball carrier named William "Refrigerator" Perry: "I don't want to think about the Refrigerator. Or the stove. I'm going to throw all my appliances out of the house."

Hugh Gallarneau

Hugh Gallarneau came to the Bears out of one of the most celebrated backfields in college football history. It was the Stanford Cardinals of 1940 with Frankie Albert as quarterback, Gallarneau at right halfback, Norm Standlee at fullback, and Pete Kmetovic at left half. Coached by Clark Shaughnessy in Gallarneau's senior year at Stanford, the Cardinals were perhaps the only team in college ball that year using the T formation.

Gallarneau was the speedy back, Standlee the powerhouse, Albert the consummate passer and scrambler, and Kmetovic the jack-of-all-trades back. With their potent offensive attack, Stanford went 10-0-0 that year and then triumphed in the Rose Bowl over Nebraska 21-13.

Shaughnessy, who was instrumental in helping George Halas institute the T formation with the Bears, kept in close touch with Papa Bear during that 1940 season, the result being that Gallarneau and Standlee were both drafted by the Bears in 1941.

In his rookie year Gallarneau returned a punt 81 yards for a touchdown and a Bear record at the time. He led the club in punt returns in both 1942 (9 for 101 yards, 11.2

average) and 1946 (10 for 99 yards, 9.9 average) and in kick-off returns in 1942 (6 for 151 yards, 25.2 average).

Gallarneau is the eighteenth leading rusher in Bear history, gaining in his five-year career 1,421 yards on 343 carries for an average gain of 4.14 yards and 26 touchdowns. He led the team in rushing in 1946 when he ran for 476 yards on 112 carries and 7 touchdowns.

Hugh Gallarneau retired after the 1947 season and went into the clothing business, first for Marshall Field's and subsequently as a top executive for Hart Schaffner and Marx. He is now retired and still living in the Chicago area.

My first actual football experience did not come until I was a freshman at Stanford. I had not played in high school. I had gone to Morgan Park High School in Beverly Hills—the one on the South Side of Chicago, not the one in southern California. I was a swimmer and a diver in high school—that's all.

I was also a Depression era kid, and as a result I had to stay out of high school for two years and work as a laborer in Chicago's famous Union Stockyards.

I had always wanted to play football in high school, but it just didn't work out. When I went back to school after the stint at the stockyards, I made the honor society and won an academic scholarship to Stanford.

The first thing I did when I arrived out in Palo Alto, California, was to turn out for football. It created a kind of problem for the coach because he got a guy who weighed 185 pounds and could run the 100-yard dash in 9:06, which was good, but had never played a lick of organized football in his life, which was bad.

The coaching staff did the obvious thing: they made an end out of me. After my freshman season, however, I decided to back off. I wasn't happy with my football career, so I became a boxer. As a sophomore I won the Pacific Coast heavyweight boxing championship. For some reason the coaches out there figured if

I could run fast and I could fight, I ought to be a halfback. They talked to me, and so in my junior year I went back out for football. This time they made a right halfback out of me, which in the Pop Warner [Stanford's legendary coach of the 1920s and early 1930s] system, which was still being used at Stanford in the late 1930s, was a blocker, an end runner, and an occasional pass receiver. I had a very undistinguished career as a right halfback in that system.

In 1940 Stanford, after firing our coach, Denny Thornhill, hired Clark Shaughnessy from the University of Chicago. It was a little discouraging to us because Shaughnessy was the only coach in the country who had a worse record than our coach the year before—the reason was that Chicago was in the process of deemphasizing football.

Shaughnessy came to Stanford with the T formation, and none of us were terribly enthusiastic about it. I'd never heard about going to the line of scrimmage without blocking, but in Shaughnessy's scheme of things faking and deception were much more important than blocking. Later it turned out he was dead right, because the installation of the T with Frankie Albert as quarterback, Norm Standlee at fullback, Pete Kmetovic at left half, and me at right half took a team that in 1939 won only one game—we beat Dartmouth—to a team that was undefeated in 1940 [10-0-0] and went on to win the Rose Bowl.

Clark Shaughnessy proved to me to be one of the great coaches in American football, and he made heroes out of all of us by installing a system that truly took advantage of our particular talents.

Playing the T formation under Shaughnessy was also my ticket to the Chicago Bears. They had instituted it in the pro game, and so George Halas drafted me in 1941. It worked out quite well because Shaughnessy, being the strict and adept type of teacher he was, had taught us the system thoroughly, and so I knew it as well as anybody on the Bears when I joined the team.

Our great fullback, Norm Standlee, was also drafted by the Bears in '41, and we were called the "Stanford twins" when we showed up at the Bears. It turned out to be quite a nice season too, because we ended up winning the NFL championship by beating the New York Giants in Wrigley Field.

Coming to the Bears was like dying and going to heaven to me, I guess, because I got to come back home and play for the champion Bears.

I had heard many things about Coach Halas before I came back to Chicago, some of which were controversial, but I learned that he was one of the truly fine owners in the NFL. He certainly treated me in such a way that I revere him today.

I first met Halas when he came out to San Francisco in the spring of 1941 to talk to Norm Standlee and me about joining the Bears. I'd read a lot about him because he was already a pro football legend. We sat and talked awhile, and I decided immediately that to have a chance to come back and play football in my hometown was very gratifying and flattering.

I was extremely impressed by the whole team, and even though we were fighting for the same position, halfback, George McAfee and Scooter McLean became good friends of mine from the start.

There were all kinds of wonderful players on that team in '41, and I can tell you they were all great guys as well as extraordinary football players. But the one man who truly stood out for me was George Halas. He was the inspiration for the whole group. A lot of people have denigrated Halas for one reason or another, but in my opinion he was one of the finest, most honest men I ever met in my life.

In those days we had training camp at St. John's Military Academy, and that was a dream place—absolutely beautiful, the weather always nice. There were nice lakes nearby, and from time to time we would sneak out and take a swim or do a little fishing. Delafield, Wisconsin, was the name of the town.

Halas always ran a tight training camp, though. There were things that you could do and others you couldn't. The great thing about Halas was that he explained his rules and his fines in advance, so you knew just what it would cost you if you were to break a rule. There was no confusion. I remember once during the season I was late for practice, and it cost me. I lived way out south in Beverly, and we practiced at nine in the morning at Wrigley Field up on the North Side. In those days there wasn't the Outer Drive, so you had to come up Michigan Avenue. And that particular day the Michigan Avenue Bridge over the Chicago River was up to let some boats through. I sat there in traffic squirming. Finally the bridge came down, and I sped on to practice, but I was fifteen minutes late when I got there.

George said, "Hugh, you're late."

"Well, George," I said, "the damn bridge was up. I can't help that."

"What's the rule?" he said. "You owe me $25."

I persisted. "George, come on, the damn bridge was up!"

He said, "You should have left earlier."

I also remember one of my teammates, who will remain nameless, who, before the College All-Star game in 1947, broke a rule, and it cost him a thousand dollars. I won't mention his name, but I guarantee it wasn't me. The rule he broke was leaving training camp and staying out till a rather late hour and coming back smashed. He got caught, and it cost him a thousand bucks.

Pro football I found was tremendously different from college ball. My first impression came when Norm Standlee and I were invited to play in the 1941 Chicago All-Star Game at Soldier Field. Our opponent was the Chicago Bears. They beat us without a great deal of trouble [37-13], and we got a taste of what was in store for us.

Two days after that game George Halas drove Norm and me up to training camp in his Buick Roadmaster. We got our rooms, and that afternoon we went out to practice. I remember Joe Stydahar and Danny Fortmann, two of our stellar linemen in those days, greeting us on the field, and I noticed neither one had any front teeth. I turned around to Standlee and said, "What in the world are we doing here? All these guys've gotten their teeth knocked out." I thought to myself, Is that some kind of mark of distinction in pro football? Well, as it turned out, it wasn't, and I still have my teeth. But my initial reaction was one of fear and trepidation.

One of the games I remember most that first season was

the playoff game against the Packers, our number-one enemy. We had beaten them in the opening game of the season in Green Bay [25-17], then they knocked us off down at Wrigley Field later [16-14]—on a controversial call, I might add. At any rate, that was the only game we lost that year [the loss to the Bears was the Packers' only loss that year, both teams ending the regular season with records of 10-1-0].

We met at Wrigley Field in what was the first playoff game in NFL history to see who would face the New York Giants, who had won the NFL East, for the championship. I remember it was a very cold day. I was one of the kickoff returners, and Green Bay kicked off to us. I fielded the ball, fumbled it, and it was recovered by Green Bay. About three minutes later Cecil Isbell, their quarterback, passed to Don Hutson and then Clarke Hinkle bulled it in for a touchdown, and it was Green Bay 7, the Bears 0. Needless to say, I felt rather bad about it, and I also knew if that score stuck, Halas would cut my salary for sure, something I couldn't afford.

A little later Isbell punted to us, and I got loose and ran it back 81 yards for a touchdown, which tied the score and managed to get George's mind off my earlier blunder. It gave us the momentum to go and win the game [33-14].

Halas had a way of getting you up for a game. A good example is the way he got us up for the Philadelphia Eagles' game that same year. It was the next-to-last game of the regular season. We were supposed to kill them that afternoon—the Eagles had won only two games all year. But at the end of the first half Philadelphia was ahead 14-0.

We went into the locker room, and Halas gave probably the best pep talk I ever heard. He said, "You guys are looking like a bunch of ham and eggers. You're doing everything wrong you could possibly do wrong. And if you don't get your act together, I hope you realize, you will not have to play in the championship game—and therefore *no playoff check*, which is a helluva lot more than you're getting paid for playing this damn game today." And then he stormed out.

Well, we were all chagrined, unhappy with ourselves, and we went out in the second half and set the highest second-half scoring record then in the NFL history. We scored 49 points and won the game 49-14. I personally scored 4 touchdowns that half because I hated the thought of losing that money. One of them was called back, though, because Joe Stydahar was holding on the play.

In 1941 we had so many worthy backs we platooned it. George McAfee and I played the same position, right halfback. Basically Norm Standlee, Ray Nolting, and I would play in the backfield in the first and third quarters, and McAfee, Bill Osmanski, and either Harry Clark or Bobby Swisher would handle the second and fourth quarters.

Going into the last game of the season that year against the Chicago Cardinals, McAfee and I had each scored 10 touchdowns, and the NFL record at the time was 11. We both were going after it. I scored the first touchdown of the game and said, "Hot damn, I got it." Tied the record. McAfee screwed the thing up, however, by scoring 2 touchdowns that day, ending up with 12 for the season, a new record. Actually it was a tie for a new record because Don Hutson of Green Bay scored 12 as well that year.

We were extremely fortunate to have George McAfee in our backfield. He was truly one of the finest broken-field runners I ever saw in my life. He was also the complete football player. He could run, pass, punt, and he was a fierce, feared blocker although he never weighed more than 175 pounds.

Bulldog Turner, on offense and defense, was the epitome of the greatest center/linebacker in the game. Not only that, Bulldog was an extremely intelligent ballplayer who knew what every player should do in his position on any given play.

Sid Luckman was truly special. He has always had humility. Sid's a highly intelligent guy, which he has proven by his life on the field and off it. Sid did what quarterbacks don't do today; he called every play on his own—combining intelligence with great athletic abilities. Sid could also punt, and he could run the football. He was, to me, probably the finest quarterback of our era.

Sid was also completely supportive, whether you were a veteran or a newcomer to the team. Another thing about Sid that made him so great a quarterback was that he made it a point to find out everything that was going on on the field. We were running the T formation with a man in motion, a relatively new formation in the pros in those days. If I'd go in motion, he'd say, "Hugh, who was covering you when you went out in motion?" Or if we spread Kenny Kavanaugh, our left end, wide, he'd say, "Kenny, when Hugh goes in motion and you're wide, who's covering you?" He would solicit information from all of the players. He wanted to know from Ray Bray [a guard] which way he thought he could take a guy, in or out.

Sid's favorite receiver in those days had to be Kenny Kavanaugh, one of the great ones. He still holds the Bear record for the most touchdowns by a receiver. He caught 50 TD passes [closest to him is Harlon Hill with 40]. And he held just about every team pass-catching record until Hill and Morris and Ditka came along. And, don't forget, Kenny was in there playing defense as well.

I played defensive right halfback too, and in some formations I would back up the line. It was a lot less sophisticated than it is today. I remember Bulldog Turner just turning and saying, "You cover outside this time; I'll cover inside," or vice versa.

We had some characters on the team as well. Dick Plasman, one of our ends, didn't like to wear a helmet and often didn't. He was a big, tough, husky guy. I remember one time he was going down for a pass and ran into the brick wall at one end of Wrigley Field. Hit it full speed—didn't hurt his head, but he broke both wrists.

In 1942, my second season, we won eleven straight games in the regular season. Then we went down to Washington to play the Redskins for the championship, and it was the most frustrating game I can remember. Nothing we tried worked. We had a great team, but everyone was flat. I scored 2 touchdowns in the game, but both were called back because of penalties. We lost to a poorer team that afternoon [14-6], and none of us were very happy about it.

After the 1942 season I went into the Marine Corps and eventually went through seven invasions in the Pacific. I was a radar night fighter director. On Okinawa I set a Marine Corps

Hugh Gallarneau (1941-42, 1945-47), finds a gaping hole in the Chicago Cardinals' defense in 1941. Leading the interference for him is center Bulldog Turner (1940-52), who was elected to the Pro Football Hall of Fame in 1966.

record at the time when the fighter planes I directed knocked down six Japanese bombers in two nights.

I was mustered out of the marines the day before the Bears' opening game of the 1945 season against the Packers. I played half a football game that day for the El Toro Marines against the Fleet City naval team at Kezar Stadium in San Francisco. I played only half the game because otherwise I wouldn't be able to catch my flight back to Chicago. As it was, we flew all night and got back to Chicago in the morning. The Bears had a plane ticket waiting for me there, and I flew up to Green Bay. I made it in time for the game, but it was a disaster. I think I fumbled three times, and we lost to the Packers [31-21]. Actually the entire 1945 season was a bad one with so many of our players still in the service or just getting out and having been away from football for a long time.

The next one, 1946, was a different story, especially for me. That year George McAfee got hurt early in the season, and so I played most of the time at right half. It was my most productive year for the Bears, and I made All-League that year. [Gallarneau was fourth in rushing in the NFL in 1946 behind only Bill Dudley of the Steelers, Pat Harder of the Cardinals, and Steve Van Buren of the Eagles.] And we got back in our winning ways, winning the NFL West and then defeating the New York Giants for the championship [24-14]. There were about sixty thousand people at that championship game, the most ever up to that time for a title game in the NFL, and we each got $2,300 as a payoff—a lot then but pretty small change compared to what the boys get today for winning a Super Bowl.

That was also the game that was tainted by a scandal just before it got under way. It had to do with Merle Hapes and Frank Filchock of the Giants, who were accused not of gambling but of having been approached by gamblers and, I guess, consorting with them. Hapes was banned from the game for life, but Filchock was allowed to play in the game. Later he was barred too. We just beat Filchock to a pulp that day, we were all so mad at him about what he was bringing down on the game. We broke his nose and just generally beat the hell out of him.

I not only played with some of the greatest football players of their time; I also played against some too. Don Hutson of the Packers gave me what gray hairs I have today. You know he was so fast and shifty you couldn't cover him with a tent. The guy had three speeds, and Don could easily fake you out of your athletic supporter, as they say. And he had hands—if the ball came anywhere near him, he'd catch it.

One of the others I'll never forget was Bucko Kilroy, a bruiser of a lineman for the Eagles. Every time I'd go through the line, he'd throw an elbow at my mouth. I remember coming back to the huddle one time bleeding like mad, and Johnny Siegal and Joe Stydahar, two of our toughest, took a look at me. They then told Luckman which play to call, one that was kind of away from Kilroy. After the play I turned around, and Kilroy was on the ground, out like a light. There was a definite camaraderie on that team.

George Halas has often been accused of being a little tight with the bucks, but I've seen the generous side of him. An example was my rookie year, 1941. I signed for a rather modest amount of money. George Halas, always the intelligent business-man, withheld 20 percent of your total compensation for the season so that when the season was over you'd have something to go home with. When I came in to see him at the end of the season, he mentioned the fact that for a short period of time I had tied the NFL record for touchdowns, at least until McAfee and Hutson beat it that year. We settled up on the 20 percent, and then he handed me a check for $500.

I said, "Well, what's that for, George?"

He said, "You did have a good season: you averaged 6.2 yards a carry. For a rookie you did a damn good job. This is your bonus."

"Well, it isn't in my contract," I said, because I was so bewildered by it.

He said, "It doesn't have to be in your contract. If some-body wants to give it to you, he gives it to you. So just shut up and take it."

Another example came much later. This was eighteen years after I retired from pro football—makes it 1965. George Connor, the great Hall of Fame tackle who played for the Bears after I left, and I both went to Illinois Masonic Hospital for shoulder operations, which were performed by Dr. Ted Fox, who was then the Bears orthopod. Both operations went well, and George and I went home after four or five days in the hospital. About a week later we came back to the hospital to have the stitches removed. While Dr. Fox was taking out the stitches, he said, "Hugh, the Old Man called the other day."

I said, "What did he want?" George and I had at that point not heard a word from Halas, and we were a little disappointed.

"He wanted to know if these operations were necessitated by injuries that occurred while you were playing for the Bears."

I brightened up and said, "Well, Ted, yes, as a matter of fact, they were. This was my blocking and tackling shoulder. The same is true with George. Why?"

"In that case, I'm to send him the bills," Fox said.

I had actually planned to retire after the 1946 season. At the time I was working off-season and part-time during the season for Marshall Field's—I was their sporting goods buyer. But after I had such a good year in '46, I thought I ought to capitalize on it and get a good contract for 1947. The people at Field's went along with it but told me this had to be my last year if I wanted to be a full-time, longtime employee of the company.

I did get a good contract from Coach Halas and played out the year, but it wasn't one of my better ones. Then I gave up the game.

I hated to quit football, but I was thirty years old then. I might have gotten another two or three years in, depending on whether I got injured or not, but I knew it was time to quit playing a game and go to work, get on with another career. But I'll never forget those five wonderful years I had with the Chicago Bears.

1941 Championship Game

At Chicago, Wrigley Field, December 21, 1941

New York Giants		Chicago Bears
Jim Poole	LE	Dick Plasman
John Mellus	LT	Ed Kolman
Kayo Lunday	LG	Danny Fortmann
Mel Hein	C	Bulldog Turner
Len Younce	RG	Ray Bray
Bill Edwards	RT	Lee Artoe
Jim Lee Howell	RE	John Siegal
Nello Falaschi	QB	Sid Luckman
George Franck	LH	Ray Nolting
Ward Cuff	RH	Hugh Gallarneau
Tuffy Leemans	FB	Norm Standlee
Steve Owen	Coach	George Halas

Giants	6	0	3	0 —	9
Bears	3	6	14	14 —	37

Touchdowns—Giants: George Franck; **Bears:** Norm
Standlee (2), George McAfee, Ken Kavanaugh
Field Goals—Giants: Ward Cuff; **Bears:** Bob Snyder (3)
PATs—Bears: Bob Snyder, Joe Maniaci, Lee Artoe, Scooter
McLean

Bill Wade

Just before the 1961 season George Halas decided he had to revamp his offense, and the first step he took to achieve that was to acquire veteran quarterback Bill Wade from the Los Angeles Rams. With Wade came a revitalized passing attack that would help carry the Bears to the NFL title three years later.

Wade had amassed some impressive passing statistics while quarterbacking Vanderbilt in the early 1950s (201 completions for 3,397 yards and 31 touchdowns). The Rams selected him as their bonus draft choice in 1952, but Wade had two years of military service before he officially joined the team in 1954.

As a Bear, Wade was the starting quarterback from 1961 through 1964 and served as backup to Rudy Bukich in 1965 and 1966. Wade holds a variety of Bear passing records. He is the only Bear quarterback to pass for more than 3,000 yards in a season (3,172 in 1962) and the only one to pass for more than 2,000 yards three times.

Wade passed for more than 300 yards in a game nine times (closest to him in the Bear record book is George Blanda with four) and also holds the mark for accomplishing that four times in a single season (1962). The 466 yards he gained passing in a game against the Dallas Cowboys in 1962 is only 2 yards shy of the club record set by Johnny Lujack in 1949. Wade is also credited with the longest touchdown pass in Bear history, a 98-yarder to Bo Farrington in a 1961 game against the Detroit Lions.

His Bear career quarterback rating of 73.4 ranks third behind Jim McMahon and Sid Luckman. In his six years with the Bears, Wade completed 767 of 1,407 passes for 9,958 yards and 68 touchdowns. And, of course, he quarterbacked the 1963 NFL champion Chicago Bears.

After football Bill Wade struck a career in the banking business in Nashville, Tennessee, until his retirement in 1990.

I began to play football in first grade in Nashville, Tennessee. I started out as a guard, moved to center, then to fullback, and finally to tailback. I expected to play tailback at Vanderbilt under Coach Red Sanders, but he took his single wing out to UCLA after my freshman year. Our new coach, Bill Edwards, instituted the T formation at Vanderbilt, and I was converted to quarterback.

I played in the College All-Star game in Chicago in 1952. We had quite a team that year. Of the fifty-two players on it, fifty went on to play in the pros. We had Hugh McElhenny, Ollie Matson, Frank Gifford, Bill George, Gino Marchetti, Bill McColl, Fred Williams, Vic Janowicz, Babe Parilli. We should have beat the Rams that year, but we lost 10-7.

After two years in the navy I played with the Rams for seven years. Near the end I asked to be traded to the Bears. I didn't like the way things were going out there in Los Angeles. We had a new coach, Bob Waterfield, and a new general manager, Elroy Hirsch, and nothing was quite settled. I wanted to be with a team that had one coach, one person you answered to, not like four or five at the Rams. And, in the league then, I thought the best of that would be George Halas of the Bears or Paul Brown of the Cleveland Browns.

So Mr. Halas was contacted, and as it turned out, he was looking for a passing quarterback, and I had had seven years' experience. He was quite familiar with me because we had played the Bears a number of times during those years, and so the trade was made and I came out to Chicago in 1961.

George Halas tried to make me feel at home right from the start. He had me come out early, in June, and start learning his system. Along with some others, I worked out for six weeks before training camp that year. It wasn't like I was a rookie. I'd played against the great defense the Bears had, and you could not easily forget players like Bill George and Doug Atkins and Fred Williams.

In Rensselaer, Indiana, where we had training camp, I roomed next door to Coach Halas, and Atkins was across the hall. They used to argue with each other all the time. Doug was a very outspoken person, and he certainly liked to agitate things. Everybody liked Doug, and that includes George Halas. I think the coach liked to have guys around who created a little stir, and Doug was certainly that. He was mischievous; so were Bill George and Fred Williams. And so was George Halas. I remember him scheduling practice several times after we lost games over in the Armory on Chicago Avenue. It was a horse arena, and there was horse manure and the smell. That was a favorite place of his to practice after we lost a game.

Ed O'Bradovich was another memorable one around there during my time. Ed was a top player, and he was very tough. I remember one game against the Giants. Phil King, who is deceased now and had been a close friend of mine from our days at Vanderbilt, was a halfback for them but a pretty big guy—6'4", 225 pounds. This particular game Phil made the mistake of hitting Ed but not knocking him out. Ed took out after him, and Phil ran and got behind Jack Stroud, one of their tackles. Well, Stroud managed to stay between Ed and Phil, and finally Ed just shouted he was going to get him after the game. And Ed even went to the hotel they were staying at after the game, but he couldn't find Phil. Ed was one guy you didn't want to get mad at you.

Mike Ditka was a rookie the year I came to the Bears. Mike

was an excitable, ferocious football player. Right from the start I always tried to figure ways to throw the football to him because I knew if he got the ball he would kick and bite and run over people and bounce off them and stiff-arm them and step on them—anything to gain some yards once he got his hands on the ball. He was one fine competitor as a player.

Mike caught 56 passes that first year [1961], which was almost a Bear record [Jim Keane had caught 64 in 1947], and 12 of them were for touchdowns, and that was a record then [tying the record Harlon Hill set in 1954]. Then he caught 75 passes in 1964. That was the same year Johnny Morris caught 93. We set an NFL record that year for combined catches for wide receiver and tight end.

We had a number of great players around that time. Willie Galimore was one of the greatest runners in Bear history. And Rick Casares—people didn't realize what an extraordinary athlete he was. In college [Florida] he was All-Southeastern Conference in both football and basketball. Mike Pyle was a great center, and Ted Karras, Herm Lee, Jim Cadile, and Bob Wetoska were very good along with him on the offensive line.

The most memorable season for me, of course, was 1963. I will never forget going to Pittsburgh the weekend after President Kennedy was assassinated. We didn't know whether we were going to play a game that Sunday or not. We did. And Coach Halas got the whole team together before it and told us we were going to go out there and play and hope we can get everybody's mind off the terrible tragedy. It was a very depressing situation.

We made the best of that day we could, and we salvaged a tie when Mike Ditka made that phenomenal run. I threw him just a short pass, and he was hit by many, many players but wouldn't go down. If we'd lost that game, we would have lost our conference and would not have won the championship that year.

It was very cold when we played the Giants for the championship in '63. It was not a day for passing the football. The Giants can attest to that: two of Y. A. Tittle's passes were picked off by Larry Morris and Ed O'Bradovich, which set up our two touchdowns. I ran the ball that day myself. I loved running the football, and I always felt I could help the team by being able to run the ball when I had to. But there were very few plays designed for me to run, although in that game our strategy had me running the ball because the Giants' defense was keying on our running backs. I carried the ball in for our two touchdowns on quarterback sneaks. Those and our great defense were just enough to beat the Giants, 14-10.

Football is a game that has so many little nuances, so many changes that happen in a game. That championship game was a good example of that. I wanted to carry the ball. And I did, but it was brutally cold, and on one play I started through a hole and thought I was going somewhere, and there was a guy behind me who I didn't know was there. He whacked me, and the ball went out of my hands, and they recovered, and they ended up scoring their touchdown as a result. But we turned it around with defense, and I got to make a couple of touchdowns. That's why football is such a wonderful American game. It makes men out of you. It stresses the great lessons of life. It makes you humble; it makes you strive. It unites people as a team. It teaches definite values and self-discipline. And we had learned all that, and it came out that freezing-cold Sunday in Wrigley Field in 1963.

George Allen was a definite influence on that team. He was a great defensive coach. I knew George from Los Angeles when he got his start in pro ball coaching with the Rams in 1957. He was young, enthusiastic. He came to the Bears the next year, and I had to play against his defenses. He was such a hard worker. There are few people coaching in professional football who I respect who haven't paid their dues by playing the game. But George Allen and Paul Brown are two exceptions. George got the game ball after the 1963 championship game, and he truly deserved it. He handled that rowdy bunch we had on defense, and he turned them into a unit, a unit that worked.

I thought early on that I would be a tailback, but instead I ended up a passing quarterback. Viewing it from different angles, I learned a lot. I saw how a quarterback could be stung. For example, he goes back to pass and lets fly, and the receiver runs the wrong pass pattern. The pass is intercepted, and it's the quarterback's fault. The tailback had more options.

I have always been a believer that the person who makes the mistake on the field should bear the brunt of it. I don't think teams should be separated so that the defense and the offense are like different teams themselves. I believe both parts of the team should sit together, be together, at team meetings, in the locker room, all the time.

Blame should be placed where blame is deserved. You miss a tackle, you miss a block, you fumble the ball. One thing that has always bothered me, and I speak from having been there, is the statistics a quarterback has to live with. There should be an official scorer who can gauge every time a receiver drops a pass or runs the wrong pattern. Like in baseball: you drop the ball, it's an error. As a receiver you should be judged on balls that you drop—your error. Instead it goes onto the quarterback's stats, although it had nothing to do with the way the quarterback threw the football. Put errors where they should be put. Why should a quarterback's rating reflect the errors made by somebody else? I definitely think that would clarify a lot in terms of true football stats.

As my career was drawing to a close, I had the opportunity to watch the beginning of two fantastic football careers. In 1965 Gale Sayers and Dick Butkus joined the Bears. They were absolutely sensational rookies. Coincidentally, they played their first pro football game in my hometown, Nashville, Tennessee. Our first preseason game that year was exhibition down there against the Los Angeles Rams.

You could tell from the very start that they were just the best at their particular positions. The only other player I remember that I could immediately tell was the best at his position when he came to the pros was Mike Ditka. Those three rookies you could tell were destined for stardom. I didn't see Walter Payton play as a rookie, but I believe you could probably say the same about him.

Mike [Ditka], I mentioned earlier, was an excitable, ferocious player. Well, he's that way as a coach too. It's great fun to watch Mike coaching the Bears; he's such a competitor, and I think he's certainly one of the best coaches in modern-day professional football. To me you have to be tough to coach professional football, and Mike is certainly that.

I especially remember Gale Sayers's 6-touchdown game that rookie year. We were playing the 49ers, and after his 4th touchdown he came over and sat down next to me on the bench. By that time I had seen a lot of pro football—I'd been in the league twelve years by then—but I'd never seen a performance like the one Gale was putting on that day. I said to him, "Don't let up. Keep going. You may never get another chance like this again. They can't stop you." He went back and scored 2 more touchdowns to tie the record. He should have broken it that day. We were on the 2-yard line late in the game, but Halas had taken Sayers out of the game and put Jon Arnett in for him. Arnett carried the ball in for the touchdown while Gale watched from the sideline. It would have been an all-time NFL record if Gale had scored it. I don't know if it was Halas or somebody else who was responsible for Gale being out of the game. But Gale never complained about it. He never said a word about it to my knowledge.

I had my first knee operation the year that Sayers and Butkus came up and consequently didn't play as much as I had the previous four years. I came back in 1966 but hurt my knee again and had a second operation. I was hoping to come back in 1967, but I was having a lot of trouble spinning, and I knew I wasn't playing the game full-speed. I figured if I couldn't play full-speed, there was just no sense in playing at all.

I talked it over with George Halas, and he agreed. He asked me to stay around and help coach the quarterbacks. We had three at the time who were fighting for the position: Rudy Bukich, Larry Rakestraw, and Jack Concannon. After that year I went back to Nashville and took a job with the Third National Bank and stayed there for the next twenty-two years.

Atkins Antics

Ray Sons, when he was sports editor of the *Chicago Sun-Times*, once wrote: "Doug Atkins stories are something like the legends of Beowulf, Siegfried, and St. George. They aren't quite believable."

One story reveals more than a little about the personality of the enormous end (6'8", 255 pounds in his heyday in the 1960s). It is told by Blanton Collier, who was an assistant coach at Cleveland the year Atkins broke in with the Browns and among whose duties was "looking after" the freewheeling rookie. At a lunch counter one day after a morning practice session, Atkins offhandedly asked Collier if his wife was in town.

Collier shook his head negatively. "I'm batching it," he said.

"Are you behaving yourself, Coach?" Atkins asked.

"Of course I am."

"It's hell, ain't it, Coach?" sighed Atkins.

Then there was the day that Atkins, as a Chicago Bear, came onto the practice field late, clad only in shorts, T-shirt, and a helmet. He raced up and down the field several times before the mystified eyes of his fellow players and the coaching staff and then trotted back into the locker room. Asked later what he had been doing, he replied, "Just breaking in a new helmet."

Bill Bishop, a tackle who played alongside Atkins with the Bears, once said about him, "If he'd had the temperament of Ed Sprinkle, they would have had to bar him from football."

They also tell the story of the time Atkins had a martini-drinking contest with tackle Fred Williams. "I drank twenty-one," Williams said, "same as Atkins. But he beat me. I figured because he drove me home and carried me in that he must have won."

And, of course, there are the incidents involving the pit bull named Rebel he kept in his dormitory room at the Bear training camp in Rensselaer, Indiana. The dog was trained to kill on command—at least that's what Atkins had all the other players convinced of. No guest would attempt to leave the room or pass by Rebel, even to go to the bathroom, it has been told, unless sanctioned by the dog's master—which is why no one ever left Atkins's legendary dorm parties, despite curfew, before the host decreed the party over.

Don Kindt

Don Kindt came to the Bears from the University of Wisconsin in 1947, a first-round draft choice that year, and stayed around for nine seasons. As a rookie halfback he joined a backfield that was quarterbacked by Sid Luckman and consisted of such stalwart running backs as George McAfee, Hugh Gallarneau, Scooter McLean, Bill and Joe Osmanski, and Bob Fenimore. He was the Bears' third top rusher that first year.

In his final year, 1955, he was in a backfield that was quarterbacked alternately by Ed Brown and George Blanda and had such other running backs as Rick Casares, John Hoffman, Bobby Watkins, and Chick Jagade.

Kindt played with many of the most exciting and interesting Bears in club history and was known as a rugged, consistent competitor on both offense and defense.

After football Don Kindt went into business in Wisconsin for a company that manufactured fluid-measuring devices. Now retired, he still resides in Wisconsin and remains a Bear fan amid a swarm of Green Bay Packer fanatics.

I was just out of the army in 1947 when I learned I was drafted by the Chicago Bears. I was in the hospital recovering from knee surgery when my coach from the University of Wisconsin, Harry Stuhldreher, who had been one of Notre Dame's Four Horsemen, came by to visit. I still had a year of college ball eligibility left at the time.

While he was there, Gene Ronzani, an assistant coach with the Bears at the time, came by and told me I was their first-round pick. He had a contract with him for me to sign. I was kind of embarrassed about the situation, but Harry said, "Don, you've gotta sign the contract. You can't turn down a first-round draft choice." I was in the engineering school at Wisconsin, and Harry wanted me to promise him, however, that I would finish school and get my degree—which I did.

I signed the contract there in the hospital. Being from Milwaukee and going to college in Madison, I'd been a Green Bay Packer fan all my life. I'd watched Don Hutson and Cec Isbell and Tony Canadeo play, and Buckets Goldenberg became a very good friend of mine. At the same time, I had always been in awe of the Bears. I knew what great teams they had in the 1940s with guys like Sid Luckman, Bulldog Turner, George McAfee, Bill Osmanski. I was a little bit nervous and excited about the prospect of playing with players of that caliber.

It was going to be a big change too because we had played from the old Notre Dame box formation at Wisconsin and of course the Bears played the T formation, which George Halas had brought into pro football.

And so I began the first of nine summer training camps down at St. Joseph's College in Rensselaer, Indiana. I spent so much time there I thought I was going to be ordained. We were out in the middle of the cornfields, the middle of nowhere, but Halas, who was a very suspicious sort, always thought the Packers or the Cardinals or somebody had scouts out there spying on us. He'd have Andy Lotshaw, our trainer, and the equipment manager and some others combing the cornfields around the training camp. He'd say something like: They're spying on us, so we're going to camouflage this play or that play.

Even when we were up in Chicago, Halas would have Lotshaw and the others walk around the upper deck of Wrigley Field to see if they could spot any spies in the apartment buildings that looked into the stadium there. They never found anybody. They never found anybody in the cornfields either.

One story I'll always remember about George Halas happened in Washington not too long after I joined the team. In the army I had been the personal chauffeur to Colonel Willis Matthews, who was a top guy on the staff of Douglas MacArthur in the Pacific. Well, after the war he was promoted to general and was the adjutant to General Omar Bradley in Washington. I had done a lot of things for him—some special missions and that when I was his chauffeur—so when we were going to Washington to play the Redskins I called him up and offered to give him tickets to the game for him and his family. Well, he was delighted and said, "Now, while you're out here, why don't you come have lunch with me?"

When we got to Washington, I talked to him again, and he said, "We're going to have lunch at General Bradley's house over at Fort Myer." So I went up to Halas and asked if I could have a little time off practice because I was going to have lunch with Omar Bradley. He looked at me funny and asked what my rank was when I was in the service. I said PFC. "And you're going to have lunch with Omar Bradley, who's head of the whole goddam U.S. Army? Get out of here, Kindt."

Well, I went, and Omar Bradley was very nice—he was like your father, treated you very well. After the lunch he said, "Don, do you think you could get me forty tickets for the Redskins' game?" and told me he'd give me a check for them. I said I'd try. Then he invited me to come to a big dinner he was having that night.

I went back to practice and asked Halas if I could get forty tickets for the game. He said, "You don't know forty people, Kindt. Why the hell would you want forty tickets?" I said they were for Omar Bradley. He thought this was the biggest hunk of BS he'd ever heard in his life. "Sure," he said. "You want forty tickets, go see my brother Walter, and be damn sure you've got the money to pay for them."

I said, "By the way, General Bradley wants me to come to this big dinner he's having tonight."

Halas just shook his head. "PFC . . . Get the hell out of here." I did and went and got the tickets.

Well, as it turned out, Halas was invited to the same dinner by Admiral Nimitz, whom he had served under in the Pacific. There was this cocktail party before the dinner. The navy people stayed together in one wing and the army in another. "They don't fraternize with us," General Bradley said. But a little while later Halas came in and saw me sitting at a table with General Bradley and General Matthews and General Hap Arnold and a couple of others. He just looked at me, shaking his head, and said, "I'll be a son of a bitch, the kid told me the truth!"

I got up and said, "Gentlemen, I want to introduce you to the man that started the NFL. He's my coach and the owner of the Chicago Bears, George Halas. Coach Halas, this is General Omar Bradley . . . " and so on down the line. Halas shook hands with Bradley, at the same time saying a couple more times, "I'll be a son of a bitch, the kid was telling the truth!"

As far as football went, we had a great backfield there. George McAfee and Hugh Gallarneau, both of whom played the right halfback position, were a very big help to me when I first got there. They showed me all kinds of things because the pro game was an awful lot different from the one I'd played in college. I was competing for the left halfback position with two other rookies—George Gulyanics, who came from some junior college, and Bob Fenimore, who was an All-American from Oklahoma State. I got to start a lot of the games that year at offensive left halfback and defensive safety.

Coach Halas didn't like the wives to come to the games. His wife, Min, had a luncheon for the players' wives before the season, and the group was referred to as the "Nothing After Wednesday Club." The rookie wives didn't know what that meant. At the luncheon they learned: give your husbands no nooky after Wednesday night, because it will sap their strength.

The game I remember the best is the very first one. We

went up to Green Bay to play the Packers. Halas told me he wanted me to start because he knew my family and all my friends from Wisconsin would be there for the game. Needless to say, it was going to be a big thrill for me.

Packer Stadium in those days was nothing but a city-owned, small-time stadium that didn't even have a locker room. We would dress in the Northland Hotel, get on a bus, and go over to a high school about a block or so from the stadium, which had a little locker room where we'd get our ankles taped and things like that. Then we'd walk over to the stadium for the pregame warm-ups, and then back to the locker room for a pregame pep talk from Halas, then back for the kickoff.

Well, I had sprained an ankle in an exhibition game a week or two earlier, and it was bothering me after the warm-ups. Back in the locker room, the trainer decided I should get a shot of Novocain in my ankle. So he went to find the doctor to give it to me. Finally the doc showed up, and I told him to hurry because I was on the kickoff team. He gave me the shot, and with that I heard the crowd from Packer Stadium roar. I put my cleats on, grabbed my helmet, and ran the block over to the stadium. And the ticket takers wouldn't let me in.

They said, no ticket, you don't get in. The game was already under way, and I guess they thought I'd come up with a novel way of trying to sneak into a game. Later I heard Curly Lambeau, the Green Bay coach, had given instructions not to let any opposing players in if they were late. I don't know whether that was true or not, but it wouldn't surprise me. At any rate my brother, who was in the top row of the stands, could see down below what was happening and managed to get a cop to come, and they finally let me in.

I had to run around the field to get to the Bears' side; about seven minutes of the first quarter had already elapsed by the time I got there. Did I ever get a chewing out from Halas when I finally made it over there. But he did eventually put me into the game.

I'll never forget one touchdown I scored. That was the following year against Detroit. I remember it exactly because it was October 17, which was my father's birthday. He came down to Chicago to watch the game, and before it I told him I had a birthday present for him—I was going to score a touchdown for him. I was playing fullback that day, and Sid Luckman called for a fullback draw, a play where he'd fake a pass and then just slip the ball to the fullback. There was a big hole, and I went 67 yards for a touchdown. After it I turned to where my dad was sitting in the stands and waved.

After the last game of that season, which was against the Cardinals and also would decide the NFL West championship that year, I went home, and the next day I had this severe pain in my back. I thought somebody must have kneed me, but I'd actually slipped a disk. And in those days, once you slipped a disk you were through playing football. Back in Wisconsin I went to an orthopedic surgeon I'd known at the University of Wisconsin. I told him I was going to play football again. He said it would never happen. But he got together with a neurosurgeon, and they performed a lamenectomy, an operation. It was the first time, I understand, that a lamenectomy was ever performed on an athlete who, after it, was able to go back and play football. I worked hard after it, especially swimming, and I managed to get seven more years of football in.

There were a lot of great and funny people I met along the way. Pat Harder, the wonderful fullback for the Cardinals, was a boyhood friend of mine. We both went to the same high school in Milwaukee. We would always holler all kinds of things at each other across the line of scrimmage in those days, but we were still great friends.

Bobby Layne was a real piece of work. He came to the Bears in 1948, the same year Johnny Lujack did. So we had three great quarterbacks—those two along with Luckman. I got to know Bobby pretty well. He was the wildest man I ever met in football. He didn't observe training rules too well, and we had a lot of great parties, and he was always the ringleader.

We had a helluva party on the train coming back from Detroit. We went over there to play the Lions on Thanksgiving Day; we did that all the time in those years. Bobby kind of took

over the party. He was up there singing about Ida Red or some
other country song, and he'd be singing away in that old Texas
twang when he wasn't swigging something down. Halas kept
coming around and sniffing all the glasses. He didn't mind if
you had a beer, but he didn't want any booze being drunk.
Layne and some of the others were always switching glasses
around, or they'd be drinking out of Coke bottles, and the booze
bottle would be hidden under a table in the dining car.

Another time in Chicago we were all staying at this hotel on
Wilson and Sheridan, and Bobby got a party going. He got some
gals, and he was up on the bar dancing and singing and raising
all kinds of hell. He and Bulldog Turner were singing all these
Texas songs. Finally Bobby and Bulldog decided they had to go
take a leak, but the men's room was crowded, so they went
outside and peed in the alley. The police caught them and took
them over to the station house. The next day the *Chicago
Tribune* ran a picture of them in jail. Bulldog had a roll of bills
in his hand, which he was waving around. And don't think Halas
didn't fine their fannies after he saw that.

We had another guy on the team who was very successful
with women, who will remain nameless. He was always telling
everybody about the joys of going down on a woman. A crotch
cannibal, I called him. Well, he was always saying he wanted to
put on an exhibition of it for us.

Word of his escapades got back to Halas. Well, I was called
in to see Halas one day, and when I got there his secretary told
me this nameless individual had just gone in there ahead of me.
She knew what it was about and said, "You've got to listen to
this, Don." So we stood next to the door, and I heard Halas
shout, "You put your face there! Oh, pooey, pooey. Agh. That's
nauseating." That ended all plans for this guy's special exhibition season.

I remember another time we were playing Detroit at Wrigley
Field. I was playing safety at the time. This was in the 1950s,
and Jug Girard, who had been my roommate at Wisconsin, was
playing halfback for the Lions. Well, the Jugger ran a post-
corner—that's where he runs toward the post and then cuts to

the corner. Bobby Layne threw it to him, and we're just about at the goal line, and I dove and batted the ball into the air and knocked Jug on his butt at the same time. Well, the ball makes this little loop in the air and comes down right in Jug's gut.

Halas was incensed, as he was known to get sometimes on the sideline. He ran all the way down to maybe the 10-yard line, where I was now standing right in front of the box where the mayor and his wife—it was [Martin] Kennelly at the time—were sitting with some other local dignitaries. And he grabbed me and screamed at me, "You lousy cocksucker, you cunt!"

And I said, "No, it's Kindt, K-i-n-d-t. You pronounce it Kindt."

I retired after the 1955 season and went back up to Wisconsin. Curly Lambeau was gone from Green Bay by that time, and my old high school football coach, Lisle Blackbourn, was now coaching the Packers. He offered me a job as an assistant to coach their backfield, but I turned it down and got out of football for good. But it was great fun while it lasted.

Where Was Abe Cohen on the Scouting Report?

Going into the 1934 NFL championship game, the Bears knew how good triple-threat tailback Ken Strong was. They knew Mel Hein was a perennial All-Pro center. They knew about everybody on the New York Giants—except Abe Cohen.

And it was the 5'2", 140-pound Cohen who turned the tide that frigid day at the Polo Grounds and enabled the Giants to defeat the Bears and claim the NFL title.

Cohen, a tailor by profession and a sports fanatic by persuasion, helped out as a kind of jack-of-all-trades for the Giants and for Manhattan College.

With the field frozen that day and both teams slipping and sliding all over it, getting nowhere, Cohen left the Polo

Grounds at the end of the first quarter, hailed a taxi, and went over to Manhattan College. With a master key, he opened the lockers of the basketball players, snatched all their sneakers, and rushed back to the game.

He got there near the end of the third quarter, with the Bears leading 13–3. The Giants shed their cleats and donned the sneakers Cohen had brought. George Halas, seeing the tactic, shouted from the sideline to his players, "Step on their toes!" But to no avail. The now well-tractioned Giants went out and scored 27 unanswered points in the fourth quarter to give themselves a 30–13 victory. It became known forever after as the "Sneakers Championship."

The following day sportswriter Lewis Burton of the *New York American* summed it up best: "To the heroes of antiquity, to the Greek who raced across the Marathon plain, and to Paul Revere, add now the name of Abe Cohen."

Gary Fencik

During his twelve years with the Bears safety Gary Fencik racked up more tackles (1,117) and snared more interceptions (38) than any other defensive player in Bear history. In 1986 he surpassed Dick Butkus in career combined takeaways (interceptions and fumble recoveries) for the club record of 50 (Butkus had 47).

A wide receiver at Yale, he set school reception records there with 82 for 1,435 yards and 7 touchdowns. A tenth-round draft choice of the Miami Dolphins in 1976, he was claimed on waivers by the Bears just after the start of that season.

Fencik had a career-high 6 interceptions in 1979 and was named All-Pro and repeated that stat in 1981, the year he also recorded his most tackles (135). In the Super Bowl season of 1985 Fencik led the team in tackles with 118 and was named second-team All-Pro and first-team All-NFC.

In five different games Gary snatched 2 interceptions, and in two games he was credited with 17 tackles each. His longest interception return was 69 yards for a touchdown against the Denver Broncos in 1981. When he retired after the 1987 season, only six players in history had played more seasons for the Bears than Gary Fencik's twelve.

Fencik now does color for the Bear games on WGN radio and has established a new career in real estate with the Hawthorne Realty Group in Chicago's western suburbs.

W hen I went off to college, playing pro football was never one of my considerations. I didn't think I was large enough. But I had a pretty good career at Yale, and in my senior year, when the scouts started sending stuff, I got my hopes up about being drafted.

In college, ironically, the two most memorable games I played in we lost. Both were against Harvard. In my junior year we went up to Cambridge, and they had Pat McInally, a wide receiver then, who later became quite a punter for the Cincinnati Bengals. We were undefeated and were winning, but they came back on a long drive and won it in the last few minutes. I had had a really good day—11 catches for something like 180 yards. In my senior year we had another excellent team, but they beat us on a field goal in the last minute of the game.

Ivy League football was different. I remember Buddy Ryan, our defensive coach with the Bears at the time, telling me on the plane coming back from an away game that he wanted me to go over and explain to Mike Singletary how difficult spring football was in the Ivy League. So I did. I told him, "The first day we come out and work out, and the scouts are there. At the end of the day we have a barbecue, which is fairly traditional at Yale, and after it Carm Cozza [longtime Yale head coach] says, 'We'll see you boys next fall.' " We were allowed only one day of spring practice in the Ivy League.

Howard Cosell invited me to come down to New York for the draft of 1976. I had taken a seminar he conducted at Yale called Contemporary Sports in America. It was limited to twelve people, and each week Howard would come to New Haven and bring a guest speaker—people like Bob Wussler, who was president of CBS Sports at the time, Bill Bradley, Pete Rozelle, some very interesting men.

So I went down and got my first taste of the glitter of pro sports. Besides draft day, it was also the day the New York Giants signed Larry Csonka after his great career with the Miami Dolphins, which was in all the newspapers. Cosell and I went out to lunch with Csonka and his agent, and it was really something. Walking down the street in New York, people would stop and say hello to Howard and Csonka—people got out of cabs, cars stopped.

That was the day the Dolphins drafted me. My freshman coach at Yale, Harry Jacunski, had contacted a friend at Miami and told them I had played defensive back as a freshman, and a scout for the Dolphins then talked to me about switching from wide receiver to safety, which was something they needed down there. I was really excited about the prospect because I always wanted to play defensive back. So I knew up front what I was going to be if they drafted me, and I was happy about it. And they took me in the tenth round.

Then I ruptured my lung in a freak accident. We were playing a scrimmage game against the New Orleans Saints in Fort Lauderdale. Bobby Douglass, his Bear career over then, was their quarterback, and he tossed a short pass, and when I tackled the receiver I ruptured my lung. I didn't know it at the time, and the Dolphins misdiagnosed it for a couple of days. I just figured I had some bruised ribs. But then when they discovered what it was, the Dolphins released me on Labor Day.

I took a job in a management training program at Citibank in New York. Then the Bears called, and so did the Steelers. I came to Chicago and met with Jim Finks and Jack Pardee, the head coach that year. They took a look at me, and Finks offered me a contract. The Bears were in the process of rebuilding, and the organization itself was being renovated under Jim Finks, and I thought it would be a good place to be for me. I had also grown up in the Chicago area, in Barrington, and still had family here. So I did not bother to go out to Pittsburgh.

Actually the Bears picked up my contract from the Dolphins, which had been drafted by Bobby Beathard, who was their player-personnel director at the time. It was a fair contract, and I was pleased with it. When the Bears decided they wanted me, Jim Finks asked me what I was making with Miami and some other details, and I told him. I didn't have an agent at the time. He said they would give me the same deal.

When I actually went in to sign the contract, I discovered that all the incentives were missing. I said to Jim, "This isn't the contract I signed with Miami." So we ended up negotiating, and I ended up getting one of the incentives, one I was pretty adamant about, which provided for an additional bonus if you made the active roster. I respect Jim Finks a lot, but I don't know whether it was my imagination or not, but I'd swear when we were negotiating his chair was a lot higher than mine and I was always looking up.

I joined the team after the first game of the '76 season. It was a real young team, and many of the players were only in their first or second year, and as a result I got along fine right from the start.

Jack Pardee was a good players' coach. He was a tough guy who had played on some great teams, and he wanted to play very physical football. Our defensive scheme was very, very simple. It did not take a week to learn it.

Doug Plank and Craig Clemons were the two starting safeties when I arrived. Doug got hurt in the last preseason game of 1977, and so they switched Craig to strong safety, and I started as free safety. When Doug came back about four weeks later, he replaced Clemons, and I remained at free safety. Doug and I started together on a Monday night game against the Los Angeles Rams. It was in that game that I got my first pro interception. That interception, incidentally, was the last pass Joe Namath threw in the NFL. After it he was replaced by Pat Haden and never played again. It was the same game Isiah Robertson was all over Walter Payton. He had a thing going, and he was trying to give Walter as much grief as he could. I have a picture at home with me and Brian Baschnagel walking off the field after that game with our arms around Walter, and Isiah is pointing a finger at him. Isiah used to talk so much, gesture, posture out there. Walter never needed to do that kind of thing. We won that game, by the way, 24-23.

I made some good friends early—Terry Schmidt, Brian Baschnagel, Bob Thomas, and, of course Doug Plank, who I really learned a lot from about how to hit and the attitude you needed to have on the field. Nobody who ever saw a game during that time could doubt that Doug Plank could hit. He made so many they heard throughout the stadium. I remember one especially he put on Jimmy Giles, Tampa's tight end, on a Monday night game. His attitude: reckless abandon, just throw your body, and take no prisoners. Have fun out there—that was his attitude—but make sure you have your head on a swivel.

Another person who taught me a lot was Doug Buffone. It was fun playing behind Buffone because he was at the end of his career and he knew all the moves, all the tricks. He would think so quickly out there that it was easy to react just off his moves. Buff was kind of the connection to what football was like in the sixties and the early seventies, the connection from the Butkus stories and the era I'd watched the Bears as a kid. Doug used to get sick before a game. He got all the linebackers to get sick before the game. I think it was like a tradition; they all just followed what Doug did.

Terry Bradshaw of the Steelers was a tough quarterback to play against. He had a great arm. I remember once he zinged a ball out there and I missed the interception, dropped it. I came back to the bench later, and Buddy Ryan was all over me. I said, "Hey, Buddy, he throws the ball so damn hard."

For the next five years at least, I heard Buddy announce every time we played Pittsburgh, "Keep in mind Fencik can't intercept the ball because Bradshaw throws it too hard."

Kenny Stabler of the Raiders [later of the Oilers and Saints] was another great quarterback of that time. He could really throw the ball too. But he was such a cool guy at the same time. I remember once I gave away a safety blitz, and after he stung us he winked at me. And Joe Montana of San Francisco. What can you say about him? Every stat speaks for itself. He was the best at making instant decisions out there on the field. But I had some good games against him. I had two picks off him in the playoff game for the NFC title in 1984, a game we ended up losing pretty badly [23-0]. Sometimes you feel like you can read a quarterback or feel the flow of what he is doing. I had that several times with Montana. Somehow I could read him better than a lot of other quarterbacks.

A game to remember was that 1977 one in New York, which got us into the playoffs. The day before it the weather was great, sunny. The day of the game it was miserable—sleeted and snowed the whole game, the worst weather conditions I played in during my entire career. Players were out there on the sideline in the second half unscrewing their cleats to get down to the screws so they could get better footing. It was one of the first times we had one of those heated benches, and it really didn't work very well. I remember Mike Hartenstine lying down in the sleet with his arms stuck in where your feet were supposed to go. It was a bizarre game with Walter [Payton] having a shot at O. J. Simpson's single-season rushing record and Bob Thomas getting yelled at by Bob Parsons for missing a couple of field goals but finally making one in overtime to give us a win [12-9]. It was the first time the Bears got to the playoffs since 1963, and it was a real thrill.

One player I used to go back and forth with a lot was James Lofton, who was with Green Bay in those days. He was one of the best you could go up against, but I always thought he was giving me a cheap shot when he got the chance. On the other hand, he thought Plank and I were doing it to him. I made the Pro Bowl one year, and we were sitting on the bench together, and I said, "I don't understand you. I don't like the way you play."

He looked at me and said, "I don't like the way you play."

After that we had a kind of silent truce. There were a couple of times I knew he could have hit me but he didn't, and there were a couple of times I had a real free shot at him and I didn't take it. We just understood each other a little better and, I guess, figured it wasn't worth it to keep going back and forth at each other.

Tight ends could be very difficult. Two of the best I ever ran up against were Dave Casper of the Raiders and later with

the Oilers and then the Vikings and, of course, Kellen Winslow
of San Diego. Casper was always looking for someone to run
over. He had great hands, and you knew in clutch situations
they were going to go to him. With Winslow it was just a matter
hopefully of not getting embarrassed by him, because the guy
had such incredible talent.

One of the best running backs I played against was Billy
Sims of the Lions. He had both speed and power, could run
power inside and the speed to go outside. He was a good pass
receiver too. It's too bad his career was shortened. And Tony
Dorsett of the Cowboys—I never saw anybody cut like that.
There were just so many different kinds of runners. Earl Campbell of Houston, for example; he wasn't graceful like Dorsett.
What he had was pure power—he was going to kill you. He ran
over so many would-be tacklers. One year when we were supposed to play the Oilers the following week, I watched their
game against Denver on television. In the last couple of minutes
Denver needed to get the ball back, and their safety, Steve Foley,
came up and hit Campbell as hard as he could, obviously hoping
to jar the ball loose. He hit him head-on, and Foley went flying
into the air. Earl just kept going and got a touchdown. The
cameraman panned back up the field to a spread-eagled Steve
Foley lying there. At that moment, I thought, I'm going to wear
a neck collar next week.

Offensive linemen are another category. They're so strong
and large, and it seems they all have these Charles Atlas bodies.
But most offensive linemen have kind of strange builds after a
while because they have to have that center of gravity, and so
they end up putting more weight on in the midsection. One of
ours, Noah Jackson, well, he might have gone a little overboard,
but he was a very talented player. He and Revie Sorey at guards
for us were almost scary to see even at practice, they were so big
and at the same time so agile.

Walter Payton was only in his second year when I joined
the team in 1976. And we both retired after the same year, 1987.
I think anybody who knows Walter is well aware of what a
prankster he was. It was either M-80s in the shower room,
pinching you, or practical jokes. A couple of years after we

retired I ran into him, and he gave me a hug and almost broke my ribs. Then he laughed, and we shook hands, and I went right down to the ground. It's like there is never anything really straight with Walter.

I think I learned to appreciate all sides of Walter by having the opportunity of playing on the same team with him for twelve years. I remember I used to go out to the New Jersey seashore with some Yale friends after each season, and I'd always bring along the highlight films from that year. When you sat down and watched those, you realized how really great Walter Payton was.

Walter was fairly quiet his first couple of years in the league. In fact I initially thought Roland Harper was his mouthpiece or ventriloquist. Later he changed and became much more open. I try to think of one story that would do justice to Walter Payton, but I really can't—not just one. To watch him play on the field was one thing. Dazzling, frightening. But his leadership was another—something that was very dramatic to everyone on the team. A perfect example of the way Walter Payton was occurred in 1987, our last year. He knew it was his last. We went on strike, and he went along with nothing to gain and a lot to lose. He could so easily have said something like "Look, this just isn't in my best interests, and I'm not going to do it." But he did it, went along with us to help the others coming along. I think that's a testimony to what Walter Payton was like as a Bear and a professional football player.

The one thing Walter did that defensive players learned to hate—he would explode into you at the moment of impact, bounce off, and continue running. A lot of runners, when they know they're going to get hit, hit hard, will just kind of relax and go down. Not Walter. I talked to Randy White, the Cowboys' great All-Pro defensive tackle, and he just shook his head and said, "Payton's the toughest, *the* toughest."

All of us got hurt in the game. Walter had his pains along with the rest of us, but he was such a superb specimen of training. I ordinarily got hurt at the end of the year. I ran out of cartilage on the left side of my nose, so they had to replace it with some from my ear. I broke an arm one year, but I missed only two weeks and played after that. I blew my knee out one

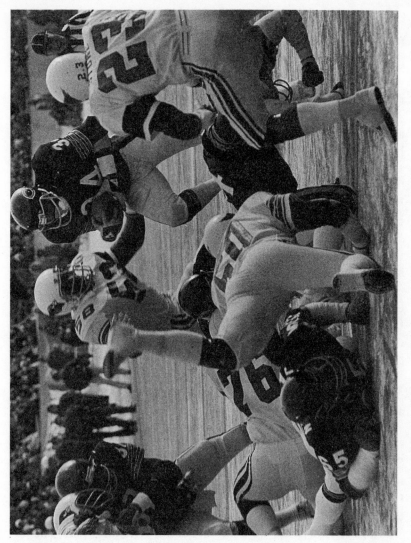

Walter Payton (1975–87) scores one of his 125 Bear touchdowns here against the St. Louis Cardinals. Payton holds practically every Bear rushing record and scored more points (750) and played in more games (190) than any other Bear in history. Payton is eligible for enshrinement in the Pro Football Hall of Fame in 1993.

year, the same year I had an ankle that had to be reconstructed after the season. Another time a dislocated shoulder. Everybody has those. You get kind of used to them. They pop out, and you get them popped back in, but they are really sore.

Mondays weren't the worst days for me. It was Tuesdays—they were really bad. Sunday night was always a good party night after the game. The next day you'd just watch film. It wouldn't set in until Monday night or Tuesday. The older you got, the longer it lasted during the week. And artificial turf had a lot to do with it. There would be points in the season when you could not sleep on your stomach. Or, like Nick Nolte in that movie *North Dallas Forty*, you would try to roll over on your right side, and it was too sore, so you'd roll over on your left side and just end up limping off to the bathroom to find some anti-inflammatory drug to get the swelling down. I ended up having three operations on my left knee. The other things went away; the knee is still a bother.

I was in my seventh year when Mike Ditka took over as head coach. All of us felt that Mike was a strange choice because he hadn't been either a defensive or offensive coordinator. We had spoken to some of the Cowboys players, and they said he was just so emotionally volatile that it seemed to them he was a questionable pick as a head coach.

To my memory Mike was, however, the first head coach I ever had who specifically laid out what the goals of the team and the organization were. And while I know it seems natural that every team wants to go to the Super Bowl, I think unless you publicly state what the goals are it's kind of tough to be held accountable as to where you are in fact going. The first time we ever met Mike was at a minicamp down in Phoenix, and he held a team meeting, and he laid it out for us.

His primary goal was not just to win the NFC Central but to win the three games following it, the last of course being the Super Bowl. And then he said, "As I look at this group of men, half of you won't be here when we get there." After we did get there, I checked the two rosters, 1982 and 1985, and between the two there had been a 60 percent turnover in players.

Under Mike there were new standards. His word was good with the players. Plus I think the organization itself got better. There was good rapport between Mike and Jerry Vainisi, the general manager, and between both of them and Mike McCaskey, the Bears' president. There was more a sense of family, a sense of purpose.

But Ditka was volatile. I remember in 1983 when we lost two overtime games in a row. The second was in Baltimore. I had gotten hurt that game; backpedaling, I hit the infield in the stadium and managed to rip my groin. I wasn't the only casu-

alty. In the locker room after the game Mike came and whacked
one of those black traveling trunks we had so hard he broke his
hand. He ordinarily led the team in prayer, but he turned to
Vince Evans and said, "Vinnie, you better lead the team." Then,
as he was walking down the hallway, I could hear him saying to
Fred Caito, our trainer, "I think I broke my fucking hand." He
wore a cast for a couple of days and then got rid of it. I think he
was a little embarrassed about it.

We really felt bad about losing in the 1984 playoffs. We just
couldn't get anything going that day against the 49ers [lost 23-
0], and we were all in the locker room crying like little kids after
it. The next summer, our first day up in Platteville, Ditka said at
the team meeting, "I don't know about you guys, but second
best isn't good enough for me." And that set the tone for the
whole 1985 season.

We opened against Tampa Bay, and at halftime it looked
like we could lose that game. Buddy Ryan changed the defense
for the second half and said to us, "We're going to fool them.
Leslie [Frazier], you're going to intercept the ball." And damn if
Leslie didn't. And right then we started to think this was
something special. [The Bears beat Tampa Bay 38-28 that day.]

Then when we beat Dallas [44-0] and the following week
killed Atlanta [38-0], I knew we were something special. It was
one of those seasons where everyone connected with the team
sacrificed a lot—their friends, families. When we got into the
playoffs, Ditka said to us, "Even though you earned the right to
be here, now you've got to take it!" And we did.

The week before the Super Bowl down there in New Orleans was great fun. It was a workweek for us, but Ditka let us
party, and there was no curfew. I think everyone was pretty
relaxed. We never even saw any of the Patriots. They were under
a very strict regimen. I think Ditka pretty much knew his team,
knew that we were really going for it. We had confidence because of our season and the two playoff games, and we had
beaten the Patriots earlier that year [20-7].

It was during that week that Buddy [Ryan] told me he had
taken the Philadelphia job. At the last defensive meeting before
the game Buddy said, "No matter what happens tomorrow, you

guys will always be my heroes." It was all pretty emotional. I turned to Mike Singletary and said, "I can't believe Buddy won't be here next year." And then, looking into Singletary's eyes, I realized Buddy hadn't told him, so I said quickly, "You've got to believe with the season we've had he'll be a head coach next year."

Everything clicked. It was just an amazing season, and we won the Super Bowl by the biggest margin in the history of the game [46-10].

I wasn't going to come back after the 1986 season. I talked to Mike Ditka and Vince Tobin [Buddy Ryan's replacement as defensive coordinator]. I told them if I wasn't going to be a starter, if I was to lose that job, I didn't want to come back. No, no, it wouldn't happen, they told me. And then I came into camp, and after the first week I was second string. They decided to switch things around. Tobin told me they felt they wanted to showcase Todd Bell. He looked so good they wanted to put him at strong safety and then move Dave Duerson to free safety. So I sat on the bench most of that year. It made the decision to retire after the 1987 season an easy one.

And I will say the Bears enabled me to retire with some sense of dignity. I had gotten a lot out of my pro football career. Now it's a new life, a new career. I'm still associated, doing the Bears games on radio. I hope the guys out there now get to experience what I did, a triumphant trip to the Super Bowl.

Notes and Quotes from a Super Bowl Season

The regular season was 1985, the Super Bowl, XX, and these were some of the words describing the Bears' magnificent season:

Otis Wilson, describing his defensive teammates: "Mike Singletary is the quiet, Christian type; I'm the wild one; Fencik is the Ivy Leaguer; Dan Hampton is the politician; Steve McMichael is crazy. It makes for a wild bunch."

Safety Gary Fencik (45) puts the shoulder to Los Angeles Ram running back Cullen Bryant. Helping out is linebacker Tom Hicks. Fencik was a mainstay in the Bear defensive backfield for twelve seasons (1976–87).

NFL Commissioner Pete Rozelle, on Jim McMahon's inscribed headbands: "I'm concerned that it will spread. I don't want our players running around like race-car drivers with patches all over them. Pretty soon, we'll have a center with a Big Mac on his fanny."

Mike McCaskey, the Bears' president, the week before Super Bowl XX: "Our secret weapon is the placebo effect. I don't know how the Patriots can counter that. That's when there's no evidence that the treatment works, but the patient thinks it works, so it does. The placebo effect and the man from Japan [Jim McMahon's acupuncturist, who was treating him for a bruised fanny] are our secret weapons."

Dick Enberg, Super Bowl XX broadcaster, during the third quarter of that game: "If it were a fight, they'd have to stop it."

Pete Brock, Patriot center assigned to block William "Refrigerator" Perry, after the effort in Super Bowl XX: "I'm not in a real talkative mood. So if you're hanging out for a quotable quote, it just ain't flowing."

The Best Days Ever

200-Yard Rushing Games:

> 275: Walter Payton, 11/20/77, vs. Vikings (40 carries)
> 205: Walter Payton, 11/30/77, vs. Packers (23 carries)
> 205: Gale Sayers, 11/3/68, vs. Packers (24 carries)

400-Yard Passing Games:

> 468: Johnny Lujack, 12/11/49, vs. Cardinals (24 of 39)
> 466: Bill Wade, 11/18/62, vs. Cowboys (28 of 46)
> 433: Sid Luckman, 11/14/43, vs. Giants (21 of 32)

200-Yard Receiving Games:

> 214: Harlon Hill, 10/31/54, vs. 49ers (7 receptions)
> 201: Johnny Morris, 11/18/62, vs. Cowboys (10 recep-
> tions)